# THE WELFARE WE WANT?

## The British challenge for American reform

Edited by Robert Walker and Michael Wiseman

First published in Great Britain in May 2003 by

The Policy Press
Fourth Floor, Beacon House
Queen's Road
Bristol BS8 1QU
UK

Tel +44 (0)117 331 4054
Fax +44 (0)117 331 4093
e-mail tpp-info@bristol.ac.uk
www.policypress.org.uk

British Library Cataloguing in Publication Data

A catalogue record for this book is available from the British Library

ISBN 1 86134 408 2 hardback

A paperback version of this book is also available

Cover design by Qube Design Associates, Bristol.
*Front cover:* photograph kindly supplied by www.third-avenue.co.uk

**Robert Walker** is Professor of Social Policy in the Department of Sociology and Social Policy at the University of Nottingham and Research Fellow at the Institute for Fiscal Studies, London, UK and **Michael Wiseman** is Research Professor of Public Policy and Economics at The George Washington University and an Affiliated Scholar with the Institute for Research on Poverty at the University of Wisconsin-Madison, US.

Printed and bound in Great Britain by Bell & Bain Ltd, Glasgow

# Contents

Acknowledgements                                                                    iv

*one*     Sharing ideas on welfare                                                   I
          *Robert Walker and Michael Wiseman*

*two*     Welfare in the United States                                              25
          *Michael Wiseman*

*three*   The British perspective on reform: transfers from, and a lesson           65
          for, the US
          *Alan Deacon*

*four*    Eradicating child poverty in Britain: welfare reform and children         81
          since 1997
          *Mike Brewer and Paul Gregg*

*five*    The art of persuasion? The British New Deal for Lone Parents             115
          *Jane Millar*

*six*     Beyond lone parents: extending welfare-to-work to disabled people        143
          and the young unemployed
          *Bruce Stafford*

*seven*   Shaping a vision of US welfare                                           175
          *Robert Walker and Michael Wiseman*

Index                                                                              193

# Acknowledgements

The editors gratefully acknowledge the financial support of the Rockefeller Foundation and the active interest and participation in the project by Julia Lopez, the Director of the Foundation's Working Communities section. The continuing enthusiasm of the contributors has been essential and is much appreciated, as is the editorial assistance of Felicity Skidmore and the excellent project management by Carrie O'Regan, our graduate assistant at The George Washington Institute of Public Policy.

Finally, without the ongoing tolerance, support and affection of Jennifer Walker and Carol Wiseman there would be no book.

# ONE

# Sharing ideas on welfare

*Robert Walker and Michael Wiseman*

## Anticlimax as prologue

By most accounts, 2002 was expected to be a landmark year for welfare reform in the United States (US). The Congress was scheduled to reauthorise Temporary Assistance for Needy Families (TANF) and the Food Stamp Program (FSP), the major safety net programmes for families with children. In truth, not much was achieved, and the intense scrutiny of the welfare programme that many predicted Congress to apply (cf Blank and Haskins, 2001, pp 3-4) never occurred. FSP was refunded with only modest change, and substantive action on TANF was put off to 2003 and beyond. After six years of experience with the system created by the 1996 Personal Responsibility and Work Opportunity Reconciliation Act (PRWORA) and what was surely the largest social policy research effort in world history, the country was left with pretty much what it had: a deeply fragmented, incoherent system neither motivated by, nor structured in light of, a vision of the social assistance Americans might want.

This anticlimax was the product of many factors. One was a gift of the economy: the decline in welfare caseloads, brought about by the longest sustained economic expansion in American history, stifled the concern about burgeoning dependency that had motivated the reform effort in the early 1990s. A second was fiscal: the 1996 reforms and subsequent legislation flooded states with federal money. No governors wanted to kill, or even redress, the treasury goose that was laying the golden grants. A third was a matter of perception: despite substantial evidence to the contrary, national opinion makers continued to claim that the laboratories of federalism, called states, were successfully mixing federal resources and grass-roots acumen to forge a new, work-oriented welfare order. To its credit, the second Bush administration attempted in its reauthorisation proposals to increase state accountability. However, in the end the administration, constrained by a burgeoning federal deficit and focused more on terrorism than social welfare, turned away from aggressive reform.

This is good news for the myriad scholars and research organisations dependent for their livelihoods on the persistence of welfare conundrums. Welfare reform, as Americans have known it, is far from dead and is probably set for a new lease on the resources of government and philanthropic institutions.

But for most of the country's citizens the prospect of another half-decade of welfare deja-stew is surely depressing. This book suggests that welfare policy malaise is best addressed by doing something that hardly comes naturally in the US: looking outside, specifically to Britain. Over the past five years, welfare reform in Britain has in many ways moved beyond what has been accomplished in the US. The results, we and our contributors will argue, are worthy of attention as a source of ideas or points of reference for the resumed US debate over welfare and connecting social assistance to work.

Richard Rose has usefully defined a lesson, interpreted in a policy context, as "a program for action based on a program or programs undertaken in another city, state, or nation, or by the same organisation in its own past" (Rose, 1993, p 21). Learning from other jurisdictions is a common and valuable aspect of policy making. The character of such exchanges varies, ranging from, in Rose's terms, simple copying to cases in which observation of initiatives in one location is used as intellectual stimulus for quite different innovation in another (Rose, 1993, p 30). We see such stimulus as the most promising possibility for exchange with Britain, and we would add that exchange occurs at various levels, ranging from the abstract rhetoric/ideology used to motivate change, through the particulars of strategy, to the very concrete details of implementation (Walker and Wiseman, 2001).

Welfare reform in the US has involved a great deal of lesson-sharing across states and between levels of government, and many agencies, both public and private, have defined their involvement in reform in terms related to the generation and exchange of lessons. Just what factors mediate the process and outcome of such exchanges is of considerable intellectual interest. Rose (1993, Chapter Six) discusses the importance of congruity of values, objectives, and structures across exchanging entities; the ease with which existing programme delivery systems can be replaced by newly learned ones; the scale of changes involved, the simplicity of the model of cause and effect underlying policy; and the presence of momentum for change. At least superficially, such considerations have much to say about welfare reform as experienced over the past decade in the United States. The new state systems, built with waivers – Federal inducements for states to innovate in welfare policy – and carried through from Aid to Families with Dependent Children (AFDC) to TANF required only modest change in existing delivery systems, the changes involved were incremental rather than revolutionary, the models motivating the changes were generally simple, and variation across states in values and objectives, never great, seemed to diminish as the momentum for change grew.

Obviously, the leap from Wisconsin to Ohio is shorter in cultural, political, and institutional distance than is the leap from Britain to Ohio or to any other American state. But in thinking about the future of the data catchment for welfare-related policy analysis, the size of the gaps may be less important than whether or not the distances are shrinking. With regard to the subset of British employment policies that address the same constellation of social problems and concerns that feature in welfare reform debates in the US, we contend that the two countries are within hailing distance at many levels of possible lesson exchange, from rhetoric to particulars. This reflects longstanding similarities: notably a preference for market solutions rather than the collective action by social partners that characterises the social democratic model, and welfare states that emphasise poverty relief above social solidarity and cohesion. Over the past decade, the active borrowing of US policy models by British policy makers has reduced the policy divide still further, making Britain's social policy terrain even more accessible to the US policy actor than it was 20 years ago (Peck and Theodore, 1998; Walker, 1999).

The focus here is to use this increased access to stimulate a flow of ideas and benefits of experience back from Britain to the US. This book specifically concerns the potential contribution of British experience to US policy perspectives on the following issues:

• how to engender and sustain political support for providing adequate benefits for those without alternatives;
• how to integrate multiple programmes to promote work;
• how to focus policy on meaningful goals;
• how to link policy evolution to programme experience.

Before offering a brief account of the development of the British policies that address these issues, it is necessary to draw attention to key differences between the US and the UK. These differences help account for ways in which US policies have been adapted and remodelled in Britain. They need to be taken into account when examining the opportunities for making the anticlimax of the TANF reauthorization debate the prologue for a reverse transfer of policy ideas. For convenience, throughout this book, we and our contributors generally use United Kingdom (UK) and Britain interchangeably, although, in fact, the institutions of Northern Ireland differ significantly from those described here.

## The limits to comparability

We begin with size and wealth: Britain is smaller (60 million versus 273 million population) and less well off than the US. Britain's 2000 per capita gross domestic product was $24,500, only 69% of the $35,600 reported for the US (OECD, 2002). (These comparisons are based on the OECD 2000 Purchasing Power Parity estimate of £1=$1.55; unless otherwise indicated, the authors and the other contributors will for convenience use £1=$1.50.) These differences are arguably less important for social policy than is the fact that Britain is a highly centralised, unitary state whereas the federal structure in the US creates a complex web of policy responsibilities that frustrates coherent policy design and implementation and produces variable and sometimes inchoate benefit provision. In Britain, almost all social policies are national in coverage; and job placement services, social assistance, and social security benefits are delivered largely by the local offices of national agencies. Local governments do provide social work and educational services, but such provision is tightly regulated from the centre. Moreover, the parliamentary and electoral systems in Britain give government largely unfettered power to introduce and implement policies without need for major compromise.

Britain conducts its welfare-to-work programmes in a context that includes two important universal benefits that are absent in the US. The country's health service is national and largely free to all comers at the point of use, so ready access to health care is not linked to welfare receipt or eligibility. This is in sharp contrast to the US, where family access to such care depends effectively on TANF eligibility. The provision in Britain of a universal Child Benefit without means testing also lessens the risk of poverty attributable to the presence of children and reduces the disincentives large families create in the US for parents attempting to move from reliance on welfare to support through work.

Both Britain and the US have non-means-tested provision for unemployed and disabled people. Unemployment Insurance (UI) in the US provides weekly benefits as a fraction of weekly earnings up to some state-determined maximum. The benefits are typically paid for up to six months, but extensions are common in locations with exceptional unemployment. There is no automatic link to other welfare systems for families that exhaust their UI claims. In Britain, insurance benefits for unemployment are payable for a maximum of six months depending on a person's contribution record and are integrated with means-tested provision in a single scheme called Jobseeker's Allowance. Many people have their contribution-based benefit 'topped up' with Income-Related Jobseeker's Allowance. In the US, disability benefits are paid to former workers who meet certain standards for employment history but have lost the ability to engage in 'substantial gainful activity' as the result of a physical or mental impairment. In Britain disabled people are variously entitled to a mix of insurance and non-contributory, non-means-tested benefits that provide income support and help meet additional costs associated with disability.

Beyond these benefits, means-tested social assistance is universally available in Britain on the basis of a statutory assessment of resources. In 2000, a single-parent family (in Britain commonly and perhaps more accurately termed a 'lone parent' family) with two children received a basic benefit of £121.30 weekly or about £526 per month, in addition to rent. On average, Housing Benefit added about £258 per month for a total annual income of roughly $1,176. This exceeds the maximum combined TANF and food stamp benefit in all US states except Alaska and Hawaii (where living costs are exceptional), and is comparable to the most generous of state benefits for the subset of TANF households that also receive rent assistance. However, in our judgment the important difference lies not in disparity in amounts but the absence of categorization. In the US, TANF is available only to families with children; adults without children must rely on a combination of other systems. In Britain, almost everyone who is not working 16 or more hours per week and lacks sufficient income is eligible for assistance within two closely aligned programmes, Income-Related Jobseeker's Allowance for those required to seek employment and Income Support for those who are not. The result is that retirement pensioners constitute the largest group of social assistance – welfare – recipients in Britain, followed by disabled people. Unemployed claimants have, until very recently, outnumbered lone parents (Walker with Howard, 2000).

Britain has a proportionately much larger public housing sector than the US. Even after almost twenty years of sales and privatisation, publicly provided units still account for 22% of the housing stock. A further 4% of dwellings are let by social housing organisations. The means-tested Housing Benefit cited in our earlier payments example is available to meet some or all the rent of almost anyone with income below a threshold level, irrespective of employment status. There are also universal means tested rebates, called Council Tax Benefits, for local property taxes.

A final difference to note is that, although disproportionate numbers of unemployed and lone parent claimants are from ethnic minorities, race is almost entirely absent from British debates on welfare. Ethnic minorities account for less than 7% of the UK population.

Tables 1.1 and 1.2 serve as reference aids for later chapters by providing an overview of British social assistance provisions presented from complementary perspectives. Table 1.1 summarises Britain's main social assistance schemes. Striking to the US reader will be the lack of categorical restrictions, with social assistance cash benefits not generally restricted to groups of people with particular characteristics (such as family type) in the way that TANF is primarily targeted toward single parents. (Readers who would like a similarly structured overview of analogous US programmes may refer to Table 2.1 in Chapter Two.) Table 1.2 lists the financial support currently available to various groups of people of working age in Britain and compares them with those available in the US. As the tables indicate, benefit programmes in both countries have categorical variation in work requirements.

## Origins of British welfare policies

A little history will help explain the different patterns of provision for each of the family status groups listed in Table 1.2.

Table 1.1: Major means-tested UK cash and in-kind benefit programmes for non-elderly persons

| Programme | Target Group | Benefit | Activity Requirement | Source of Funds/ Operating Agency | Benefit Expenditures* (£ Billions, FY1999/2000*** unless otherwise noted) | Recipients (in millions, 1998 unless otherwise noted) |
|---|---|---|---|---|---|---|
| Income Support (IS) | Low-income, non-working individuals and families | Cash grant, varying by income, age, family size and age of children, and presence and severity of disability | Lone parents and disabled people have no work requirements. (From 2002 all recipients will be obliged to attend an initial work-focused interview.) Voluntary New Deal welfare-to-work schemes exist for lone parents and on a trial basis for disabled people | Centrally funded<br><br>Benefits Agency | £ 8.41 | 3.8 |
| Working Families' Tax Credit (WFTC) | Low-income workers with child dependents working 16 or more hours each week | Earnings subsidy delivered as a wage supplement by employers or, if so chosen, as a cash benefit by Inland Revenue (the tax agency) to child's (children's) caretaker. Self-employed workers are paid directly by Inland Revenue | Must work 16 hours or more each week | Centrally funded<br><br>Inland Revenue | £ 1.22 | 0.79 |

**Table 1.1: contd.../**

| Programme | Target Group | Benefit | Activity Requirement | Source of Funds/ Operating Agency | Benefit Expenditures* (£ Billions, FY1999/2000** unless otherwise noted) | Recipients (in millions, 1998 unless otherwise noted) |
|---|---|---|---|---|---|---|
| Jobseeker's Allowance (JSA) | Low-income unemployed workers and their families | Cash grant, varying by family size, contribution record, and/ or income | Unemployed adult recipients are required to seek and be available for work. People aged 18-24 unemployed for 6 months and others unemployed for two years are required to engage in New Deal welfare-to-work programmes | Centrally funded | Contribution based: £ 0.52 | Contribution based only: 0.187 |
| | | Depending on their contribution record, recipients receive contribution-based or an income-based JSA or both | | Benefits Agency and Employment Service | Income based: £ 2.93 | Income based: 1.2 |
| Social Fund | Very needy persons receiving certain means-tested benefits | Interest-free loans and, in special circumstances, grants. Allocations made by local Benefits Agency offices from a cash limited fund | As main programme | Centrally funded Benefits Agency | £ 0.205 | 2.01 million crisis and budgeting loans made in FY1999/ 2000 |
| Housing Benefit | Needy persons | Cash grant, varying by family size, income, and rent. (Received as a rent rebate by tenants in public housing) | As for JSA if unemployed, otherwise, none | Centrally funded Local authorities | £ 11.49 | 2.7 |
| Council Tax Benefit | Needy persons | Tax rebate, varying by family size, income, and tax obligation | As for JSA if unemployed, otherwise, none | Centrally funded Local authorities | £ 2.58 | 5.3 |

**Table 1.1: contd.../**

| Programme | Target Group | Benefit | Activity Requirement | Source of Funds/ Operating Agency | Benefit Expenditures* (£ Billions, FY1999/ 2000** unless otherwise noted) | Recipients (in millions, 1998 unless otherwise noted) |
|---|---|---|---|---|---|---|
| Free School Meals | Children aged 0-16 in families receiving Income Support or income-based Jobseeker's Allowance and 17- and 18-year-olds receiving these benefits in their own right | Vouchers | None | Funded by local authorities with central government assistance | Local authorities | Data not available |
| **Related programmes without means tests** | | | | | | |
| Incapacity Benefit | Blind, and otherwise disabled persons incapable of work who have (or have been credited with) adequate contributions | Three levels of cash grant, increasing in value with time on benefit | None as person has to be assessed incapable of work. Voluntary New Deal welfare-to-work scheme is being trialed and is to be extended nationally | Centrally funded<br><br>Benefits Agency | £ 7.03 | 2.3 |

**Table 1.1: contd.../**

| Programme | Target Group | Benefit | Activity Requirement | Source of Funds/ Operating Agency | Benefit Expenditures* (£ Billions, FY1999/ 2000** unless otherwise noted) | Recipients (in millions, 1998 unless otherwise noted) |
|---|---|---|---|---|---|---|
| **Child Benefit** | All children aged 0-16 and 17- and 18-year-olds in full time education | Means tested cash grant varying by birth order (more for first or eldest child) | None | Centrally funded Benefits Agency | £ 8.29 | 12.6 |

*Note:* Universal healthcare is provided free at point of use

* OECD purchasing power parity for 2000; £1=$1.55 (OECD, 2002).

** Since the British fiscal year begins April 5; FY1999/2000 lies primarily in calendar 1999.

*Sources:* DSS (2000b), Walker and Howard (2000)

Table 1.2: Benefit packages and work obligations, US and UK (Adults without disabilities)

| Family status | | Means-tested Benefits available if not employed | Work obligation | Means-tested Benefits available if employed | Notes |
|---|---|---|---|---|---|
| **Lone Parents** | UK | Income Support<br>Housing Benefit<br>Council Tax Benefit | Voluntary access to New Deal for Lone Parents programme of support for movement to work<br><br>Attendance at initial work-focused interview to become compulsory in 2002 | Working Families' Tax Credit (includes Child Care Tax Credit)<br>Housing benefit<br>Council tax benefit | Healthcare is free at point of use<br><br>Interest free loans are available to recipients of Income Support from the Social Fund, as are grants for a restricted set of circumstances |
| | US | Temporary Assistance for Needy Families (TANF)<br>Food stamps (FS)<br>Medicaid | TANF obligation varies by state. All states can require participation in work activities for virtually all recipients. Actual activity rates are much lower<br><br>FS applicants or recipients must register for work with employment service; can be required to participate in employment and training programmes | Earned Income Tax Credit (EITC)<br>TANF (access varies by state; generally time-limited)<br>Food stamps | Federal contribution to TANF has 5-year time limit; states have option for reduced or greater limit. TANF benefits are not entitlements, but most states assure access |

**Table 1.2: contd.../**

| Family status | | Means-tested Benefits available if not employed | Work obligation | Means-tested Benefits available if employed | Notes |
|---|---|---|---|---|---|
| **Parent in Two-Parent Family** | UK | Income Support<br><br>Jobseeker's Allowance (JSA)<br><br>Housing Benefit<br><br>Council Tax benefits | Recipients of all benefits are likely also to be in receipt of JSA unless disabled (when no work obligations apply)<br><br>JSA is conditional on:<br><br>Being available for and actively seeking work<br><br>Signing and adhering to a Jobseeker's Agreement (checked every two weeks)<br><br>Attendance at New Deal for 18- to 24-year-olds if JSA recipient for 6 months<br><br>Attendance at New Deal for Long-Term Unemployed for persons aged 25 or more if JSA recipient for 18 months | Working Families' Tax Credit (includes Child Care Tax Credit)<br><br>Housing Benefit<br><br>Council Tax benefit | Healthcare and Social Fund Access same as for Lone Parents |
| | US | Temporary Assistance for Needy Families (most states)<br><br>Food stamps<br><br>Medicaid | TANF obligation varies by state. Stringency and incidence of obligations much greater for two-parent than for single-parent families | Earned Income Tax Credit<br><br>Food stamps<br><br>TANF (some states; may be time-limited) | Federal contribution to TANF has 5-year time limit; states have option to reduce or raise limit |

**Table 1.2: contd.../**

| Family status | | Means-tested Benefits available if not employed | Work obligation | Means-tested Benefits available if employed | Notes |
|---|---|---|---|---|---|
| **Adult without Child Depend- ents** | UK | Income Support<br>Jobseeker's Allowance<br>Housing Benefit<br>Council Tax benefits | Same as for "Parent in two-parent family" except after 6 months if aged 18-24 and partner of claimant is not working<br><br>Attendance of partner at New Deal for Partners | Housing Benefit<br>Council Tax benefit | Healthcare access same as for all other citizens |
| | US | General assistance (GA)(some states)<br>Food stamps | State GA programmes, where available, typically have work requirements.<br><br>Able-bodied adults age 18-50 without dependents (ABAWDs) lose FS eligibility after three months if not working or active in employment and training programmes for at least 20 hours per week | Food stamps<br>EITC | No national public health benefit |

*Sources:* For US, principally Committee on Ways and Means (2000).

For UK, miscellaneous documents of Department of Social Security (2000a).

British social assistance evolved as a response to mass unemployment rather than to the needs of dependent children in one-parent households (Beveridge, 1909). Labour exchanges and unemployment insurance were introduced in 1909 and 1911, respectively; exchanges came first to ensure that jobsearch obligations could be adequately policed (Price, 2000). Mass unemployment in the aftermath of the First World War led to the introduction of what was intended to be a temporary form of unemployment assistance – the Dole – for those workers who had exhausted any entitlement to insurance benefit. Despite this original intent, much of the combination of unemployment insurance and means-tested residual benefit remains in place, although the details have been substantially modified by reforms made at the end of the Second World War, in response to recommendations of the Committee on Social Insurance and Allied Services (generally called the Beveridge report, after its chair, Sir William Beveridge), and by subsequent developments (Beveridge, 1942). It was fear that the US might follow a similar trajectory that kept unemployment insurance and relief separate in the Roosevelt era (Handler and Hasenfeld, 1991).

The Beveridge reforms extended unemployment insurance to most full-time workers and consolidated social assistance provisions into a single National Assistance scheme covering all adults without work and adequate income. The labour exchanges retained responsibility for payment of unemployment insurance claims, but did so on an agency basis for the new Ministry of National Insurance. The Beveridge report recommended fixing insurance benefits at subsistence level rather than on the basis of prior earnings. The consequences of this (largely inadvertent) policy choice were profound, for in so doing Beveridge ensured that Britain would rely heavily on means testing and not follow the social insurance route taken by social democratic countries in continental Europe. One result is that the policy debate about welfare reform in Britain is commonly couched in terms of means-tested benefits, as it is in the US, although as already noted the main beneficiaries are not the same.

As in the US before the advent of the Work Incentive Program in 1967, in Britain employment and social assistance policy developed along separate tracks for much of the post-Second World War era. In 1974 benefit administration was split from job placement, a change that underscored the passive nature of the benefits system. Until well into the 1980s, British employment policy was to tackle mass unemployment by limiting labour supply, and diverting older workers into de facto retirement and young people into training and work experience schemes. Thereafter, under a Thatcher government much influenced by monetarist economics and somewhat in awe of US economic achievements, UK employment policy shifted towards deregulation and increasing labour market flexibility. Direct taxation was reduced, in-work benefits – wage subsidies – such as the means-tested Family Credit were extended and increased, the out-of-work benefit level was pegged to enhance work incentives, and jobsearch obligations were rigorously enforced. The 1986 introduction of Restart – regular interviews for unemployed claimants supported by threat of benefit sanction – was credited by the operating agency with increasing the annual outflow from unemployment by 8.5% (UK Department of Employment, 1986).

The pace of policy development quickened in the 1990s and broadened in scope, as concern about benefit dependency (a term first used by UK government ministers in 1987) and the possible growth of an underclass increased. The direct and indirect role of US ideas in feeding these concerns is well documented. The thought of Charles Murray and Lawrence Mead was particularly influential, published through prominent right-of-centre think tanks in Britain, such as the Institute of Economic Affairs and the Adam Smith Institute. The US-inspired *Jobs study* published by the OECD in 1994 further broadened political support for stimulating labour market flexibility and tackling poverty by employment-led reforms (OECD, 1994).

In 1996, job-placement and benefit payment were reunited by the Conservative government with the creation of a new programme, Jobseeker's Allowance, that made benefit receipt conditional on signing a contract specifying the steps claimants are expected to take to find work. It also combined unemployment insurance and assistance benefits into a single scheme. In the same year, the first British 'workfare' scheme (Project Work) was piloted for 18- to 24-year-olds unemployed for two or more years. Growing fear that rising claims for Invalidity Benefit (now called Incapacity Benefit) – the approximate equivalent of US Disability Insurance – were masking unemployment and reflected increased benefit dependency led in early 1997 to tightened eligibility requirements and a review of all existing cases.

The reappraisal of the policy stance towards lone parents occurred a little earlier than that relating to disabled people. Once again the debate resonated with US ideas and policies (Walker with Howard, 2000). Prior to the mid-1980s, policy was a constrained response to evidence of severe and widespread poverty among lone parents. Non-working lone parents were entitled to receive National Assistance, and when later versions of the programme (currently called Income Support) were remodelled in 1980 and 1987, lone parents received extra benefit. Also, from 1977 to 1999 a small non-means-tested addition to Child Benefit was available that benefited lone parents in work. By the early 1990s, however, a 50% increase in the number of lone parents, a nine-point fall in the percentage in paid work, and high levels of non-payment of child support (called maintenance in the UK) by absent parents had helped change the parameters of the policy debate. The tenor of the debate became much more shrill – with Charles Murray's journalistic predictions of a growing British underclass fed by the un-socialised offspring of lone mothers according well with Mrs Thatcher's moral indignation and fervent espousal of 'traditional family values' (Murray, 1990; Land and Lewis, 1998).

Following reviews of US and also Australian child support policy, a new system of support collection from non-custodial parents was established in 1993, and a new Child Support Agency (CSA) was created to carry it out. Collections were initially restricted to absent parents of children receiving social assistance. Establishing the CSA to collect these payments was arguably the most ambitious piece of social engineering introduced into the UK since the aftermath of the Second World War. The new policy faced vocal opposition from many quarters, and its implementation proved chaotic. Measures were also introduced to create financial incentives to encourage lone parents to take jobs. Until 1999, benefits paid for households with earnings mostly came through the Family Credit programme and its predecessor, Family Income Supplement. Both programmes included a substantial marginal disregard of earnings in benefit computation (which Income Support has never done) that acted essentially as an earnings subsidy. Families' eligibility for Income Support or Family Credit depended on hours worked. Originally the threshold for transferring to Family Income Supplement was 30 hours; this was reduced to 24 hours with the introduction of Family Credit in 1988 and then to 16 hours in 1992. In addition, the Government introduced into the calculation of Family Credit entitlement a partial disregard of child support (maintenance) received from non-custodial parents.

The proportion of lone parents employed increased from 39% to 44% between 1993 and 1998. However, despite the shrillness of the policy debate, lone parents retained much public sympathy, and there was little vocal support for making work compulsory. The public seemed to accept the profound changes in gender and sexual relations, the availability of divorce, and the rise in cohabitation that contributed to the growth in lone parenthood, and were divided as to the wisdom of creating a generation of latchkey children through the imposition of work requirements.

In sum, despite important differences, commonalities between the US and the UK in the patterns of welfare provision were already well established before the Labour government was elected in 1997: the low-tax, deregulated economy and labour market; the residualist nature of welfare; the heavy reliance on means testing and policy focus on poverty relief rather than the maintenance of living standards; the acceptance of proactive welfare and the importance of employment as a route out of poverty; and the emphasis on obligations and personal responsibility. Moreover, these similarities did not arise by accident or as an independent response to common problems. Rather, there was a substantial importing of both ideas and strategy, with Britain adapting and making their own policies that had their origins in the US.

## New Labour

The reforms of the 1997 Labour government constitute an extension of, rather than a break with, the policy developments of the previous fifteen years. Moreover, the influence of US policy thinking at all levels, from rhetoric and strategy to implementation, has been even more marked. As described by Mike Brewer and Paul Gregg in Chapter Four, the unique contribution of the Labour government has been to elucidate the strategic objectives of welfare policy and to present them in positive, integrative terms rather than in negative and polarizing ones. Welfare reform is recognised to be less important in itself than as one interrelated element in a coordinated policy response to social and economic change. Reform is part of modernizing government and the labour market to equip individuals and society better to succeed in an increasingly open and global economy.

New Labour's approach is well illustrated with reference to four packages of policies that have grabbed the headlines. The first two – 'welfare-to-work' and 'making work pay' – sound familiar to US ears, the second pair – 'tackling social exclusion' and 'ending child poverty' – much less so.

In 1997 a British government was elected for the first time in 50 years on a manifesto promoting welfare reform (echoing the Clinton election promise to "end welfare as we know it"). The centrepiece of the Labour government's welfare-to-work agenda was a commitment to return 250,000 young people back to work within the tenure of the first parliament. Although aimed at the young unemployed, the influence of US thinking is clearly evident in the structure of the flagship programme, New Deal for Young People, described in detail by Bruce Stafford in Chapter Six. It comprises a period of active jobsearch (Gateway) followed by a suite of Options, graded according to distance from labour market readiness and a Follow-Through phase for those people who have failed to secure employment. The options – subsidized work, education and training, voluntary and environmental work, and self-employment bear a striking resemblance to those offered under Wisconsin's 'Wisconsin Works' (W-2) scheme. It is no coincidence that UK ministers, civil servants, and Members of Parliament all visited that state in 1997/98. New Deal for Young People is a clear adaptation of a US policy, simply changing the target group and incorporating the objective of raising the minimum threshold of accredited training.

Ironically, given that young people are largely excluded from the US welfare system, even this focus on young people can be traced to US influences. HM Treasury papers reference US research documenting the link between youth unemployment and crime (Freeman, 1996; Treasury, 1997), and in his first set-piece speech after assuming power, Prime Minister Tony Blair spoke the language of the underclass debate:

> For a generation of young men, little has come to replace the third of all manufacturing jobs that have been lost. For part of a generation of young women early pregnancies and the absence of a reliable father almost guarantee a life of poverty. (Blair, 1997)

The difference in policy approach was that Britain mandated employment for men before mandating it for lone mothers. Moreover, while compulsory involvement in New Deal was extended rapidly, the next targets were, again, not lone parents but the long-term unemployed and, later, the partners of the unemployed. Involvement of lone parents and disabled people was initially on an entirely voluntary basis, with an emphasis on work-oriented advice rather than active work experience. This reflects the more inclusive nature of British social policy and public opinion. The New Deal family of welfare-to-work schemes is summarised in Table 1.3.

The 'making work pay' agenda was also generalised in its target, but again was influenced by US thinking. Key elements included the introduction of a minimum wage, set at a level informed by US experience, and the conversion of Family Credit into a positive tax credit, Working Families' Tax Credit (WFTC), available to all low income families with a member in paid work for more than 16 hours each week. The design of Working Families' Tax Credit is a hybrid. Like Family Credit, the WFTC is paid fortnightly and includes an option for routing payment to the principal caretaker for the wage earners' children. But like the US Earned Income Credit, the main US policy of comparison in the debate about implementation, the WFTC is assessed in conjunction with wage payment and is the province of the tax and not the benefits agency (Walker and Wiseman, 1997).

Labour's commitment to tackle social exclusion reflects European influences on British policy learning. However, Labour has used the phrase as shorthand for multiple deprivations but with an emphasis on the processes that generate deprivations rather than, as is common elsewhere in Europe, on the immediate circumstances of individuals and families. In so doing, Labour has sought to shift action and expenditure away from dealing with immediate problems and more to preventing problems in the future. The underlying analysis identified a number of facets to the issue: lack of opportunities to work and to acquire education and skills; childhood deprivation; disrupted families; barriers to older people living active, fulfilling and healthy lives; inequalities in health; poor housing, poor neighbourhoods, and crime. It also recognised that many living on and within the margins of poverty had not benefited from economic growth. Instead, they had often been negatively affected by economic and social change, cycles of economic boom and bust, failure of the education system, inequitable delivery of health care, poor housing design, and top-down models of policy making.

Labour's approach to date has been on three tracks. First, cross-departmental policy institutions and project teams have been established to develop policy approaches to address specific forms or manifestations of social exclusion: rough-sleeping, truancy and exclusions from school, teenage pregnancy, and neighbourhood decay. Second, area-based strategies have been developed that focus resources on local communities, seeking to coordinate the activities of agencies and to engage the local populace in the process of reform. The names given to these initiatives – Sure Start (loosely modelled on the US Head Start), Health Action Zones, Employment Zones, Education Zones, New Deal for Communities, and Single Regeneration Budget – signal different policy emphases within a common approach of 'joining up' policy planning and service delivery. Third, national policy strategies have been put in place to enhance opportunities in the short, medium, and longer term. Central to this approach are the creation of a framework for macroeconomic stability and growth and promotion of a flexible and adaptable labour market in which

**Table 1.3: New Deal 'welfare-to-work' programmes in Britain**

| Target Group | Required duration of worklessness for eligibility | Year 2000 Funding (£ millions[a]) | Compulsion | Content | Remuneration | Subsidy to Employer[b] | Implementation |
|---|---|---|---|---|---|---|---|
| **Young people aged 18-24** | More than 6 months | £2,620 | Yes | *Gateway:* Intensive help, advice, and guidance *Options:* Subsidized employment Voluntary work Environmental Task Force Self-employment Full-time education/ training *Follow-through:* Renewed intensive help | Rate for job<br><br>All pay wage or an allowance equal to JSA plus £15.83/ week Allowance equivalent to JSA | £60/wk for 6 months Training contribution of £750 | Pathfinder areas: January 1998 Nationwide: April 1998 All options to include accredited training of 1 day/ week |
| **Long-term unemployed aged 25+** | More than 2 years | £450 | Yes | *Gateway:* As above *Options:* Subsidized employment Full-time education/Training *Follow-through:* As above | Rate for job Allowance equivalent to JSA | £75/wk for 6 months | June 1998 |

**Table 1.3: contd.../**

| Target Group | Required duration of worklessness for eligibility | Year 2000 Funding (£ millions[a]) | Compulsion | Content | Remuneration | Subsidy to Employer[b] | Implementation |
|---|---|---|---|---|---|---|---|
| **Partners of the unem- ployed** | Duration of partner's unemploy- ment | £60 | Yes for childless couples aged 18-24; otherwise voluntary | Similar to New Deals for young people and long-term unem- ployed above, but requires joint application | As for young people aged 18-24 | As for young people aged 8-24 | April 1999 as a voluntary initiative; compulsory in early 2001 |
| **Lone parents** | No restriction by duration | £190 | No | Advice Access to programmes Follow-up | Not applicable | Not applicable | Pilots: July 1997 Nationwide: October 1999 |
| **People with disabilities** | 28 weeks of benefit receipt on grounds of incapacity | £200 | No | Test schemes | Not applicable | Not applicable | Pilots: October 1998; variant nationwide July 2001 |

*Notes:*

[a] 2000 OECD purchasing power parity: £1 = $1.55

[b] Participants who do not receive a wage continue to receive an allowance equal to the Jobseeker's Allowance. Travel grants may be made.

*Source:* Authors' construction

both firms and employees are enabled to respond effectively to structural change. These are complemented by investment in education and skills to enable people to learn through life and remain employable as the market changes, and by measures such as the national minimum wage and a tax and benefit system that promotes work incentives. By keeping people in touch with work in the short run, raising incomes, and increasing opportunity, the goal is to break the intergenerational transfer of disadvantage. Whether these measures are on a scale large enough, whether the institutions of government can be engaged to work together in a way that is both cumulative and long term, whether the positive effects anticipated from the reforms on the macroeconomy in fact occur, or whether the management of the economy continues to be (seen to be) effective are still open to doubt. Nevertheless, the coherence of Labour's policy is impressive and in many senses admirable.

The explicit commitment to eradicate child poverty in twenty years did not emerge until February 1999, although it was foreshadowed by changes in the family size increment in out-of-work means-tested benefits and by increases in the universal Child Benefit (Blair, 1999). Prime Minister Blair coupled announcement of the new goal with both the modernization agenda and a goal to make welfare popular. Equally, though, it was a response to the high and growing level of child poverty (a phenomenon that until recently the UK has almost uniquely shared with the US among advanced OECD countries; See UNICEF, 2000), and new evidence that childhood deprivation had long-term implications for life course development. While President Clinton referred to ending child poverty as a "pledge to 21st-century America" in his January, 2000 State of the Union speech, Blair made the objective specific: end child poverty in 20 years. Subsequent government publications have reiterated and refined this pledge to include intermediate objectives (Department of Social Security, 2000a). The bedrock of the strategy relies on the success of the welfare-to-work and making work pay policies. But it also comprises additional elements to boost family incomes – higher benefit rates and increased collection of child support from absent parents – and measures to reduce the scarring effect of childhood deprivation – Educational Maintenance Allowance to encourage over-16s to stay in school, new career-oriented advice and support schemes, and a Children's Fund to underwrite local anti-child-poverty initiatives.

## The rest of the book

UK governments have been borrowing US ideas on welfare reform for some time. Now, however, the commitment of the current Labour administration to fundamental reform as part of its modernization agenda offers US policy analysts and policy makers an expanded perspective on common problems of programme design and management. Chapter Two, by Michael Wiseman, establishes the lookout point for this survey: welfare as Americans now have it. One benefit of looking at Britain is that so doing will force a wider perspective. Welfare, in the US sense, refers to means-tested cash assistance or its equivalent, and often to just one programme: Temporary Assistance for Needy Families (TANF), which is received mostly by single parents. The 2002 US welfare reform debate reached beyond TANF only in including the Food Stamp Program, which was addressed in the 2002 Farm Bill. To match the span of the discussion of British policy, Chapter Two also takes account of Supplemental Security Income, the Earned Income Credit (EIC), and the myriad general assistance programmes operated by states or local governments to provide income of last resort to those not qualifying for other benefits. Chapter Two argues that the impact of TANF reform on both families and institutions has been substantially overstated, and that reauthorisation is likely to leave many key problems unaddressed. Among these problems are: provision of funding, integration of multiple programmes, assessing programme performance assessment, and building systems for translating experience into useful management information. But the transcending issue is the 'vision thing': what sort of social assistance system should the United States seek to attain?

Chapter Three, by Alan Deacon, demonstrates that there is enough commonality at the level of ideology and strategy – agreement as to the purpose of reform, the centrality of paid work, and the enforcement of obligations – for the UK to have successfully adopted many features of the US system: proactive policy, welfare-to-work, work-first, casework, tax-based earnings subsidies, a minimum wage, alliances with business, public–private partnerships, one stop service delivery and so on. Thus the congruity of values, objectives, and structures cited by Rose (1993) as a catalyst for lesson exchange seems to be growing.

The UK experience is made particularly instructive because, while British policy makers have clearly drawn from American experience, they have shaped the insights gained in the US to serve a much more ambitious agenda. This agenda addresses issues of labour market efficiency and international competitiveness and commits the UK to enhancing individual opportunity and eradicating child poverty in 20 years. Deacon argues that despite very real differences in administrative structures and policy details, and equally profound cultural differences, the shared understanding at the level of objectives and policy instruments means that both what Labour has set out to achieve and its way of accomplishing its goals are pregnant with possibilities for the US.

Chapter Four, by Mike Brewer and Paul Gregg, documents the strategic vision underlying Labour's reforms: a response to increased earnings inequality, lower income mobility, more workless households, rising lifetime inequality, escalating child poverty, and evidence of links between childhood deprivation and lifetime achievement. Chapter Four describes the UK battle plan on three fronts: raising direct financial support for children, reducing the number of children in non-working households, and lowering the incidence and severity of scarring factors in childhood. It synthesises evaluative evidence on the success or otherwise of those programmes and shows how the strategic agenda is being updated and reshaped in light of achievements so far. If US administrations have intended to achieve a once and for all reform, it is clear that New Labour has embarked on a long-term incremental project in which learning from experience is a key component.

Chapter Five, by Jane Millar, focuses on lone parents – notably the welfare-to-work scheme New Deal for Lone Parents and reforms of the childcare and child support systems. Given that welfare in the US is almost synonymous with policies aimed at single mothers, this is the chapter to which most American readers may turn first. They will learn that, in the British context of universal means-tested provision, lone parents do not dominate the policy reform debate. However, Britain has begun to wrestle with the same issues that have exercised the US debate: balancing mothers' obligations at home and at work, providing quality childcare, sustaining employment once obtained, and enforcing the financial obligations of absent parents. To date Labour's welfare-to-work reforms have been voluntary, but concerns about low uptake are leading to increased obligation. Even so, the impact of voluntary schemes on welfare roles and employment may have been comparable with pre-PRWORA demonstrations in the US, although the reliability of effect assessments is, as Millar indicates, suspect.

Chapter Six, by Bruce Stafford, demonstrates just how much further it is possible to extend proactive work-based policies once one jettisons the narrow US conception of welfare. The two New Deal programmes he describes and evaluates are, respectively, targeted on young unemployed claimants and recipients of social insurance incapacity benefits. The former is the flagship of Labour's welfare-to-work schemes and reflects recognition of the disadvantaged position of unskilled young workers, the lifetime scarring effects of limited labour market attachment, and possible links with crime and out-of-wedlock births. It is mandatory and, as noted above, closely modelled on US programmes for lone parents. New Deal for Disabled People addresses the same rapid increase in the number of working age people claiming incapacity benefits that has occurred in the US. It challenges the presumption of incapacity as a permanent and complete bar to employment and begins to extend work obligations into the social insurance system. Chapter Six also compares and contrasts the design and implementation of the two programmes and asks whether the differences are a logical and necessary consequence of the target groups and varied institutional legacies.

Our afterward in Chapter Seven reviews the book's contributions and returns to the issue of where in this agenda the most promising opportunities for collaboration and learning lie. Promise depends on where the US system is heading, a prospect befogged by the debate over reauthorisation. We close with a summary of features that a new American welfare reform initiative inspired by British accomplishments might have. Of course, this vision differs from the system that is emerging in Britain. But like the New Labour programme and in contrast to reform as Americans have come to know it, our vision has both direction and ambition.

## References

Beveridge, W. (1942) *Social insurance and allied services* (Beveridge Report), Cmd 6404, London: HMSO.

Beveridge, W. (1909) *Unemployment: A problem of industry*, London: Longmans Green.

Blair, T. (1997) 'The will to win', Speech on the Aylesbury Estate, Southwark, 2 June.

Blair, T. (1999) 'Beveridge revisited: A welfare state for the 21st century', in R. Walker (ed) *Ending child poverty: Popular welfare for the 21st century?*, Bristol: The Policy Press, pp 7-18.

Blank, R. and Haskins, R. (eds) (2001) *The new world of welfare*, Washington, DC: Brookings Institution Press.

Committee on Ways and Means (2000) *2000 Green book: Background material and data on programs within the jurisdiction of the Committee on Ways and Means*, Washington, DC: United States House of Representatives.

DoE (Department of Employment) (1986) 'Evaluation report of restart pilots', Unpublished DoE file 11/RP 366/86.

DSS (Department of Social Security) (2000a) *Opportunity for all – Second annual report 2000*, Cm 4865, London: The Stationery Office.

DSS (2000b) *The changing welfare state: Social security spending*, London: DSS.

Freeman, R. (1996) 'Why do so many young American men commit crimes, and what do we do about it?', *Journal of Economic Perspectives*, vol 10, no 1, pp 25-42.

Handler, J.F. and Hasenfeld, Y. (1991) *The moral construction of poverty: Welfare reform in America*, Newbury Park: Sage Publications.

HM Treasury (1997) *Employment opportunity in a changing labour market: The modernization of Britain's tax and benefit system*, no 1, London: HM Treasury.

Land, H. and Lewis, J. (1998) *The emergence of lone motherhood as a problem in twentieth-century Britain*, London: London School of Economics and Political Science.

Murray, C. (1990) 'Underclass', *Sunday Times Magazine*, 26 November 1989, reprinted in C. Murray, *The emerging British underclass*, London: Institute of Economic Affairs.

OECD (Organisation for Economic Co-operation and Development) (1994) *The jobs study: Facts, analysis, strategy*, Paris: OECD.

OECD (2002) *Main economic indicators*, Paris: OECD.

Peck, J. and Theodore, N. (1998) 'The limits of policy transfer: Innovation and emulation in welfare to work', Paper presented to APPAM Twentieth Research Conference. New York, October.

Price, D. (2000) *Office of hope: A history of the Employment Service*, London: Policy Studies Institute.

Rose, R. (1993) *Lesson-drawing in public policy: A guide to learning across time and space*, Chatham, NJ: Chatham House Publishers, Inc.

UNICEF (2000) *A league table of child poverty in rich nations*, Florence: UNICEF, Innocenti Research Centre, International Child Development Centre.

Walker, R. (1999) 'The Americanisation of British welfare: a case study of policy transfer', *International Journal of Health Studies*, vol 29, no 4, pp 679-97.

Walker, R. with Howard, M. (2000) *The making of a welfare class? Benefit receipt in Britain*, Bristol: The Policy Press.

Walker, R. and Wiseman, M. (1997) 'The possibility of a British Earned Income Tax Credit', *Fiscal Studies,* vol 18, no 4, pp 401-25.

Walker, R. and Wiseman, M. (2001) *Looping back and joining up: Britain's New Deal and the next round of US welfare reform*, Institute for Research on Poverty Discussion Paper 1223-01, Madison, WI: IRP.

# TWO

# Welfare in the United States

*Michael Wiseman*

The Personal Responsibility and Work Opportunity Reconciliation Act of 1996 (PRWORA) ended 'welfare as we knew it', replacing Aid to Families with Dependent Children (AFDC) with Temporary Assistance for Needy Families (TANF). PRWORA did not end the debate on welfare; indeed the requirement that TANF be reauthorised by 30th September 2002 intensified it. This chapter reviews the American social assistance system, its recent history, the changes brought about by PRWORA, and the debate over reauthorisation. What was missing from that debate was a sense of what Americans want the experience of social assistance to be and what changes in organisation might move the reality closer to the political ideal. British experience, Chapter Seven will suggest, has much to offer on both fronts. Like other contributions in this book, this analysis concentrates on policy for persons of working age, their families, and their children.

## The system

The United States is a residual welfare state in which most income support is means tested and only the state pension (Social Security) system for older people and the associated national health insurance programme (Medicare) are genuinely universal. What is provided for poor and near-poor households is constructed from a number of building blocks – components that are administered by various national, state, and local agencies. The result is that assistance available to poor people and the terms under which such assistance may be obtained depend in part upon where such people live and very much on age and family circumstance.

### Major means-tested programmes

A recent Congressional Research Service (CRS) study counted 84 means-tested antipoverty programmes, ranging from Medicaid to assistance with home weatherproofing.[1] Seven of these programmes – Temporary Assistance for Needy Families, the Food Stamp Program, the Earned Income Tax Credit, general assistance, Supplemental Security Income, housing assistance, and Medicaid/children's health insurance – are particularly pertinent to comparison with British social assistance. These programmes are summarised in Table 2.1.

For each the responsible national agency, target group, and benefit are listed as well as the source of funds. Much recent reform in the US has been about linking benefits to recipient obligations, and these obligations generally involve work or preparation for work. The table identifies this work connection where present. A sense of scale is provided both by funding and by number of recipients.

These programmes differ in a number of ways, including the nature of assistance provided and the group (focal unit) for which means are tested. Four of the seven programmes provide general cash assistance, and three provide benefit tied to specific purchases: food for food stamps, shelter for housing assistance, and health care for Medicaid. The focal unit for the Earned Income Tax Credit (EITC) is the taxpayer and associated dependants on whose behalf federal taxes are paid and the EITC is returned. For the Food Stamp Program the unit is the household sharing cooking facilities. For TANF it is needy children and their parents, and so on. Benefits from the programmes is listed in Table 2.1 are not confined to those who meet the federal poverty standard, but most of the benefits listed go to families with incomes less than twice this level.

These seven programmes accounted for 40% of all national outlays for low-income assistance in federal fiscal year (FY) 2000. (The federal fiscal year begins in October of the preceding calendar year and ends in September.) The lion's share of the remainder was for medical care for groups other than low-income families with children. The total federal budget for FY2000 was $1.8 trillion, so everything in the table amounts to about 7% of federal outlays. Total outlays for all means-tested benefits equalled 4.1% of gross domestic product (GDP) (Burke, 2001, p 1).

## Benefit and family category

The implications of Table 2.1 are better illustrated by translating what one sees in the table into what recipients experience on the ground. Table 1.2 in the previous chapter outlines benefits available to adults in various situations. Consider a needy lone parent. For such a person the core US system generally works like this: a single mother seeking assistance goes to the local office of the state social services agency. She provides information on her income and assets and, if she is not receiving child support from the father of her children, she is required to provide information necessary for establishing a court order for such payments. Her eligibility for aid is assessed by the agency. She may be required to seek work during the period over which her application is processed, and efforts may be made to 'divert' her from benefit receipt, if this can be accomplished by employment or by meeting her immediate needs in other ways. If her need is acute, she will qualify for an emergency allocation of food stamps and, possibly, other types of emergency assistance. If she meets the various eligibility criteria, she receives a monthly TANF cash grant and an electronic benefits transfer card that can be used when purchasing food. In all states the food stamp allocation will vary by family size; in most states the TANF grant does as well.

**Table 2.1: Major means-tested US cash and in-kind benefit programmes for non-elderly persons, 2000**

| Programme/ [Agency] | Focal Unit | Benefit | Activity Requirement | Source of Funds | Expenditures (in billions of dollars; for FY2000 unless otherwise noted) | | Recipients (in millions, 2000 unless otherwise noted) |
|---|---|---|---|---|---|---|---|
| | | | | | Federal | State | |
| Earned Income Tax Credit (EITC)/ [Department of the Treasury] | Low-income workers with child dependants; a small benefit is available for workers aged 25-64 who do not have children | Earnings subsidy delivered as reduction in tax liability or, at very low earnings, as cash payment | Must have earnings | Uniform benefit federally funded; 10 states supplement | 32.3 (Made in FY2000 for calendar year 1999) | not available | 19.4 (Number of families with children) |
| Temporary Assistance for Needy Families (TANF)/ [Department of Health and Human Services] | Low-income families with children | Cash grant, varying by family size, location, and income | With some exceptions, adults are required to participate in work or work-related training activities | Federal block grant to states, plus state contribution | 6.9 (Cash benefits only) | 7.6 | 2.2 (Average monthly caseload) |
| Food Stamp Program (FSP)/ [Department of Agriculture] | Low-income households | Electronic debit cards restricted to use for food purchase (and in some instances, cash); amounts vary by household size | With some exceptions, unemployed adult recipients are required to seek work | Federal government pays all benefit costs, half of local administration costs | 15.0 (Total amount of benefits provided, all recipients, including elderly) | 1.1 (State-funded supplements for legal immigrants) | 7.3 (Number of households, all ages) |

**Table 2.1: contd.../**

| Programme/ [Agency] | Focal Unit | Benefit | Activity Requirement | Source of Funds | Expenditures (in billions of dollars; for FY2000 unless otherwise noted) | | Recipients (in millions, 2000 unless otherwise noted) |
|---|---|---|---|---|---|---|---|
| | | | | | **Federal** | **State** | |
| General Assistance (GA) | Very needy persons ineligible for TANF or SSI; not universally available | Varies by state | Varies by state; work requirements common | State and local funds; no federal contribution | None | 2.6 | 0.6 (Average monthly caseload) |
| Supplemental Security Income (SSI)/ [Social Security Administration] | Needy aged, blind, and disabled persons; data here are for non-elderly | Uniform national cash grant, with supplementation in some states | None | Uniform benefit federally funded and administered; state supplements funded by states | 25.7 (Amount spent on cash benefits for non-elderly) | 2.9 | 4.6 (85 thousand children) |
| Public Housing and Rent Subsidies/ [Department of Housing and Urban Development] | Low-income persons; data here are for families with children | Covers share of rental costs | None | Federal funds; some states support similar activities | 14.9 | N.A. | 4.7 |
| Medicaid and State Children's Health Insurance Program (S-CHIP)/ [Department of Health and Human Services] | Low-income families with children; pregnant women; aged, blind, or disabled persons. Data here are for children and their families. | Covers cost of medical care within insurance framework | None | Federal and state funds; federal share exceeds half of all costs and is based on state per capita income | 29.9 | 21.1 | 33.4 |

*Source:* The programme descriptions are based on information in Burke (2001). The expenditure, recipient counts, and population data are from a variety of sources, including Burke (2002). Details are available from the author on request.

The TANF recipient receives a card that authorises health care providers to bill the state for medical services received by her or other members of the family. If she is working or when she begins work, the food stamp and TANF benefits are reduced according to the amount of earnings she has. This reduction is in part offset by an earnings subsidy, the EITC, which is most often collected when she files her income tax claim at the beginning of the following year. If she is not working (and, in some cases, if she is working only part-time), she will be required to participate in various programmes intended to assist in preparing for and finding work. In some circumstances she will be required to do work without additional pay in a 'community service' or 'work experience' job. If required, such employment cannot exceed the number of hours per month obtained by dividing her TANF grant by the minimum wage ($5.15 per hour).

Given the ballyhoo surrounding reauthorisation, the $6.9 billion cited in Table 2.1 for federal outlays for TANF may seem small, especially when compared to outlays for the Food Stamp Program, the EITC, SSI, and Medicaid. In fact, total federal outlays for TANF are much greater – roughly $16.5 billion per year in FY2002. Since 1996, states have shifted federal funds from use for benefits (what Table 2.1 tabulates) to use for work programmes and in-work supports such as childcare subsidy.

## The combined benefit

Because state TANF benefits differ, so do the incomes received by families in similar financial circumstances but living in different states. This variation is apparent both in benefits received by families with no incomes of their own and in the way the TANF benefit changes if family members begin work.

Table 2.2 shows how the benefits combined to effect total income for a family of three in 1999.[2] Benefits are illustrated for California, a state with relatively high TANF benefits, and Texas, a state with very low benefits. Three different situations, defined by different assumptions about wage and hours of work, are presented. In all cases monthly amounts are calculated, because for all benefits except the EITC, eligibility is assessed and benefits paid on a monthly basis. (Total income is shown for New York and South Carolina at the bottom of the table, for intermediate comparisons.)

The first calculation assumes the parent is not working. In California the TANF benefit for such a family was $626 in 1999; Texas provided $188. The difference in total income is also substantial, but the gap is not, in proportionate terms, quite as great. The reason is that the food stamp benefit is calculated on the basis of income from other sources, including TANF. Since a family receiving only TANF has a lower income in Texas than would the same family in California, the food stamp payment is larger. Nevertheless, the Texas combined benefit is 40% lower than what is paid in California.

As earnings increase, the state-to-state difference declines. For a woman working 35 hours per week, total income in Texas would be just 12% lower than if she

**Table 2.2: Family income under alternative work assumptions selected states, 1999**

This table shows the composition and amount of income for a single-parent family of three in which the parent works at a $6.00 per hour job. It is assumed that the household has no income from sources other than earnings and benefits. State taxes and additional state transfers are not included. For programme definitions, see Table 2.1.

| State | Income | Hours of work per week @ $6.00/hour | | |
|---|---|---|---|---|
| | | 0 | 20 | 35 |
| California | Total Income | $892 | $1,310 | $1,533 |
| | Earnings | $0 | $516 | $903 |
| | TANF | $626 | $481 | $287 |
| | FSP | $266 | $146 | $94 |
| | FICA* | $0 | ($39) | ($69) |
| | Federal Tax Liability | $0 | $0 | $0 |
| | EITC | $0 | $206 | $318 |
| Texas | Total Income | $523 | $1,015 | $1,345 |
| | Earnings | $0 | $516 | $903 |
| | TANF | $188 | $0 | $0 |
| | FSP | $335 | $332 | $193 |
| | FICAª | $0 | ($39) | ($69) |
| | Federal Tax Liability | $0 | $0 | $0 |
| | EITC | $0 | $206 | $318 |
| California | Total Income | $892 | $1,310 | $1,533 |
| New York | Total Income | $862 | $1,257 | $1,475 |
| South Carolina | Total Income | $536 | $1,114 | $1,390 |
| Texas | Total Income | $523 | $1,015 | $1,345 |

ª Federal Insurance Contributions Act. FICA amount is the employee's social insurance contribution.

Source: Calculated using the Urban Institute's 'State TANF Income Calculator' (see www.urban.org).
See text for explanation of table.

were residing in California. What is happening is that the mix of assistance shifts from TANF, with its substantial state-to-state variation, to the nationally uniform combination of food stamps and the EITC. Indeed, with earnings of $903 (4.3 weeks x 35 hours x $6.00), the woman would not be eligible for *any* TANF benefit in Texas. Because of variations in the structure of state TANF programmes, which will be discussed later, the reward for increasing work varies.

Several caveats are in order concerning the numbers in Table 2.2. The impression of simultaneity of benefit receipt given by the table is incorrect. First, while food stamp and TANF benefits are paid monthly, most households do not collect the EITC until they file their federal income tax reports; typically such payments are not received until March of the following year. Second, because of lags in reporting and adjustment, the woman who moves from no work to 20 hours per week will often not see adjustment in TANF or food stamp benefits until as many as four months have passed. Finally, the table presumes that the family in question receives all the benefits to which it has claim. Actual take-up rates of TANF and food stamp benefits, discussed later, imply that many eligible families do not receive what they are entitled to.

## Benefits and poverty

The US poverty standard in 1999 was $13,410 for a family of three. The monthly equivalent of $13,410 is $1,118; none of the states listed provided this level of benefit for families with no other income. (Recall, however, that all TANF families have comprehensive medical care provided through the Medicaid programme.) Even 35 hours of work at $6 did not produce enough earnings to take the family above the 1999 poverty line without cash assistance, and $6 is more than the $5.15 minimum wage.

But given the nature of the benefit system, work in all cases makes a difference. In South Carolina, a relatively low benefit state, a half-time job at $6 raised a family of three to the poverty line in 1999, given the associated food stamp, TANF, and EITC benefits. In Texas, more work was required to cross the line.

## Observations

Tables 2.1 and 2.2 contain a lot of information. Here are five points that are particularly relevant to drawing workfare-related distinctions between British and American social assistance systems:

- *The state/local core differs by family type.*

The major programme, TANF, is available only to families with children. This is the programme that replaces what was called, until the beginning of the 1997 federal fiscal year (October 1996), Aid to Families with Dependent Children. If adults in such families are disabled, they may receive SSI, but payments for children will come out of TANF. Individuals without children are eligible under certain circumstances for food stamps and the EITC, but basic cash assistance is available for people in this group only if they live in a state or locality that offers general assistance. In 1998, only 18 of the 51 states (including the District of Columbia, which is treated throughout this chapter as a state) offered cash assistance to able-bodied adults without children. Thus a second target of New Deal policy, young people without dependents, is virtually excluded from social assistance in the US.

- *None of these benefits is explicitly linked to job loss.*

In the US there is no means-tested unemployment benefit. It is possible for persons receiving Unemployment Insurance (UI) benefits to receive food stamps and, in some cases, TANF payments. However, food stamp and TANF benefits will be adjusted downward to account for UI payments. For those covered, UI benefits last up to 39 weeks in states with high unemployment rates, and a few states provide benefits for 52 weeks. Once benefits are exhausted, needy workers must seek food stamp, TANF, or other benefits under common programme rules. Long-term unemployment is not a direct focus of the American welfare-to-work effort, because long-term unemployment per se does not qualify a person for benefits. At any point between 1990 and 1996, for example, only about one third of all unemployed individuals in the US received unemployment benefits.

- *Much of the American social assistance system is nationally uniform. The widest variation occurs at the bottom, with the programmes of last resort featuring greatest state discretion.*

Base benefits for three of the major programmes – the Food Stamp Program, Supplemental Security Income, and the Earned Income Tax Credit – are the same everywhere, although some states do supplement both SSI and the EITC. In contrast, eligibility standards and benefit amounts for the core income support system, TANF, are established by states.

- *Despite the dominant role of federal programmes and, especially, federal finance, the assistance a poor person receives depends very much on where that person lives.*

This is especially true if he or she is not working, as is evident in Table 2.2. This dependence is obvious in the case of general assistance, since most states have no such programme at all. All states have TANF as a last resort for families with children, but programmes differ widely both with respect to benefits paid and in the terms under which assistance is given.

Because the role of TANF in social assistance diminishes with earnings, state-to-state variation in household treatment does as well.

- *Lots of cooks are in the kitchen.*

At the federal level the assistance system involves five different cabinet-level departments. This number increases to six when the important role of the Department of Labor in the conduct of work programmes is included. Federal agencies have counterparts in state government and even at the local level, so that, for example, the US Department of Health and Human Services (DHHS) is connected through its regional offices to state departments of social services, which in turn typically link to county social service agencies. This diversity of 'stovepipes' might be expected to lead to coordination problems, and it does.

## Welfare politics

American attitudes towards social assistance are notoriously ambivalent (Weaver, 2000, Chapter Seven). On the one hand, public opinion polls reveal a remarkably consistent and general public commitment to helping the poor. On the other hand, questions about 'welfare' evoke considerable hostility. To campaign for "ending welfare as we know it", as Bill Clinton did in 1992, was a stroke of genius. The slogan offered the public the sense of fixing one wrong while leaving open the door to doing something better.

### AFDC in the dock

The welfare Americans knew (or at least recognised as such) was AFDC. The indictment of AFDC included several counts, with relative emphasis changing over time. Generally opponents claimed that the welfare system (1) encouraged dependency, (2) rewarded irresponsible behaviour, and (3) invited fraud and abuse. The notion of 'dependency' seems at times to be sufficiently broad to include any welfare use, but when pressed, welfare critics associate dependence with long-term reliance upon benefit as the sole or major source of visible family support (US DHHS, 2002b). AFDC fostered dependence, it was argued, by discouraging work. Moreover, welfare encouraged other behaviours that also led to dependence, including improvident childbearing. And fraud and abuse involve a combination of deliberate misrepresentation of income as well as use of assistance in lieu of exploiting opportunities for self support, either through employment or by seeking assistance from absent parents, families, or others.

Given the indictment, several responses were available.

One response, posed in a famous 'conceptual experiment' in Charles Murray's influential 1984 book *Losing ground*, would be to genuinely end welfare, or at least means-tested social benefits, on grounds that the social costs of the system's perverse incentives were too great to justify continuation and that these costs could not be reduced in a way that would be efficient (Murray, 1994; see Chapter Three below for a discussion of Murray's role in the British welfare debate). While elimination of AFDC was never seriously considered, *Losing ground* became an important point of reference in the debate. Murray's argument contained two important propositions. One was that welfare fostered behaviours that were contrary to what are commonly perceived as the goals of public assistance. The other was that government programmes could not do otherwise and that government should therefore leave the social assistance field or at least retreat to defensible positions on the perimeter.

An alternative response was to argue that programmes could be modified to improve incentives and that the benefits of assistance programmes, especially for children, outweighed the costs. The 'new paternalist' version of the government-can-do faction moved beyond strengthening the invisible hand of financial incentives to arguing for a guiding hand of government in the lives of the long-term dependent. Paternalist policies, Lawrence Mead writes, "assume that the people concerned need assistance but that they also need direction if they are to live constructively" (Mead, 1997, p 2).

## Waivers and reform

From the Nixon through the Carter administrations, reform efforts concentrated on expanding the role of national government. This emphasis was propelled by the fact that national law established many of the parameters of AFDC. Appreciation of the long history of state resistance to providing assistance, especially in the South and West, also taught advocates to look to Washington. State penuriousness could be overcome, it was thought, by a combination of national mandate and federal assumption of costs.

Beginning with the Reagan administration in 1981, perceptions of the competence of states in the engineering and implementation of reform began to change as the results of a number of 'demonstrations' of work-oriented changes in welfare rules were published and promoted. These demonstrations involved experimentation with intensive enforcement of jobsearch requirements and, in some instances, with requiring unpaid public service work by recipients in exchange for benefits – a practice that came to be known as 'workfare' (Walker, 1991). In most cases these demonstrations were not, for logistical and budget reasons, implemented statewide. This potentially created problems, for federal law required AFDC programmes to be available on the same terms to all state residents. However, federal law did include provisions for granting exceptions – waivers – for investigating the consequences of changing programme rules in ways judged by the Department of Health, Education, and Welfare (now DHHS) to further the ends of the law. Generally evaluations are required for experiments conducted under waivers, and the results of some of the waiver-based state experiments have come to play a significant role in the US welfare policy debate, as well as in discussions of welfare strategy in Britain.

Action on welfare was not limited to governors and the executive branch. A renewed effort at welfare reform within Congress produced, in 1988, a substantial but incremental reform of AFDC called the Family Support Act (FSA). FSA established a new welfare-to-work programme, called JOBS (for Job Opportunities and Basic Skills), included provisions expanding support for two-parent families, and substantially increased the federal role in promoting collection of child support from non-custodial parents. The law's proponents used the results of the earlier welfare-to-work demonstrations to gain support for more stringent work obligations for recipients and requirements that states raise the proportion of recipients involved in employment-related activities. New demonstrations were authorised, including a national evaluation of JOBS. However, funding for the JOBS programme was very modest, and for reasons still not well understood, the national welfare caseload began to grow almost immediately after the Family Support Act was signed by President Reagan.

The average monthly assistance caseload grew by 17% between 1988 and 1991 (Wallace and Blank, 1999).

## The 1992 Campaign and the Clinton administration strategy

This resurgence of caseload growth did two things. One was that it kept welfare policy on the national agenda. The other was that it seemed to demonstrate that the incremental approach to reform contained in the Family Support Act, that is reform pretty much as the country had long known it, was still not working. In contrast, activist policies in some states, notably as practiced in Wisconsin by Governor Tommy Thompson, appeared to directly address work and behaviour issues and to produce results (Wiseman, 1996). In late 1991 the first Bush administration began encouraging states to apply for more waivers for welfare demonstrations.

The Bush waiver strategy came too late. By 1992 Arkansas Governor Bill Clinton had managed to seize the reform issue with the slogan "Ending Welfare as We Know It" and by emphasising time limits, although just which feature of AFDC was to be time-limited was left unclear. Once elected, however, the new president chose first to address national health insurance policy and tax reform, including expansion of the EITC. By the time the administration's welfare reform proposal, the 1994 Work and Responsibility Act, was introduced, momentum had been lost. Congressional Republicans were considering much more substantial changes to welfare as one part of the 'Contract with America', the party's manifesto for the fall 1994 Congressional campaign.

While the Clinton administration was slow in introducing its own reform proposal, it quickly adopted and liberalised the Bush waiver strategy. Governors were encouraged to experiment. Over time, the demonstrations approved by the Clinton administration became increasingly diverse and multifaceted. By 1996, 43 states had been granted approval for some sort of welfare demonstration. However questionable these initiatives may have been on substantive grounds, they added to the push for more devolution of programme authority from the federal to state governments. The enthusiasm with which governors pursued such demonstrations is testimony to the political popularity of reform.

Ultimately a new welfare law, PRWORA, did pass and was signed by President Clinton in August 1996. Implementation began in October.

## Welfare (as we knew it) ended

PRWORA ended the Aid to Families with Dependent Children programme (AFDC) and replaced it with a block grant to states for Temporary Assistance to Needy Families (TANF).

The stated purpose of the legislation was to:

1. aid needy families so that children may be cared for in their homes or those of relatives;
2. end dependence of needy parents upon government benefits by promoting job preparation, work, and marriage;
3. prevent and reduce out-of-wedlock pregnancies and establish goals for preventing and reducing their incidence; and
4. encourage formation and maintenance of two-parent families (Committee on Ways and Means, 2000, p 354).

PRWORA is complex, but six features are central: (1) the shift to block grants; (2) the expansion of state latitude in programme design; (3) time limits; (4) loss of entitlement; (5) work requirements; and (6) constriction of federal authority. Each feature is discussed in more detail below. Their effects were difficult to forecast in 1996, and some critics predicted quite dire consequences for children. Two prominent executives in DHHS resigned in protest when President Clinton signed the bill.

## Block grants

Federal assistance to states for provision of AFDC benefits was *open-ended* and *matching*. *Open-ended* means that once a state plan was established and approved, the federal government would pay a fixed share of benefit costs and administrative expenditures no matter how many eligible families were identified. *Matching* means that at least half of all costs were paid by the federal government (the actual share depended on state per capita income), so assistance was, from the states' perspective, relatively cheap. PRWORA committed the federal government to maintaining the grant made to each state for its TANF programme at a measure of the highest level established in the three years prior to 1996 (Falk, 2002a). The aggregate grant came to $16.5 billion, compared with $15 billion paid in the last year before PRWORA implementation. While PRWORA increased state resources, it created a powerful incentive to reduce outlays. Unlike the situation with a matching grant, under the new regime every dollar saved at the state level released funds for other uses, including tax reduction. This incentive was in part offset by a maintenance of effort (MOE) requirement penalising states that reduced their own social assistance outlays by more than 25% of levels established in 1994.

## Expansion of latitude

Under PRWORA, states were no longer required to obtain federal approval for implementation of many of the innovations adopted in the early 1990s. The ability of states to require work-related activity by both applicants for and recipients of social assistance was increased, as was states' ability to sanction those failing to comply. States were also given more latitude in defining the categories of individuals eligible for assistance and the procedures to be used for benefit calculation.

## Time limits

The statutory manifestation of the 'Temporary' in Temporary Assistance for Needy Families was the time limit. The new law prohibited states from using federal TANF funds to provide aid to families that included any adult who had received 60 months of TANF benefits. However, states were allowed to exempt up to 20% of their caseload from this time limit, and nothing precluded the use of own state revenues for assistance to families after five years. In addition to the overall time limit, PRWORA encouraged states to impose various time-related work requirements on recipients, including involvement in 'community service' jobs after two months of receipt; but states could opt out. States could also exempt adults on various other grounds (including having infant children) as long as certain general requirements for rates of work participation were satisfied for the caseload as a whole. Thus while the time limits introduced by PRWORA drew, and continue to draw, considerable attention, their consequence in practice was a matter of considerable uncertainty. This uncertainty was magnified by the fact that the federal five-year limit was a maximum, not a minimum. States could impose time limits more restrictive than 5 years, and some, using waivers, already had.

## The end of entitlement

No feature of recent developments in the US more dramatically contrasts with European social assistance concepts than the provision in the PRWORA that eliminated the *right* of categorically eligible families to obtain cash assistance. "This part shall not be interpreted to entitle any individual or family to assistance under any State program under this part", the law stated, and "this part" was the section of the bill (401(b)), that replaced AFDC with TANF. In principle, this provision allowed states to have no TANF programme at all. The practical significance lay largely in the latitude it created for states in changing eligibility requirements, imposing obligations, and sanctioning applicants and recipients who fail to comply. PRWORA specifically denied benefits for the first five years of legal residence to persons who entered the US after the bill's signing. The law also eliminated food stamp eligibility (without time limit) for most legally resident aliens. States were given the option of extending TANF benefits to non-citizens legally resident in the country, with outlays for this purpose to be counted towards maintenance of effort requirements.

## Work requirements

PRWORA called for states to achieve certain levels of recipient involvement in 'work activities'. This requirement was cast in terms of a specified minimum percentage of all adults participating at least a minimum number of hours each week in a set of work and work-related activities named by the law. Both the definition of participation and the required participation rate were to escalate over time. In the first year of TANF operation, FY1997, at least 25% of adults were to be participating in approved categories of activities for at least 20 hours per week. By the last year, 2002, the standard was 50% of adults engaged for at least 30 hours per week. Higher minimum hour and participation rates were set for two-parent families. States failing to meet these standards faced a financial penalty.

While the levels of activity envisioned by the PRWORA participation standards were consistent with governors' reform rhetoric, there is no evidence that prior to 1996 any state had ever achieved anything like what was to be required. However, the legislation created an 'out': states were allowed to reduce annual targets for participation, per cent for per cent, by any caseload reductions achieved between 1995 and each of the six years of the PRWORA horizon (1997-2002). (The caseload reduction credit excluded changes in caseload brought about by alteration in federal or state law.) Moreover, states were permitted to count recipients who combined benefit with work in unsubsidised jobs as meeting the participation requirements. Thus, while the participation and activity standards created some incentive for active creation of employment and training activities for TANF recipients, pressure to do so would be diminished insofar as the caseload contracted and some recipients combined welfare and unsubsidised work.

## The Federal role

The logic of PRWORA was to diminish the role of national government in the operation of the programmes of last resort. If Washington was to do less, it made sense to cut the size of what had been the responsible agencies. Accordingly, PRWORA mandated a 75% reduction in DHHS jobs "that relate to any direct spending program, or any program funded through discretionary spending" converted to a block grant by PRWORA (Section 416). To make certain the 'federal bureaucrats' got the message, the law expressly prohibited "officer(s) or employees of the Federal Government" from regulating "the conduct of States ... except to the extent expressly provided" by the new law (42 USC 617).

These changes posed a political problem for the Clinton administration. In the wake of PRWORA, just what role was national government to play?

## Outcomes

PRWORA did not immediately affect most AFDC recipients. (The exception was the small group of legally resident aliens denied federal assistance by the new law; states assumed responsibility for many of these recipients.) However, PRWORA did change incentives and opportunities for both federal government and the states, and these changes produced policies that make a difference at ground level.

### Caseload decline: effect and cause

Logically it would make sense to defer discussion of trends in the number of families receiving assistance until reviewing the response of government to the new legislation. Both the federal and state government responses determine the terms under which assistance is ultimately offered, and it is this intermediate outcome, combined with the conditions that lead families to seek assistance, that produce the caseload. However, the rapid decline in the AFDC/TANF caseload, already apparent in 1996, itself clearly influenced the pattern of government response to PRWORA and, ultimately, the system as the country had it by 2002. Figure 2.1 illustrates the caseload story. As already discussed, the caseload began to rise in 1988. The increase accelerated with the 1990-91 recession. The national peak occurred in 1994, thus predating PRWORA. The slowdown in caseload growth coincides with economic recovery, but it is also roughly coincident with the introduction of a substantial increase in the Earned Income Tax Credit and a wave of implementation by states of waiver-based

**Figure 2.1: The AFDC/TANF caseload and the economy, FY 1980-2001**

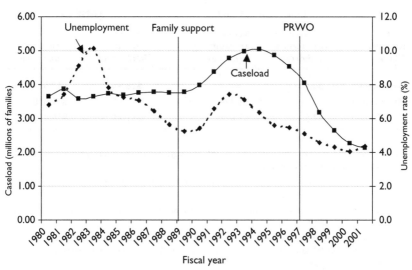

AFDC reforms approved either late in the first Bush administration or early in the Clinton first term. It is not surprising that causality for the decline remains a matter of dispute.

What is not disputed is that PRWORA provided a fiscal boost for states. State grants for PRWORA were established based on the federal contribution to AFDC at each state's caseload peak. When TANF implementation began (October, 1996), most states received an increase in federal funds over what would have been expected under AFDC, and this boost grew as the caseload fell. However, the gain from decline was greater for high-benefit states than low, with the consequence that disparity in resources available for assistance beyond the benefit structure in place in 1994-95 has grown.

Table 2.3 illustrates the problem. This table reports results of sorting states along two dimensions: (1) TANF resources divided by the estimated number of children living in low-income families in the state, and (2) TANF resources per TANF case. 'Resources' is the sum of the state's basic federal TANF block grant, any federal supplement, and the state contribution expected as a result of the TANF maintenance of effort requirement. The average resources per low-income child among the bottom 20 states amounts to only slightly more than a quarter of the resources available among the top 20. Considered per TANF case, resources available for the bottom 20 states are less than half what is available to the top 20. The full range of variation is even more dramatic. Personal income per capita in Michigan ($29,000) is 20% greater than per capita personal income in South Carolina, yet in Michigan total TANF funding is twice as great per case and four times as great per-low income child as in South Carolina.

**Table 2.3: The distribution of TANF resources FY2000**

| | TANF Resources Per: | | | |
| | Low-Income Child | | TANF Case | |
| State Resource Class | Share of all low-income children | Average amount per child | Share of all TANF cases | Average amount per case |
|---|---|---|---|---|
| Bottom 20 | 33.4% | $702 | 28.9% | $7,564 |
| Median state | | $1,374 | | $11,830 |
| Top 20 | 47.5% | $2,623 | 51.1% | $15,462 |

Definitions:

'TANF resources' is the sum of the state's basic TANF block grant, the federal supplemental grant (if received) and required state contribution.

'Low-income child' means a child living in a family with income < 125% of the relevant federal poverty standard.

'State Resource Class' is defined separately for the distribution of TANF resources per low-income child and distribution per TANF case

*Source:* Calculated by author using expenditure and caseload data from US Department of Health and Human Services (2002b), low-income population data from the Bureau of the Census website www.ferret.bls.census.gov.

---

These resource disparities are surely one factor influencing variation in state response to the federal reforms.

## Responding to PRWORA

The Clinton administration's PRWORA response involved spin, support, defence, and multiplication. The *spin* recast PRWORA as almost a victory for the administration, the culmination of reforms fostered through its waiver policy. *Support* was provided by encouraging both private and public organisations to reduce welfare rolls by hiring recipients. On the private side, the president supported the establishment of the Welfare to Work Partnership – a business-based organisation that guided and publicised corporate initiatives (Welfare to work Partnership, 2000). On the public side, the president ordered federal agencies to hire TANF recipients into available jobs, including jobs generated by the conduct of the 2000 census. *Defence* emphasised preservation of the Food Stamp and Medicaid programmes as entitlements and promotion of expanded access to health insurance.

But perhaps the most dramatic feature of the Clinton administration's strategy was *multiplication*, the effort to promote federal programmes ancillary to welfare reform. Legislation passed in 1997 established a welfare-to-work (WTW) grant programme intended to support employment services for TANF recipients with multiple barriers to employment. The 1998 Federal Transportation Equity Act authorised funding for federal matching grants for state programmes to enhance job access for welfare recipients. In 1998 the president proposed tenant-based housing assistance to help eligible TANF families move to work and to reduce disincentives for employment. By involving virtually every federal agency in highly visible welfare reform efforts, the Clinton administration managed to turn the tables on the governors, most of whom were, conveniently, Republican. Before PRWORA, the states could do reforms on the edges of the system, but ascribe responsibility for failures to the structure of AFDC. After PRWORA, the states became, in a way never true before, responsible for the core, and the president could work on the margins.

Following PRWORA, governors found themselves with reins in hand, but little evident sense of where to take their wagons. With a few exceptions, what followed, at least in the short run, was not much different from what came before. This lent some credibility to the administration's claim that most of the changes of the system were actually accomplished through the waivers it granted (Council of Economic Advisors, 1999). But while changes may not have been immediately apparent, PRWORA did change incentives and constraints faced by states, and over time the consequences of the changes could be expected to emerge.

### The stealth contraction

Both before and after PRWORA became law, hypotheses abounded about the consequences of the new legislation. Proponents argued that greater latitude in assistance programme design could allow states to better respond to applicant's particular needs and to better utilise available local resources in promoting movement to self-support. The most common concern of sceptics was that the response of the states to the combination of loss of entitlement, block grant funding, and interstate competition would produce a contraction of the system and a diminution of policy ambition – a 'rush to the bottom' (Chernick and McGuire, 1999). This downward trajectory of benefits and access was expected to be accompanied by diversion of federal funds to tax relief or to support programmes with broader local political appeal than social assistance. The sceptics' concerns turned out to be not far from the mark, but many of the manifestations of contraction are subtle, and some features of state assistance programmes have in fact been liberalised.

### Benefits

Benefits did contract, at least when assessed in terms of purchasing power. Between 1996 and 2001, 7 states reduced the maximum nominal cash benefit available to families, 27 held dollar benefits constant, and 17 increased benefits.[3] If evaluated in terms of consumer prices, the no-change-in-benefits policy pursued by the remaining 27 states is equivalent to a decline in real purchasing power of about 12.5%. This was a period of rising family and per capita income, so the fall relative to median family income was greater still (Council of Economic Advisors, 2002, Tables B-62 and B-33). Under the new law, few politicians promoted increase in benefits as one of the payoffs from reform.

### Access

The elimination of entitlement did not produce a wave of egregious examples of exclusion of families from assistance. Some features of state eligibility standards were actually liberalised, especially those related to assets. Most states increased access to assistance by two-parent families. About half the states exempt lone parents with infants from work obligations. Most states also exempt victims of domestic violence from TANF rules. At the same time, 28 states have introduced 'diversion' programmes intended to offer applicants alternatives to regular TANF receipt. The intention of these programmes may indeed be benign, but they do signal a strong state interest in keeping people from full assistance, and they often carry restrictions that deny access to benefits for some subsequent period for families diverted.

Other policies adopted are more clearly restrictive. Between 1996 and 2001, 29 states made no change or reduced the nominal value of the maximum earnings level allowable for a family seeking assistance. By 2000, in most parts of the country it was harder for a lone-parent household with earnings to establish welfare eligibility than it was in 1995. As of 2001, 22 states had established time limits for benefits shorter than the 60-month federal standard. Almost a dozen required work or job search immediately, rather than after 24 months as TANF requires. Penalties for failure to comply with required work activities can be quite severe: some 19 states penalise recipients for their first failure to comply with required work activities by suspending the family's whole benefit. Twenty-two states impose so-called 'family caps'. Under a family cap, children born to recipients more than nine months after case opening do not lead to an increase in benefits (Wiseman, 2000).

Much hinges on how such changes are applied – whether what is produced is tough love or gruff shove. Evidence is hard to come by, and what is available is generally mixed and in many instances suspect. It does appear that very few cases have been closed due to time limits; families that reach time limits are typically either granted exemptions or transferred to alternative programmes operated with state funds (Bloom et al, 2002; Wilkens, 2002).

## Funding

Broadly speaking, two important changes occurred in the pattern of welfare expenditure as a result of the block grant. First, the share of TANF annual expenditures devoted to cash benefits went down, from 73% of federal and state funds in AFDC in 1995 to 51% in TANF in 2000. Second, combined federal and state expenditure on TANF fell below the level of outlays for AFDC and its associated programmes before the 1996 reform. In FY1995 federal and state expenditures on the three programmes TANF replaced – AFDC, the JOBS (Job Opportunities and Basic Skills) programme, and Emergency Assistance – amounted to $30.1 billion. In FY2000 federal and state expenditure on TANF was $22.6 billion, in current dollars (Falk, 2002b, p 8). Over the same interval, the share of TANF outlays nominally attributable to federal funds increased only slightly, from 54% to 55%. At first blush, this is a surprise, since the federal grant is fixed, states are allowed a 25% reduction in outlays from pre-reform levels, and caseloads have fallen. This would normally be expected to increase the federal share. What has occurred is that the composition of expenditures has changed. A sizable share of federal funding has been set aside to support future expenditures or transferred to two ancillary programmes that are not limited to provision of services to social assistance recipients: the Child Care and Development Fund (CCDF) and the Social Services Block Grant (SSBG). These changes are illustrated in Figure 2.2.

Despite the decline in caseloads, states are still required to spend at a rate of at least 75% of that established pre-PRWORA. Thus expenditures per case have gone up, but not, as we have seen, because of increasing cash benefits. Instead, the additional funds have gone for supporting 'work activities', childcare, and a host of other programmes. By the end of FY2000, the unexpended portion included an accumulated $5.4 billion in obligated expenditures and

**Figure 2.2: Comparison of state AFDC outlays for FY1995 to outlays (including funds transfers) in FY2000**

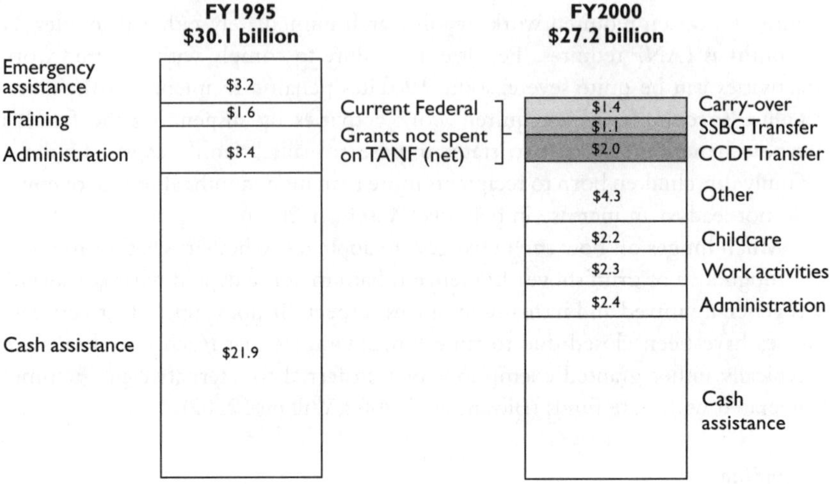

|  | FY1995<br>$30.1 billion |  | FY2000<br>$27.2 billion |  |
|---|---|---|---|---|
| Emergency assistance | $3.2 |  |  |  |
| Training | $1.6 | Current Federal ⎤ | $1.4 | Carry-over |
|  |  | Grants not spent ⎬ | $1.1 | SSBG Transfer |
| Administration | $3.4 | on TANF (net) ⎦ | $2.0 | CCDF Transfer |
|  |  |  | $4.3 | Other |
|  |  |  | $2.2 | Childcare |
|  |  |  | $2.3 | Work activities |
|  |  |  | $2.4 | Administration |
| Cash assistance | $21.9 |  |  |  |
|  |  |  |  | Cash assistance |

*Note:* 'Training' in FY1995 is outlays for Job Opportunities and Basic Skills (JOBS) programme.
*Source:* Falk (March 2002b); US DHHS (2002a).

$3.2 billion in unobligated funds preserved for 'rainy day' use (Falk, 2002c, p 4). Clearly, as of FY2000, the rainy day reserve was small in comparison with annual programme requirements.

In 2000-01 the US General Accounting Office (GAO) conducted the most credible study of the extent to which the federal block grant *supplanted* what states were previously spending (US GAO, 2001). The GAO 'followed the money' in 10 major states: California, Colorado, Connecticut, Louisiana, Maryland, Michigan, New York, Oregon, Texas, and Wisconsin. GAO's conclusion was that in many instances these states had used federal funds to replace state expenditures on 'basic welfare services' (notably benefits), but that "over time most states have maintained or even increased their own investment to address the overall needs of low-income families" (US GAO, 2001, p 12). What makes this assessment extraordinary is the standard GAO sets for evaluating states' responses: *any* increase in state effort to "address the overall needs of low-income families" is counted as a plus, even in an era in which state and local government revenues from all sources increased, in real terms, by over 18%.[4]

Given the decline in the caseload, some diversion of money to supportive services could surely be justified. What is evident is that a far larger share of the total assistance budget now goes to administration and services. Beneficence, if present at all, does not show up as cash in the hands of the needy.

## Running helter-skelter

Though the trends in generosity are at best ambiguous, diversity in programme details, as revealed by regulations, has clearly grown.

A good example of these changes is provided by procedures for treatment of recipient earnings (Wiseman and Giannarelli, 2002). Under AFDC, although basic benefits varied, all states followed essentially the same procedure in adjusting benefits for cases with earnings, with some states using waivers to experiment with changes in that procedure. PRWORA allows states to choose virtually any formulation. The result has been great divergence and a growing structural problem. In 2001, only 1 states continued to use the old AFDC procedure in calculation of benefits for cases with earnings. The remaining 47 states (including the District of Columbia) were using variants, and no two of these states were doing the same thing.

Many of these schemes are inequitable in that they provide more generously for working families previously on assistance than they do for families in the same current situation but lacking a history of recent welfare use. This comes about because one standard is applied to earnings in determining initial eligibility and another standard is employed in determining the level of earnings at which eligibility is lost. Thus, for example, in California a working lone parent with two children might be eligible for TANF assistance if her earnings are less than $900 per month (as of 1999). But once she has achieved eligibility, her earnings can rise beyond $1,500 per month (also as of 1999) before she loses it.

The introduction to PRWORA's third year report states that PRWORA "... provide(s) States with flexibility to create the best approaches for their individual circumstances" (US DHHS, 2000, p 1). It is not clear which dimension of the individual circumstances of states justifies 48 variants of the assistance guarantee and benefit reduction rate. One possible suspect for motivation is the PRWORA participation requirement. Without amelioration, the TANF participation requirement calls for states to attain unprecedented levels of involvement of assistance recipients in welfare-to-work activities. The 2002 standard requires that half of the caseload be involved for 30 or more hours per week in work or work-related programmes; for two-parent families the standard is 90%. Given the substantial administrative and logistical burdens posed by such a target, it would have been extremely difficult, if not impossible, to attain.

In fact, for 2000 (the last year for which data were available at this writing), all states met their participation standards, for two reasons. One was that the standard itself is reduced each year by the amount of caseload decline since 1995. For FY2000 the highest overall requirement thus adjusted was 27.5%, faced by Connecticut; in 31 states the caseload decline was sufficiently great that the effective participation requirement was zero (DHHS, 2002a, p III-89). Two, the remaining participation requirements were in most cases more than covered by a growing rate of employment of TANF recipients in unsubsidised jobs. Combining of work and assistance in this way is facilitated by state earnings 'disregard' policies.

Nationally in FY2000 approximately two thirds of the adults counted by states towards achievement of TANF participation requirements were in unsubsidised employment. If those families mixing work and welfare are removed from the overall participation data, the implication is that only about 20% of recipients who were not in unsubsidised employment were engaged in welfare-to-work activities (Wiseman and Giannarelli, 2002). The suspicion is that at least some states used a combination of restricted entry and generous treatment of some working recipients to avoid the effort and expense required to address the needs of those left behind. In some instances such strategies may have been adopted because the state lacked resources (recall the disparities evident in Table 2.3). Regardless of motivation, what seems evident from both expenditures and programmes is a failure to use the opportunity provided by TANF resources to create institutions capable of genuine activation of cases. In fact, neither workfare nor training is a common experience of TANF participants. What has been accomplished is to provide greater opportunities for some families to combine welfare and work but at a cost of considerable inequity in access to TANF in-work support.

## What has happened to families?

Given this survey of intermediate outcomes, the stage is set for data on changes in welfare receipt, employment, income, and poverty that have occurred in the wake of the various changes in national policy.

### Benefit receipt

Between March 1994 and the end of 2000, the number of families receiving AFDC/TANF declined by 57%, from a peak of 5.1 million to 2.2 million. By the end of 2000, 5.8% of American children were in families receiving TANF; this was down from a peak of 14.1% receiving AFDC in 1993 (US DHHS, 2002a). This fall is unprecedented. A growing body of evidence indicates that part of the caseload decline is the result of declining take-up, not declining need. Estimates from the Urban Institute's Transfer Income Model (TRIM) imply a decline in participation among eligible families from 84% to 52% over the interval 1995-99 (US Department of Health and Human Services, 2002a, p II-19). Similarly, food stamps receipt has fallen. In 1994, 71% of lone (female) parent families with gross incomes below the Food Stamp Program qualifying limit of 130% of the poverty standard reported receiving food stamps. By 2000, just 50% of such families reported such receipt (Gabe, 2000, p 34; see also Wilde et al, 2000). Rosso (2001, p xii) estimates that food stamp take-up rates for eligible married-couple households with children fell by 25% between 1996 and 1999.

## Employment

The big story here is the increase in employment among lone female parents (Gabe, 2001, p 32). Beginning in 1993, employment among all single mothers with children under age 18 began to rise, reaching a record 73.1% by March 2001. The employment rate for single mothers with children now marginally exceeds that for married mothers. The increase in employment among mothers with children under age 3 is even more dramatic. In March 1993, 35% of single mothers in this group were working, compared to 53% of married mothers. By March 2000 the employment rates for the two groups were virtually identical, 59% for single mothers and 57% for married ones.

## Income distribution

This increase in lone parent employment rates is associated with major changes in the composition and distribution of income in the lower reaches of the income distribution. These developments have been studied most carefully by Thomas Gabe of the Congressional Research Service. Gabe's calculations for the bottom two quintiles of the income distribution for single female parent families in 1995 and 2000 show a substantial change in both levels and sources of income. In 1995 families in the bottom quintile reported incomes at levels less than or equal to 53% of the poverty standard; by 2000 the analogous statistic had increased to 70% of the poverty standard. Similarly, whereas in 1995 the upper demarcation for the second quintile was almost exactly the poverty standard, by 2000 this had increased to 125% of the poverty level. While average incomes grew in real terms within both quintiles, the increase in the second (17%) was substantially greater than in the lowest (9%).

The source of this change is principally earnings, because the real value of benefits reportedly received from food stamps, AFDC/TANF, and general assistance has declined for both quintiles – most dramatically for the second. Whereas in 1995 earnings and the Earned Income Tax Credit accounted for about half (49%) of income for the second quintile, by 2000 this share was almost three quarters (74%). Thus the dramatic increase in women's labour force participation during the 1990s has produced a substantial reduction on average in the role of assistance as an income source.

## Poverty

Overall, US poverty rates have fallen since passage of PRWORA. The aggregate poverty rate fell from 13.8% to 11.3% between 1995 and 2000; the rate for families with children from 14.4% to 11.4%; the rate for children from 20.8% to 16.2%. Measures of poverty that include a more comprehensive measure of resources, notably food stamps and the EITC, show lower poverty levels and similar trends. The poverty rate for married-couple families with children in 2000 was 5.2%; for families headed by single mothers it was 30.9%. While still large, the gap between poverty rates for these two groups closed between 1995 and 2000: in 1995 the rate for female headed households, 40.2%, was 8.4 times that for married couples; in 2000 the corresponding ratio was 7.4.

The driving force behind these changes is work. Figure 2.3 illustrates the connection, and some problems. The analysis is based on data from the March 2001 Current Population Survey and covers the status of lone parent families in the preceding year. Starting at the top and moving downward, note that the proportion of single mothers who report having worked at some time during the reference year has increased, reaching almost 84% by 2000. But note as well that the upward trend was established well before PRWORA. The second line down shows that the poverty rate fell by almost one third between 1993 and 2000. But, as shown by the third line, the proportion of single mothers who reported receiving cash assistance fell by over twice as much.

The bottom line in Figure 2.3 is perhaps the most intriguing. This is the subset of mothers who reported both cash assistance and earnings during the year. As a proportion of persons reporting welfare receipt, those with earnings is going up. At the same time, the share of women who combine assistance with work is declining. Thus, TANF has not improved upon the role of AFDC as a work support; the incidence of combining work and welfare among all single parents is, if anything, diminishing. It is misleading to claim, as is common, that the increase in the incidence of work among welfare recipients is itself evidence of a change in behaviour among lone parents. What has changed in many states is policy toward continuing eligibility for recipients who take jobs.

**Figure 2.3: Welfare, work, and poverty status among single mothers, 1987 to 2000**

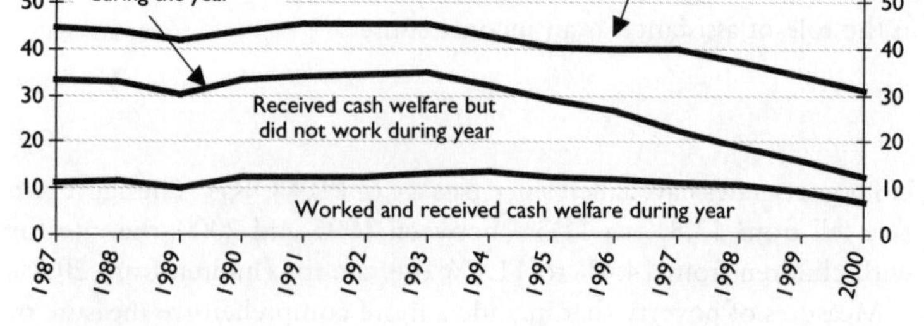

*Source:* Gabe (2001)

## Summary and implications

What happened post-PRWORA can be summed up as follows:

- The focus of levels of government changed. Federal government attention has shifted toward support of entitlements and supplemental programmes surrounding TANF; states have assumed less equivocal responsibility for the safety net.
- Benefits have declined, and with some exceptions eligibility for assistance has been constricted.
- Programme diversity has grown, with little evidence of convergence.
- Resources have been shifted from cash support to other uses.
- Despite the exceptional growth in outlays for support services, the actual incidence of work-related activities among unemployed TANF recipients appears low and may be declining.
- The share of the poor who receive TANF and food stamp benefits has declined. On average the decline in cash and food stamp assistance has been offset for single mothers by increased earnings.
- Among lone female parents, the incidence of combining work with welfare has declined.
- The poverty rate has fallen for all types of households.

These developments have many implications. Here are four:

First, those who work are financially better off; those who do not or cannot work have lost ground. This trend increases the importance of eliminating barriers to employment for jobless parents as a means of improving the well-being of their dependent children. Lowering of the safety net has increased the vulnerability of low-income families to economic downturn.

Second, the fact that working people are less likely to combine work and TANF raises the importance of the EITC and the FSP as work supports. While more money is spent on the former, it is the latter that is the more responsive to short-run changes in earnings and job loss. Thus declining food stamp take-up by working households is a matter of concern.

Third, the changing use of assistance funds affects the politics of welfare. When a large share of assistance dollars went for cash benefits, the number of persons other than recipients who had a personal material interest in sustaining the status quo was small. And voting among welfare recipients is low. Now more than half of federal funds and state contributions are going for support services. Such services are likely to be produced by adults from middle-income households. Thus while the number of recipients has fallen, the number of persons interested in continuing the current system – and active at the ballot box – has likely increased.

Finally, over time as the caseload declines, the block grant worsens the system's inequalities in ways that are not offset by food stamps and other benefits. This is because a reduction in caseload in a low-benefit state releases fewer dollars for use on support services (and more general outlays) than does the same reduction when it occurs in a high-benefit state. Thus the caseload decline in high-benefit states has produced greater gain in resources available for services than is true for such changes in low-benefit ones. The consequence is a growing bifurcation between the kinds of programmes available for actual and potential TANF recipients in high-benefit states and the programmes available in the traditionally low-benefit ones. This exacerbates the divergence already noted in benefits.

## Reauthorisation

In contrast to 1992 and 1996, welfare reform was not an issue in the 2000 election; the prevailing sentiment was that welfare reform had 'worked', and both parties claimed credit. Once elected, President George W. Bush signalled his support for state initiative by appointing Wisconsin's Governor Tommy Thompson as Secretary of the Department of Health and Human Services. However, because of delays in obtaining Senate confirmation of various DHHS appointments, the wide range of issues other than welfare to be addressed, and the terrorist attack on September 11, announcement of the Bush administration's reauthorisation proposals was delayed until early 2002.

### The White House proposal

By no accident, the second Bush administration chose to announce its proposals for reauthorisation in conjunction with the winter meeting of the National Governors' Association (NGA). Doing so allowed the president to exhibit fraternal camaraderie with the governors and to appropriate, for his own use, much of the governors' symbolic language.

Prior to the winter meeting, the NGA issued a policy brief on welfare reform that cited three objectives for reauthorisation: (1) maintain flexibility (translation: no additional intervention in state use of TANF funds); (2) maintain investment (translation: do not reduce the TANF block grant); and (3) move toward greater programme alignment (translation: take steps to eliminate inconsistencies between the programme choices states make for TANF and federal regulations for food stamps and other programmes related to TANF).[5] The administration's proposal, outlined in a policy manifesto entitled *Working toward independence* (White House, 2002) addressed all three objectives, but not in ways always satisfying to the governors. While not acknowledged by the president, the major thrust of the proposal was an assertion of greater federal influence on the evolution of state welfare systems.

#### Funding

The administration proposed continuing the current funding level for TANF and related programmes for the coming five years, thus at least nominally meeting the governors' 'maintain investment' requirement. However, a continuing nominal commitment means that in real terms federal support would decline, probably in the order of 20% over the life of the law unless the budget commitment was raised. The administration's proposal avoided addressing the issue of division of the overall TANF grant among states. States were to be required to continue maintenance of effort spending based on pre–TANF outlays.

### Federalism

*Working toward independence* points out that "the Federal Government devolved a great deal of authority and responsibility for social programs" in 1996 (White House, 2002, p 2). Nevertheless, the Federal Government's responsibilities are stated forthrightly:

> Now the Federal Government's primary responsibilities are to set broad goals for social programs, help fund them, evaluate their efficiency and effectiveness, and provide assistance to states trying to implement programs that have a proven track record. (White House, 2002, p 2)

If made by the Clinton administration, such a declaration would have been lambasted for usurpation of state authority and unwarranted presumption of competence in managing implementation. The Bush proposal pushed resumption of federal authority still further by calling for discontinuance of "outdated state program waivers", carried over from AFDC, since "flexibility under current law allows states to accomplish all the purposes of TANF without waivers", and "the requirements of TANF no longer represent an experiment" (White House, 2002, p 18). These waivers had been used by some states to avoid TANF work requirements and time limits.

The proposal's approach to enhancing 'flexibility' was to establish a new, cross-department waiver programme to facilitate state efforts to coordinate cash, housing, nutrition, and workforce programmes "so that more adults can achieve independence from welfare while attaining greater financial and social security for themselves and their children" (White House, 2002, p 2-3). This waiver programme addresses the NGA 'alignment' goal. But the federal interest in evaluation was emphasized:

> Integrated programs for which waivers are granted will be operated as demonstration programs and participating states will be required to evaluate the program [*sic*]. (White House, 2002, p 35)

Moreover, states applying for such waivers were required to demonstrate cost neutrality, that is to ensure that Federal Government costs would not increase as a result of the innovation.

## Eligibility

The proposal retained the five-year time limit and the provisions for exemption, as included in the 1996 reforms. With regard to non-citizens, the proposal is something of a halfway house: the administration proposed continuing to deny TANF benefits to non-citizens legally resident in the country for less than five years. Food stamp eligibility, more restrictive than under TANF, was to be aligned to TANF.

## Participation

*Working toward independence* called for replacing TANF participation requirements with "a new universal engagement requirement", drawn from a location not long known as a source of inspiration for reform – New York. When the appointment of Governor Tommy Thompson as Secretary of the Department of Health and Human Services was announced, many observers expected reauthorisation to bear a Wisconsin stamp. Britain's Chancellor of the Exchequer Gordon Brown dispatched a junior minister to Wisconsin and Minnesota (in frigid January!) to collect impressions. In fact, the administration's reauthorisation proposal shows greater influence from practices developed by the administration of Mayor Rudolph Giuliani in New York City (Nightingale et al, 2002; Wiseman, 2002). A hallmark of the New York City reforms was emphasis on 'full engagement' of the city's recipient caseload in community service jobs and other programmes aimed at promoting welfare-to-work. The Bush administration proposal on participation reflected the New York practice, but stepped beyond it. The minimum requirement for participation in "work or other activities that lead to self-sufficiency" was to rise from the 2002 TANF standard of 50% to 70% of all cases by 2007. The definition of participation was to be escalated from the PRWORA standard of 30 hours per week to 40. Of these 40 hours, 24 were to be in actual jobs, either subsidised or unsubsidised.

In 2001, New York City's engagement standard for social assistance recipients was 35 hours per week, with 24 in actual employment. While exemptions to the requirement were common, among recipients classed as 'engageable' the actual employment part of the participation standard was achieved by assignment of a significant share of TANF and general assistance recipients to unpaid Welfare Employment Program (WEP) jobs in various agencies. If New York's system was the model, the implication was that the new Bush administration was calling for more workfare. The operation of such systems is difficult and expensive, so whether or not they endorsed workfare, most governors saw the proposals as increasing costs.

The special participation standard applied to two-parent households by PRWORA, 90%, was eliminated in the Bush proposal. The case reduction credit that vitiated the participation requirement under PRWORA was to be phased out. As in current law, states failing to meet the participation standard were to be penalized with higher requirements for spending from own revenues.

## Performance

Before PRWORA, states were required to demonstrate conformance with federal AFDC law as a condition for receiving federal matching funds. The conformance was established by gaining federal approval for a State Plan that set out details of programme operation and choices made by the state among permissible alternatives. Under TANF, the role of the plan was diminished: the Federal Government was only allowed to certify whether or not plans were 'complete' and the requirements for this certification were minimal. The new proposal significantly expanded these requirements:

> States will be required to establish [in their state plans] program goals and report annually on their success in meeting those goals. This new emphasis on information systems and accountability will have the added benefit of further increasing states' flexibility because reporting systems will allow the Federal Government to exercise necessary oversight without falling into the trap of micro-management. (White House, 2002, p 24)

The resurrection of state plans was apparently intended to send a strong message – that what counts is engagement by the state agencies. Thus within bounds, what was important is not the specific goals that are set, but the *glasnost* that accompanies efforts to measure and requirements to report.

## Marriage and the family

'Strengthening families' is identified in *Working toward independence* as a 'pillar of reform' (White House, 2002, p 1). There is considerable uncertainty about what might work toward this end. The administration's proposal called for financial incentives to states "to develop and implement innovative programs" for promoting marriage. The proposal included numerous provisions for increasing child support collections from non-custodial parents and encouraging the pass-through of such collections by states to custodial parents receiving TANF benefits. (Most states do not pass on child support paid for children in TANF families, considering such payments as partial compensation for the states' assumption of responsibility for family support.) Teenage pregnancy was to be combated by promoting abstinence, but not on religious grounds: "The goal of federal policy should be to emphasize abstinence as the only certain way to avoid both unintended pregnancies and STDs [sexually transmitted diseases]" (White House, 2002, p 20).

*Working toward independence* was deemed a 'principles document' by the White House administration. The actual statutory proposal was introduced in the Republican-controlled House of Representatives as the 2002 Personal Responsibility, Work, and Family Promotion Act. The law passed the House in May. In general the content of the House bill was consistent with the programme outlined by President Bush. The bill included minor adjustments in the definition of participation, retained a modified (and updated) version of the caseload reduction credit, expanded funds for childcare, permitted existing state waivers to continue, and authorised $200m for programmes "to promote and support responsible fatherhood and healthy marriages."

### Food stamps

Three days before passage of the House Welfare Reform Bill, both the House and Senate accepted the 2002 Farm Bill. In addition to major and controversial subsidies for agricultural production, the Farm Bill included substantial changes for the Food Stamp Program, many of which had been endorsed in *Working toward independence*. The new law made FSP consistent with TANF by extending FSP eligibility to all aliens legally resident in the country for five or more years. Food stamp benefits were increased for larger families and states were given options for simplifying budgeting and eligibility reviews for working families.

Somewhat inconsistently, while *Working toward independence* called for tightening of rules for state TANF operation, the administration proposed relaxing penalties imposed on states for errors in eligibility and benefits determination processes for food stamps. The Farm Bill included such changes. Overall, the administration appeared willing to change the FSP in ways intended to promote access, while concentrating effort for change on TANF. The food stamp reforms brought about by reauthorisation were very consistent with the legislative agenda of groups advocating larger benefits and expanded access. The one threat to this agenda appeared in the president's super waiver proposal to allow governors more latitude in experimenting with alternatives to federal rules. The House version of the administration's reform proposal specifically included provision for converting all food assistance to block grants on an experimental basis in five states. The super waiver and the specific idea of changing FSP to a block grant became major points of contention.

### The opposition

In 2002 the Senate was under control of the Democratic Party, and by early summer development of the Senate alternative to the House (administration) version became the focus of attention of both Governors and advocate organisations. Opponents targeted three things: the participation requirements; costs; and the super waiver proposal.

Most informed observers recognised that, without the reductions allowed by the caseload reduction credit, the participation standards proposed by the administration would be quite difficult to meet. However, participation has obvious symbolic importance, and since the typical person on the street has not run a welfare-to-work programme, it is not generally understood just how difficult, costly, and counterproductive such mandates can be. Various alternative proposals introduced in the House and the Senate left the nominal standard of 70% participation intact. What was altered was the set of recipients over which the rate was to be calculated, the standard for participation, the activities to be counted, and the exemptions to be allowed. One early Democratic proposal, while nominally requiring the same participation rate as was included in the administration's proposal, was estimated to require in practice only a 6 percentage point increase over levels attained by states in 2000 (Thomas, 2002).

Opponents willing to address the proposed participation requirements more directly questioned the degree to which additional use of workfare was justified by research. In this regard considerable attention was paid to the results of the Minnesota Family Investment Plan (MFIP), an initiative undertaken in the 1990s under federal waiver (Knox et al, 2000). MFIP had only a minor workfare component; the centrepiece was a very generous incentive for combining work and welfare. In addition to raising labour-force participation, MFIP produced surprising effects on the stability of two-parent families. When compared to outcomes under AFDC, three years after programme initiation MFIP participants were 39.5% more likely to be married, 40.8% less likely to be cohabiting without benefit of matrimony, and 58.4% less likely to be divorced or separated from a partner initially present. Critics argued that the reauthorisation proposal would force states to abandon a strategy that had been proven effective not only at raising work effort but also at strengthening marriages – an avowed administration goal.

A second tack was to emphasise costs. By 2001 states had managed to find ways to spend their TANF money. If they were to raise participation, additional work experience slots would be required, and funds for childcare would have to be obtained. In the absence of additional federal grants, current funding would have to be reallocated to basic welfare services. Such changes would possibly be counterproductive and would certainly be politically difficult, given the constituency for the status quo.

The third feature, the 'super waiver proposal', was perhaps the most politically astute element of the administration's proposal, and it split the opposition. On the one hand, the super waiver offered the governors an opportunity for even more experimentation. If one believed that (a) states were motivated to secure the safety net with every available dollar, (b) the 1996 reforms were a success, and (c) by virtue of proximity state governments knew best how social assistance should be operated, it follows that experimentation with more discretion should be attempted. On the other hand, if one was sceptical of propositions (a) – (c) and believed that programme segmentation increased funding by building separate constituencies for the various welfare building blocks, the super waiver appeared to offer a fast track for restarting the race to the bottom.

It was difficult for opponents to directly challenge the NGA and its ally – the American Public Human Services Association (APHSA: an organisation dominated by state social agencies directors who are for the most part governors' appointees) – on the super waiver issue. To do so was to question what was gospel to both organisations. Instead, the strategy followed by opponents was to point to consequences for the power of Congress. A letter of opposition signed by over 300 advocacy, union, and related organisations was circulated to

Senators in May warning that the proposal would "Represent a massive and unprecedented transfer of power from Congress to the executive branch and the governors".[6]

Before 1996, welfare reform rarely faced deadlines. The 30 September 2002 deadline established in PRWORA for TANF reauthorisation spurred, by its extraordinary teleology, a remarkable outpouring of research, writing, and pundit convocation. In the end, most of this activity proved inconsequential. The debate that emerged following announcement of the administration's proposal featured very little substantive discussion about the consequences of the 1996 reforms, the emerging character of the nation's safety net, or the direction of social assistance policy. Instead, all focus was upon the details of just how many hours of what kinds of activities for which participants were to count, the need for more childcare money, and resisting the super waiver. The influence of research was hard to find.

### The Senate proposal

In the Senate, TANF fell within the province of the Senate Finance Committee (SFC). The defection from the party by one Republican Senator in 2001 shifted Senate control to the Democrats. As a result of the change, Democratic Senator Max Baucus of Montana became the SFC chair. Congressional procedures allowed the committee to either act on a separate proposal (including a Senate version of the administration's proposal) or to 'mark up' the bill already passed by the House. The Democrats enjoyed a one-vote SFC majority, and this allowed the chairman to report out of committee his own version of the House bill.

There were similarities between what the administration had proposed and the SFC mark up. Like the administration's proposal, the Senate bill retained the TANF block grant at current funding levels. Like the administration's proposal, the Illegitimacy Reduction Bonus was to be replaced with a grants programme oriented toward promoting healthy marriages. Like the administration's proposal, the Senate bill called for an increase in participation rates to 70% by 2007. But as usual, the devils and the differences lay in the details. The changes started with the title. The 2002 Personal Responsibility, Work, and Family Promotion Act became the 2002 Work, Opportunity, and Responsibility for Kids Act, or (get it?) the WORK Act. The Senate bill created so many exceptions, to the participation requirement in particular, that it was effectively eviscerated. The hours requirement for participation was reduced, and the range of activities satisfying the work requirement was increased. A loophole was created whereby states, by re-labelling TANF payments as housing assistance, might avoid the federal five-year limit. The activities permitted under the Senate version of promoting healthy marriage covered everything from grants for running programmes like the MFIP to distributing condoms to teenagers. Rather than end current waivers, the Senate bill authorised their continuation and required DHHS to approve waivers that are 'similar or identical' to those still in force. In practice this would have offered states an additional option for avoiding the federal time limit and certain work requirements.

Many of the particulars of the Senate bill were arguably improvements over the administration proposal. But together their intention seemed to be more aimed at satisfying various liberal constituencies than creating a cogent response to the administration's plan. The strategy of combining nominal acceptance of many features of the administration's proposal with a host of steps to undermine their effect backfired: instead of thoughtful and concerned, the committee's Democratic leadership came across as disingenuous. The bill gave administration spokespersons the material needed to shift public attention from the deficiencies of its own approach to the occasionally bizarre extremes of the Senate bill.

## The outcome

By mid-summer it appeared that conflict between House and Senate approaches to reauthorisation could lead to a stalemate and possibly a vote by Congress to simply extend TANF funding for another year with a 'continuing' resolution. For opponents, such a development initially appeared desirable: a continuing resolution would leave the block grant untouched, forestall any increase in the participation requirements, preclude the super waiver, and hold out promise for a refreshed and broader approach to reauthorisation in 2003.

However, by late July 2002, the impetus for resolution had grown because of economic developments. Both the federal and especially the state fiscal situations were rapidly deteriorating, and there was prospect of a military invasion of Iraq. Data released in June 2002 by the Fiscal Studies Program of the Nelson A. Rockefeller Institute of government indicated that state revenues had declined by an unprecedented 7.9% between the first quarter of 2001 and the same interval for 2002 (Jenny, 2002). The contraction of state revenues was continuing despite some indications that the national economy was improving. Then in July came the rapid downturn in the stock market that resulted in part from widespread revelation of corporate accounting scandals. Most econometric and anecdotal evidence indicated that the contraction in wealth reflected in the stock market would produce a reduction in consumption and investment and, thereby, either another recession or at least slower growth. The concern was that if the TANF appropriation was simply continued, the administration's offer of a sustained block grant would be 'off the table'. The developments strengthened the administration's bargaining position.

The problem was that the press of other legislation, and the struggle over Iraq, left little opportunity for bargaining from any position. Moreover, the Republicans began to sense a significant opportunity for regaining control of both houses of the Congress in the November 2002 elections and little chance of significant loss in bargaining power. The upshot was that reauthorisation was foregone in favour of a continuing resolution that preserved the existing structure of TANF through to December; the post-election 'lame-duck' session of Congress extended the authorisation into the new year. What was billed as the 'grand welfare debate' came in the end, to nothing.

## The issues

In the end, disappointment: continuation produced no substantive change, and the reauthorisation proposals that were fielded left many problems to be addressed. These include: (1) funding, (2) rationalisation, (3) performance, (4) learning, and (5) vision.

### Funding

In a metaphor alien to the configuration of electric trains in Europe, reform of the social security system is commonly called the 'third rail' of American politics: touching it is political suicide. If there was a 'third rail' in the 2002 welfare debate, it was the issue of funding. Basing the initial allocation of federal funding in 1993-95 made very little policy sense in 1996; it made none whatsoever by 2002.

Of course, part of the variation in state grants reflects state choices about spending under AFDC. For example, today South Carolina receives a small TANF grant and has a small maintenance of effort requirement because that state spent little on welfare in 1994. The price to South Carolina's taxpayers of increasing AFDC benefits was very low (less than 24 cents on the dollar), but the state simply chose not to do so. Nevertheless, that grant decision was made long ago, and it concerned principally the level of cash benefits under AFDC. TANF supposedly ended welfare as it was then known, and, as Figure 2.2 illustrates, a far smaller share of TANF monies is now going for cash benefits. Most TANF money is going for other uses – childcare, job placement, and the like. There seems little justification for allowing the resources available for these purposes to be governed largely by the cash benefit choices states made in the distant past and in a much different policy environment. Further, despite this variation in resources, all states are now subject to the same participation requirements, and if the Bush administration has its way, these requirements will grow. For a state like South Carolina, increasing participation may require reducing access to benefit, tighter time limits, and diversion of money from what are already low cash grants to job services.

### Rationalisation

The system overview presented at the beginning of this chapter discussed the (perhaps surprising) coherence in abstract of the national system of social assistance. In principle TANF provides the safety net, the last resort for families with children. As a last resort, TANF is the most intrusive, and the most paternal. Once families begin to work, the character of support changes, shifting from basic income to earnings supplementation, both through food stamps and the

EITC. The food stamp benefit, with its short budgeting period, provides a relatively quick response to fluctuation in income, while the EITC provides a mode of modest asset accumulation and a longer time horizon.

The reality has fallen short of the ideal. TANF benefits continue to decline in real terms, lowering the bottom of the safety net. And the actual level of work-related activity among recipients is much lower than popularly perceived or politically claimed. TANF treatment of families moving from assistance to work seems to have been motivated more by programme participation requirements than by either equitable treatment of families in like circumstances or by any thought-out strategy for promoting self-support. Use of food stamps by working families has declined, and rules for food stamps appear not to mesh well with rules applied to TANF recipients. The collection of ancillary federal programmes for poverty relief continues to grow. But such programmes tend to be piecemeal and operated with little connection to other parts of antipoverty strategy, especially the agencies responsible for the conduct of TANF. Contrary to claims of proponents, the retreat of the federal government from TANF control to the conspicuous but irresponsible periphery has exacerbated the degree of incoherence in the system.

However defined, coherence is just one of many goals of reform, and the cost of reweaving to gather up all loose ends likely exceeds the benefits. Nevertheless, the payoff to further integration of the system's major components and finding some method of birth control for new add-ons is likely to be high.

## Performance

PRWORA took a major step toward linking federal support for state programmes to both the process of social assistance and to outcomes associated with such programmes. These efforts have fallen short, in three ways. First, the incentives for state compliance are weak, and the data reported often lack credibility, both because of difficulties encountered in development of uniform standards for data collection and because for the most part what states report is not audited. Second, the performance measures related to process have generally failed to produce the information needed to link state-to-state variation in outcomes to variation in the experience for recipients that different state policies produce. While the accumulating evidence supports the notion that raising the level of activity of recipients in work-related activity does lead to higher rates of employment and case termination, effects of varying the combination of activities – an important issue in programme management – are less clear. The benefits of participation requirements would be enhanced if the process of measuring participation also produced data needed for assessing the consequences. Third, the various TANF bonus payments have in recent years rewarded states for outcomes without establishing connections between these outcomes and state efforts or between the outcomes measured and the objectives of national policy.

As was true for perfect programme rationalisation, the ideal portfolio of performance measures may not be worth the effort required to devise or implement. There is nonetheless ample room for improvement, and doing so seems technically feasible.

## Learning

As of mid-2001, the 51 states and the District of Columbia had produced 48 different procedures for calculation of TANF benefits for families with earnings. Forty-eight variants might be worth the nation's while if what is learned could even conceivably lead to some convergence of opinion about how best to calibrate incentives. Deriving common benefit from the activities of the Laboratories of Democracy requires a mechanism for comparing outcomes across these regimes and sorting out the effects of the particular choices made for outcomes that are important. Before PRWORA, states that wished to deviate from the national norm for earnings disregard were required, as a condition for deviating from federal requirements, to conduct an evaluation. Virtually all the evidence on programme effects that figured in the reauthorisation discussion, including the highly touted MFIP, was produced by waiver-based demonstrations. Now such evaluations are not required, and few states are conducting them. Waivers, once an opportunity for learning, are now a shelter from scrutiny.

The reason for this is a mismatch between the distribution of gains from serious evaluation and the distribution of costs. States and their operating agencies bear most of the operational costs of experimentation; when done well, the benefits spill-over nationally and in some cases, as British experience attests, internationally. For the most part, waivers went out when PRWORA came in, and the motivation for states to participate in careful, let alone rigorous, evaluation of alternatives in a way designed to contribute to national understanding of reform effects is diminished. Those waivers that endure serve principally to exempt states from federal requirements.

More is involved here than simply arranging more tests of broad programme alternatives like those carried out in the National Evaluation of Welfare-to-Work Strategies (NEWWS) that was spawned by the Family Support Act (Hamilton, 2002). These surely attract media attention, and the results are pertinent to state and national policy choice. But for the yeoman work of managing social assistance, it is very important also to improve understanding of the consequences of the nuances – things like variations in approach to casework, the efficacy of alternative assessment tools, and the consequences of disregarding child support payments in calculating benefit payments. To the credit of the second Bush administration and the Congress, the reauthorisation legislation included substantial funds for experimental innovation and evaluation. The challenge will lie in building a consensus around a research agenda and in finding ways to motivate states and local agencies to participate.

---

## Vision

While general agreement existed concerning what was wrong with the old system, far less agreement exists, and far less attention has been paid, to 'building welfare as we want it'. The collapse of the caseload removed welfare as an issue in the 2000 Presidential campaign, but structural problems with PRWORA remain. There are many loose ends; what is needed to wrap them up is a new ideology that focuses not on the problems of the old system but ambitions for the new. Neither the president nor any of the governors seems to have such a vision now, and none was produced by what was supposed to be the 'great reauthorisation debate'. The prospect is that until a way can be found to focus on a system for the future, the national debate on welfare policy seems doomed to repeat the sad experience of 2002.

## Notes

[1] Burke (2001). This chapter makes extensive use of work by the Congressional Research Service (CRS) of the Library of Congress. The CRS, the Congressional Budget Office, and the General Accounting Office constitute the three major agencies providing research and analytical support for the Congress. CRS publications are not generally distributed and are not posted on the web, but they are available on request. The *Green book* produced by the Committee on Ways and Means, of the House of Representatives, and publicly distributed by the US Government Printing Office is almost completely written by CRS staff. See Committee on Ways and Means (2000).

[2] At the time of this drafting, 1999 was the latest date for which the necessary data on state taxes and benefits could be assembled on a consistent basis. More recent data for system components are presented elsewhere in the chapter. No changes have occurred since 1999 in the systems represented that materially affect the discussion.

[3] All tabulations of features of state TANF programmes are drawn from the Urban Institute's Welfare Rules Database (WRD). The WRD is described and data through 1999 are presented in Rowe (2000). The numbers in the text are based on this source plus unpublished information for subsequent years.

[4] Calculated from National Income and Products accounts data, using state and local government purchases deflator. See Council of Economic Advisors, 2002, Table B-7 and B-82.

[5] The items in this list are taken from the NGA website (www.nga.org; the 'translations' are the author's.

[6] This letter was distributed under many agency letterheads. For a sample, see the letter posted on the website of the Food Resource Action Center (FRAC), the leading advocacy organisation promoting Food Stamp Program access, at www.frac.org.

## References

Bavier, R. (2000) 'Accounting for increases in failure to report AFDC/TANF receipt', unpublished manuscript, Washington, DC: Office of Management and Budget.

Bloom, D., Farrell, M., Fink, B. with Adams-Ciardullo, D. (2002) 'Welfare time limits: state policies, implementation, and effects on families', New York, NY: Manpower Demonstration Research Corporation.

Burke, V. (2001) *Cash and noncash benefits for persons with limited income: Eligibility rules, recipient and expenditure data, FY1998-2000*, CRS Report for Congress RL31228, Washington, DC: Congressional Research Service.

Burke, V. (2002) *Welfare reform: An issue overview*, CRS Report for Congress IB93034, 19 February, Washington, DC: Congressional Research Service.

Chernick, H. and McGuire, T.J. (1999) 'The states, welfare reform, and the business cycle', in S.H. Danziger (ed) *Economic conditions and welfare reform*, Kalamazoo, MI: W.E. Upjohn Institute for Employment Research, pp 275-303.

Committee on Ways and Means (2000) *2000 Green book: Background material and data on programmes within the jurisdiction of the Committee on Ways and Means*, Washington, DC: US Government Printing Office.

Council of Economic Advisors (1999) *Technical report: The effects of welfare policy and the economic expansion on welfare caseloads: An update*, Washington, DC: Executive Office of the President of the United States.

Council of Economic Advisors (2002) *Economic report of the President, 2002*, Washington, DC: The White House.

Falk, G. (2002a) *Welfare reform: Federal grants and financing rules under TANF*, Report RL30723, Updated 5 April.

Falk, G. (2002b) *Welfare reform: FY2000 TANF spending and recent spending trends*, Report RL31087, Updated 20 March, Washington, DC: Congressional Research Service, Library of Congress.

Falk, G. (2002c) *Welfare reform: TANF funding and major financing issues*, Report RS21087, Updated 18 March, Washington, DC: Congressional Research Service, Library of Congress.

Gabe, T. (2001) *Trends in welfare, work and the economic well-being of female-headed families with children: 1987-2000*, Report RL30797, Updated 21 December, Washington, DC: Congressional Research Service, Library of Congress.

Giannarelli, L. and Alderson, D. (2000) 'How has TANF changed the number and types of families eligible for cash aid? A microsimulation analysis', paper presented at the 40th Annual Workshop of the National Association for Welfare Research and Statistics, Scottsdale, Arizona.

Hamilton, G. (2002) *Moving people from welfare to work: Lessons from the national evaluation of welfare-to-work strategies*, Washington, DC: US Department of Health and Human Services and US Department of Education.

Jenny, N.W. (2002) 'Worst quarter of state tax revenue decline', *State Revenue Report no 48*, Albany, NY: Nelson A. Rockefeller Institute of Government.

Kaplan, T. (2000) 'Wisconsin's W-2 programme: welfare as we might come to know it?', in C.S. Weissert (ed) *Learning from leaders: Welfare reform politics and policy in five midwestern states*, Albany, NY: The Rockefeller Institute Press, pp 77-118.

Knox, V., Miller, C. and Gennetian, L.A. (2000) *Reforming welfare and rewarding work: Final report on the Minnesota Family Investment Programme*, Summary Report vol 1: Effects on adults; vol 2: Effects on children, New York, NY: Manpower Demonstration Research Corporation.

Mead, L.M. (ed) (1997) *The new paternalism: Supervisory approaches to poverty*, Washington, DC: Brookings Institution Press.

Murray, C.A. (1994) *Losing ground: American social policy, 1950-1980*, New York, NY: Basic Books.

Nightingale, D.S., Pindus, N., Kramer, F.C., Trutko, J., Mikelson, K. and Egner, M. (2002) *Work and welfare reform in New York City during the Giuliani Administration: A study of programme implementation*, Washington, DC: The Urban Institute.

O'Hara, B.J. (2002) 'Work and work-related activities of mothers receiving Temporary Assistance to Needy Families: 1996, 1998, and 2000', *Household Economic Studies*, P70-85, Washington, DC: US Census Bureau.

Rosso, R. (2001) Trends in *Food Stamp Program participation rates: 1994 to 1999*, Washington, DC: Mathematica Policy Research, Inc.

Rowe, G. (2000) *The Welfare Rules Databook: State Policies as of July 1999*, Washington, DC: Urban Institute.

Thomas, A. (2002) *Analysis of participation rate options*, Washington, DC: The Brookings Institution.

US Department of Health and Human Services (DHHS) (2000) *Temporary Assistance for Needy Families (TANF) Programme: Third annual report to Congress*, Washington, DC: The Department.

DHHS (2002a) *Indicators of welfare dependence,* Washington, DC: The Department, (http://aspe.hhs.gov/hsp/indicators02/) retrieved 23 July 2002.

DHHS (2002b) *Temporary Assistance for Needy Families (TANF) Program: Fourth annual report to Congress,* Washington, DC: The Department [in full?].

US General Accounting Office (GAO) (2001) *Welfare reform: Challenges in maintaining a federal-state fiscal partnership,* Report GAO-01-828, Washington, DC: The Agency.

Walker, R. (1991) *Thinking about workfare: Learning from US experience,* London: HMSO.

Wallace, G. and Blank, R.M. (1999) 'What goes up must come down?', in S.H. Danziger (ed) *Economic conditions and welfare reform,* Kalamazoo, MI: W.E. Upjohn Institute for Employment Research, pp 49-90.

Weaver, K. (2000) *Ending welfare as we know it,* Washington DC: The Brookings Institution.

Welfare to Work Partnership (2000) *The Welfare to Work Partnership's report to the President on welfare to work.*

White House (2002) *Working toward independence,* Washington, DC: The White House (www.whitehouse.gov/news/releases/2002/02/ welfare-reform-announcement-book.pdf), retrieved 28 March 2002.

Wilde, P., Cook, P., Gundersen, C., Nord, M. and Tiehen, L. (2000) *The decline in Food Stamp Program participation in the 1990s,* Food Assistance and Nutrition Research Report no 7, Washington, DC: US Department of Agriculture Economic Research Service.

Wilkens, A. (2002) *Time-limited TANF recipients,* Denver, CO: National Conference of State Legislatures.

Wiseman, M. (1996) 'State strategies for welfare reform: the Wisconsin Story', *Journal of Policy Analysis and Management,* vol 15, no 4, pp 515-46.

Wiseman, M. (2000) 'Welfare's children', Institute for Research on Poverty Discussion Paper 1212-00, Madison, WI: University of Wisconsin Institute for Research on Poverty.

Wiseman, M. (2002) 'The New York City public assistance process', typescript.

Wiseman, M. and Giannarelli, L. (2002) 'The working poor and the benefit doors: entrance and exit policy in TANF', paper presented at the 24th annual research conference, Association for Public Policy and Management, Dallas, Texas.

# THREE

# The British perspective on reform: transfers from, and a lesson for, the US

*Alan Deacon*

Chapter One discusses some of the ways in which Britain's welfare regime differs from that of the United States. These differences are important, but they have not prevented what Robert Walker (1998) has termed the "Americanisation" of the British welfare debate. Indeed there is now an extensive literature on the impact of American ideas upon New Labour thinking on welfare reform, especially its welfare-to-work programmes (Theodore and Peck, 1998; White, 1998; King and Wickham-Jones, 1999). More than anything else, this Americanisation has served to heighten New Labour's preoccupation with the problem of welfare dependency. It has meant that the British debate is less dominated by economic considerations than it would otherwise have been and more concerned with issues of individual responsibility and personal behaviour. In this way the American influence has enhanced and sustained a moralism that the New Labour government shares with its Conservative predecessors, but which distinguishes it from previous Labour governments – and indeed from social democratic governments in continental Europe (Deacon, 2000).

It follows from this that there are now important commonalities between the British and American approaches to welfare reform. They have both been formulated in response to conservative critiques of welfare, and both seek to reach an accommodation with aspects of those critiques. In consequence, the central features of welfare reform in both countries have been an emphasis upon the obligations rather than the rights of welfare claimants, the introduction of work requirements, and the attempt to 'make work pay'. Both approaches have been influenced strongly by the evidence of so-called dynamic analyses of welfare and incomes, and both have sought to address popular anxieties about welfare. Most importantly, the two approaches share a common perception of the purpose of welfare reform, and draw upon and articulate similar understandings of human nature and of the relationship between welfare and human behaviour (Deacon, 2002). It is these similarities that make it reasonable to talk of policy transfer between the two countries, despite the different institutional and cultural contexts within which those policies operate.

There is, however, one significant difference between the objectives of welfare reform in Britain and the US. This is the commitment that New Labour has made to the immediate reduction and eventual elimination of child poverty. This commitment is in turn a reflection of New Labour's belief that it is the experience of poverty in childhood that holds the key to the transmission of deprivation across generations.

This chapter reviews welfare reform in Britain in light of these similarities and this difference. Before doing so, however, it is important to distinguish between New Democrat and New Labour thinking on welfare and the policies adopted in the two countries. The reforms implemented in the US in the 1990s emerged from a complex political process brilliantly chronicled by Kent Weaver (2000). They owed as much to the ideas and concerns of Republicans in Congress as they did to those of Democrats in the White House. One consequence is that the election of the second Bush administration has led to a shift of emphasis rather than a dramatic reversal of policy. It is true that the new administration's proposals for the reauthorisation of TANF place a greater priority upon the promotion of "healthy two parent married families and responsible fatherhood" (White House, 2002, p 21), a change signalled by the appointment of Wade Horn, a founder and former president of the 'National Fatherhood Initiative', as Assistant Secretary for Planning and Education (Horn and Sawhill, 2001). In general, however, the reauthorisation debates reflect what Blank and Haskins have termed the "detoxification of the debate about welfare, welfare reform and poverty" (Blank and Haskins, 2001). There is, they note, a broad measure of agreement among observers regardless "of which side of the aisle they were on in 1996" (Blank and Haskins, 2001, p vi).

New Labour's position in Britain has always been very different from that of the New Democrats. Its huge majority in Parliament has meant that the Blair government has faced few political obstacles to the implementation of its programme. Even so, New Labour is not monolithic and there are significant differences between individual ministers and departments – most importantly between Tony Blair himself and the Chancellor of the Exchequer Gordon Brown (Naughtie, 2001). In David Marquand's words, "if thought influences action, action also influences thought":

> Belief and behaviour, ideas and policies, visions of the future and legacies of the past, form a seamless web; attempts to unpick it, to give primacy to thought over action, or to action over thought, confuse more than they illuminate. (Marquand, 1996, p 6)

## An integrative approach

Perhaps the most obvious point of similarity between the approach of New Labour and the New Democrats was that both presented welfare reform as a central element in the development of a new 'third way' for centre-left politics.

There is, of course, an enormous literature on the third way, and no little irritation with an idea described by Klein and Rafferty as "a chameleon phrase whose appeal lies in its conceptual versatility" (Klein and Rafferty, 1999, p 44). Moreover, the election of a Republican president appears to have marked the end of the third way debate in the US. Nevertheless, the idea of the third way remains important for the present discussion. As Klein and Rafferty again note, there are two dimensions to the third way:

> Politically the Third Way is a strategy for repositioning left-of-centre parties in order to ensure electoral survival. Intellectually, it is a strategy for justifying that repositioning with a coherent programme of action. (Klein and Rafferty, 1999, p 46)

Welfare reform has been central to both of these dimensions. Clinton's pledge to "end welfare as we know it" and Blair's commitment to tackle benefit fraud and to enforce work requirements for young people were not just electoral stratagems. They also represented a new, more integrative approach to welfare policy.

In the US the most widely cited claim for the third way has been Clinton's assertion that it has ended the sterile debate between the advocates of big and small government. In Britain Prime Minister Tony Blair has argued that the defining feature of third way politics is that it reconciles "themes which in the past have wrongly been regarded as antagonistic – patriotism and internationalism, rights and responsibilities, the promotion of enterprise and the attack on poverty" (Blair, 1998b, p 1). He believes it can combine policies in ways that cut across traditional political divides. In the case of welfare this requires recognition that there is a need both for the redistribution of income and for policies focused upon and demanding more of the long-term poor in terms of changes in behaviour including labour market participation. Debates about dependency and inequality are no longer seen as mutually exclusive but as addressing different dimensions of the same problem.

New Labour's approach to welfare reform, then, is an integrative one in that it is explicitly seeking to draw upon and encompass elements from hitherto conflicting perspectives on welfare. As Stephen Teles has argued, it is this integrative quality that is common to the British and American third ways:

> The core of New Democrat and New Labour thinking is a shared cognitive perspective that sees the essence of moral reasoning to be the integration of equally necessary social goods, rather than the process of choosing between them. (Teles, 1997, p 55)

This is, of course, a very big claim. In addition to its conceptual ambiguities, critics on both sides of the Atlantic have argued that the third way is an attempt to square circles. In Britain, for example, Driver and Martell have pointed to the "essential and irresolvable tensions between" the "counterpoised options of

Left and Right, social democracy, liberalism and conservatism" (Driver and Martell, 2000, p 155). In practice, they argue, third way policies such as the British New Deals represent an attempt to strike a new balance between "the demands of competing political values" at "the policy coal-face" (Driver and Martell, 2000, p 155).

This is a powerful argument. Nevertheless, it is argued here that there is more to the third way than this "pragmatic and limited notion of politics" (Driver and Martell, 2000, p 155). The point is not just that New Labour and the New Democrats have produced a new mix of incentives, authority and moral exhortation. It is that in order to arrive at this new mix they have both had to disregard long established taboos on judgementalism and on discussions of personal behaviour.

In Britain this meant abandoning the left's long-standing commitment to the provision of welfare as entitlement, and its fierce opposition to conditionality (Deacon, 2002). In the US, it meant discussing the nature and causation of social pathology in ways that had been constrained since the furore surrounding the Moynihan Report of 1965 (Rainwater and Yancey, 1967; Teles, 1996; Wilson, 1987, 1996). Above all, it meant responding to the attacks on welfare mounted by conservatives such as Charles Murray and Lawrence Mead.

In both Britain and America, then, welfare reform took the form that it did because it represented, at least in part, a response to the impact of conservative ideas about welfare dependency. Moreover, at the heart of that response was a new emphasis upon the obligations of claimants.

## The enforcement of obligations

Alongside Tony Blair himself, the most prominent advocate of a third way in Britain is the social theorist Anthony Giddens, a man sometimes described as the Prime Minister's 'favourite guru'. Giddens has recently suggested that "a prime motto for the new politics" might be "no rights without responsibilities" and just such "a redefinition of rights and obligations" (Giddens, 1998, p 65), lies at the heart of welfare reform in Britain.

This is, of course, an extremely familiar argument in the US. Back in 1988, David Ellwood observed that the "notion of mutual responsibilities" was "not controversial any more". There was, he said, widespread acceptance among liberals and conservatives that it was "legitimate to ask people to fulfil some obligations" and to expect governments to provide some jobs or training "in exchange" (Ellwood, 1988, p 226). In some respects this consensus proved to be more apparent than real, and the first Clinton plan was bedevilled by arguments over the precise nature of these mutual obligations (Ellwood, 1996; Weaver, 1998, 2000). These differences remain, but the principle of enforcing work and other obligations has not been seriously challenged in the reauthorisation debates. A similar consensus exists in Britain, at least in respect of young people. The element of compulsion in the New Deals was opposed by some leading Labour politicians when in opposition (King and Wickham-

Jones, 1999), but is not now subject to serious challenge. It has already been noted that this represents a significant shift in centre-left thinking, and one that owes much to the influence of American ideas and especially of communitarianism and the new paternalism.

In 1995 Tony Blair delivered a speech entitled 'The rights we enjoy reflect the duties we owe'. In it he declared that an incoming Labour government would combine new opportunities to work with a "reasonable obligation to take the chances offered":

> A society geared to extending opportunity is one then able to demand ᵣₑₛₚₒₙₛᵢbility with some realistic prospect of it being given. It allows us to be much tougher and hard headed in the rules we apply, and how we apply them. (Blair, 1995, p 7)

Other examples of this tough-minded approach were the introduction of home/school contracts which would set out the obligations of parents in respect of "attendance and time-keeping, homework and standards", and the requirement that tenants in social housing meet new conditions regarding their behaviour. He insisted that the government would not be "squeamish" about passing judgment on people who failed to fulfil their obligations to their immediate neighbours or the wider community in which they lived:

> Families have the right to be housed. But they do not have any right to terrorise those around them, be it with violence, racial abuse or noise. If tenants do not fulfil their side of the bargain, particularly after repeated warnings, the contract is broken. (Blair, 1995, p 9)

In this, New Labour has been true to its word, and the element of compulsion in the New Deal for Young People is only one of the ways in which an individual's entitlement to benefits or services is now dependent upon his or her behaviour (Dwyer, 1998; Dwyer and Heron, 1999). This emphasis upon the duties and responsibilities of claimants, however, is only one side of the coin. The other is the importance now placed upon paid work.

## The centrality of paid work

In March 1998 the New Labour government finally published a long-delayed consultation document, or Green Paper, entitled *A new contract for welfare* (DSS, 1998). This was short on policy detail, but it provided an important statement of the government's intentions in welfare. It did so, moreover, in language that echoed almost exactly that of Tony Blair himself. It spoke, for example, of ending a welfare system that "chains people to passive dependency instead of helping them to realize their full potential", and of the need for services which were active not passive and which pushed people to "achieve independence". The experience of the past 50 years has shown that "cash hand outs alone can lead to a life of dependency". In short, the government's aim was to "rebuild the welfare state around work" (DSS, 1998, p 9, 71, 19, 23).

> Our ambition is nothing less than a change of culture among benefit claimants, employers, and public servants – with rights and responsibilities on all sides. (DSS, 1998, p 24)

The argument that the answer to poverty lay in the redistribution of opportunities rather than in higher benefits had been made in 1994 in the influential report of the Borrie Commission, an informal group set up by Blair's predecessor John Smith to inform Labour thinking on social and economic policy (Borrie Commission, 1994). At the time the Commission's emphasis upon paid work owed more to its scepticism regarding the willingness of the British taxpayer to fund more generous benefits than it did to any optimism regarding prospects for the labour market. That said, there is a striking resonance between the arguments of the Green Paper and the analysis of the welfare conundrums, which David Ellwood put forward in *Poor support* (1988), and which underpinned the first Clinton reform plan (Ellwood, 1996; Bryner, 1998; Weaver, 1998). It is an analysis that starts from the premise that poverty among those capable of work cannot be alleviated through cash assistance without generating unsustainable disincentives to work. There are, Ellwood argued: "inevitable conflicts of incentives and values that undermine the credibility and effectiveness" (Ellwood, 1988, p 7) of cash based systems. The only way to avoid these conflicts is to redefine welfare as transitional assistance. The goal would be to equip recipients with the capacities and skills to enter or re-enter the labour force – and then require them to do so. A further goal would be to 'make work pay' by providing those in low paid jobs with supplemental support through the tax and child support systems. Remaining on welfare, however, could not be an option: "the long-term support system is jobs" (Ellwood, 1996, p 181).

This message was reinforced in the UK by the findings of so-called dynamic analyses of incomes and poverty. A considerable number of British scholars have now studied the techniques employed by Ellwood and Mary Jo Bane, and have begun to apply them to longitudinal data on income mobility in the UK (Hills, 1998; Leisering and Walker, 1998; Jenkins, 1999). In so doing they have traced the trajectories through which people move into and out of poverty, and the events – or triggers – that precede a significant change in income. The results have confirmed the overwhelming importance of work. Between 1991 and 1995, for example, almost 80% of those who moved from worklessness to work had escaped from the bottom fifth of the income distribution as a result. Put the other way round, of those leaving the bottom fifth, nearly 66% did so because someone in the household either got a job or increased his or her earnings (Jenkins, 1999). It is statistics such as these that have led New Labour ministers to describe the benefit system they had inherited as having become "part of the problem; not the solution":

> The benefits system has failed to adapt to changes in the labour market and
> society. It has ... increasingly concentrated solely on paying benefits to
> people, rather than providing them with active help to get off benefits.
> (DSS, 1999, p 29)

There is, of course, a considerable element of party politics in this. The
Conservatives had introduced a range of measures to increase the pressure
upon unemployed claimants to accept the jobs that were available. What New
Labour has done is to widen the scope of such programmes. As Bruce Stafford
shows in Chapter Six, New Labour has begun to shift the boundary between
those who are expected to look to the labour market and those who are not.
David Price, a former senior official in the Employment Agency, has recently
provided a balanced assessment of the extent to which the New Deal
programmes represent a departure from the approach of the Conservatives:

> The philosophy of 'welfare-to-work' which underlies these programmes is
> broadly consistent with the approach of Conservative governments over the
> previous ten years, but the concept of welfare has been broadened from the
> claimant unemployed to include groups such as single parents and those on
> incapacity benefit. (Price, 2000, p 311)

What is most important here is the reason why New Labour has broadened
the concept of welfare-to-work in this way. It was noted earlier that the focus
upon work and the rhetoric about the obligations of claimants are two sides of
the same coin. Taken together they should be seen as an attempt to restructure
welfare in ways that minimize the value conflicts identified by Ellwood and so
provide a basis for rebuilding popular support for welfare.

## Rebuilding popular support for welfare

As explained in Chapter One, welfare in Britain is received by a far broader
range of people than claim TANF or food stamps, and this helps to explain
why it has not aroused the virulent and often racialised hostility directed at
welfare in the US. Even so, the New Labour government has been preoccupied
with the need to rebuild popular support for welfare. In part it has sought to
do this through a high profile campaign to "build a consensus for modernising
social security" (Blair, 1998a, p 3). In launching this campaign, Blair argued
that the welfare state was no more tailored to people's needs than a car or
television set designed 50 years ago:

> More women now work. Most people change jobs at least six or seven
> times in their career and there is no such thing as a job for life. People live
> longer, in some cases for thirty years after retirement. These are big changes
> in the way we live. The welfare state must adapt to them. (Blair, 1998a, p 3)

Much more controversial is New Labour's belief that public confidence in the integrity of the welfare system has been undermined by the failure of successive governments to respond adequately to popular concern about the problem of benefit fraud.

This has led ministers to reverse Labour's previous stance on fraud and to introduce a series of well-publicised initiatives to detect and deter such abuse.[1] Moreover, New Labour's scepticism about the honesty of claimants is matched by its scepticism about the motivation of the electorate. It places little store on appeals to the altruism of the voters.[2] Instead the appeal is to their "enlightened self interest". In a speech in South Africa in 1996, for example, Blair argued that "in a society in which opportunity is extended we have greater security, our streets are safer, our young people more motivated, our ambitions better fulfilled" (Blair, 1996, p 9).

This notion of enlightened self-interest not only forms the basis of New Labour's appeal to the wider electorate. It also provides the rationale for the use of compulsion within welfare-to-work and other programmes. On the one hand welfare is to be used to encourage, cajole, and compel people to act in ways that may be unattractive in the short run but can be expected to enhance their prospects in the longer term. On the other hand, the public is to be persuaded that the money spent on welfare is not being wasted, and that the recipients are meeting their obligations.

> I think that matching opportunity and responsibility is the only way in the modern world to obtain consent from the public to fund the welfare state. It has to become the new deal for 21st-century welfare. (Blair, 1996, p 10)

Blair, however, was also at pains to emphasize that this New Deal had to be "something deeper than merely a contractual relationship" between government and voters. A "decent society" had to be "founded on duty". It required that people accept "a significant degree of responsibility" for others. Enlisting popular support for welfare, then, was not simply an end in itself. It was an essential first step, if those collective responsibilities were to be recognized and met. In the Beveridge Lecture of March 1999, Blair returned to the "great challenge" of how to "make the welfare state popular again". It was also in this lecture that he declared that it was the "historic aim" of his government "for ours to be the first generation to end child poverty" (Blair, 1999, p 17).

### An end to child poverty as we know it?

It is clear that New Labour's explicit commitment to end child poverty is by far the most important difference between the British and American approaches to welfare reform. What may be less clear is that the announcement of this commitment also marked a significant shift of emphasis within New Labour rhetoric.

Both in opposition and in the early days in government Blair and his senior colleagues had spoken little about poverty. They had chosen instead to employ language very familiar to American readers. Blair himself insisted that "our collective duty as a society" was first and foremost "to tackle the growing underclass" which was "cut off from society's mainstream" (Blair, 1996, p 9). Peter Mandelson, one of the prime architects of New Labour, spoke of "today's and tomorrow's underclass", which consisted of "people who have lost hope" and are "trapped in fatalism". The "people we are concerned about", he added, "will not have their long-term problems addressed by an extra pound a week on their benefits" (Mandelson, 1997, pp 6, 7).

On other occasions ministers did talk about processes of social exclusion, by which they meant the mutually reinforcing effects of low incomes, poor health, inadequate housing and discrimination on the grounds of race and gender. Very rarely, however, did they focus specifically upon low incomes, and hardly ever did they use what came to be known as the 'p-word'. Not, that is, until Blair so dramatically set a target of eliminating poverty in 20 years.

It is far from clear what prompted this change of emphasis. One important factor, however, was growing recognition of the extent to which the opportunities open to people during their lifetime are diminished by the experience of poverty in childhood. In the words of a recent government document:

> The key to tackling disadvantage in the future is the eradication of child poverty. Children who grow up in disadvantaged families generally do less well at school, and are more likely to suffer unemployment, low pay and poor health in adulthood. This poverty of opportunity is then more likely to be experienced by the next generation of children. (DSS, 1999, p 5)

Mike Brewer and Paul Gregg note in Chapter Four that the recognition that childhood deprivation had longer-term consequences was "probably crucial in assembling the political will to address childhood poverty". They also note that US evidence of the effectiveness of child-based interventions was "perhaps as influential". The important point for the discussion here is that ending child poverty came to be seen and presented by New Labour less as an objective in itself and more as a first step towards the broader aim of reducing inequalities of opportunity. Social exclusion came to be seen as exclusion from opportunities, and child poverty came to be seen as a root cause of that exclusion. In some respects there is nothing very remarkable about this. The pursuit of equality had long been the central objective of Labour politics. What is more surprising is that the Chancellor of the Exchequer – Britain's chief finance minister – played the crucial role in bringing it to the top of New Labour's welfare agenda.

Just before the 1997 election Gordon Brown, then Shadow Chancellor, had argued that an incoming Labour government must retain the party's traditional commitment to equality. The starting point had to be "a fundamental belief in the equal worth of every human being". This meant that all must have "an equal chance" to "develop the potential with which they were born" (Brown,

1999, p 40). In order to fulfil their potential, individuals require opportunities to work, to learn and train, and to exercise some control over the decisions that affect their lives. Moreover, the denial of such opportunities is not only an affront to social justice but also an obstacle to economic management. What is "right on ethical grounds" is now "good for the economy too":

> Today, in an economy where skills are the essential means of production, the denial of opportunity has become an unacceptable inefficiency, a barrier to prosperity. (Brown, 1999, p 41)

A Labour government, Brown argued, should take a "demanding view of equality of opportunity" and work "to prevent the permanent entrenchment of privilege from whatever source it came" (Brown, 1999, p 43). A very similar view of equality has also been put forward by Tony Blair and Anthony Giddens in their contributions to the third way debate. Blair, for example, spoke of the need to "tackle the obstacles to true equality of opportunity" (Blair, 1998b, p 3), while Giddens has argued that any talk of equality of opportunity "still presumes redistribution of wealth and income" (Giddens, 2000, p 89). This is because a market economy inevitably generates wide disparities of income and wealth. In the absence of redistribution, the wealthy will be able to confer such advantages upon their own children as to negate any possibility of equality of opportunity (Giddens, 2000, p 89).

It was against this background that in March 1999 the Treasury, now headed by Brown, published what it described as "shocking conclusions" about the "passage of inequality from generation to generation" and about the "persistent and scarring nature" of childhood poverty.[3] These conclusions were drawn largely from analyses of panel data that had been presented at a workshop organized by the Treasury in the previous November. The central message was that "people's life chances are determined by who their parents were rather than their own talents and efforts" (HM Treasury, 1999, p 31):

> Childhood disadvantage frequently leads to low educational attainment, low educational attainment leads to low pay and low employment, which in turn leads to low income and denial of opportunity for the next generation. (HM Treasury, 1999, p 27)

The key transmission mechanism was education. Studies of the educational development of children born in 1970 showed that those from privileged backgrounds were markedly ahead at the age of 22 months, and that the differential between them and children from poor backgrounds continued to widen thereafter (HM Treasury, 1999, p 29). This was not the whole story, however, since statistical research showed that poverty "has a further, distinct effect, over and above its impact on education" (HM Treasury, 1999, p 33). All of this was further compounded in the most deprived areas, in which "whole communities find themselves trapped outside mainstream society" (DSS, 1999, p 138) by high rates of worklessness and crime, poor health and low educational achievement.

It is interesting to examine New Labour's response to this data in the context of the long-standing debate in the US about the relative importance of social structure and individual behaviour in explaining the persistence and transmission of deprivation. There is no doubt New Labour's understanding of the causes of poverty is primarily a structural one. It does not deny that behaviours and attitudes help to explain why some people are unemployed for long periods, or why poverty affects successive generations of the same family. In essence, however, that behaviour is seen as a consequence rather than a cause of social deprivation.

The Treasury report is quick to point out, for example, that the slower educational development of poor children cannot be ascribed to poor parenting in problem families, but is linked to a "series of factors that are more likely to occur in disadvantaged families" (HM Treasury, 1999, p 29, 30). These include large family size, poor and overcrowded housing, low birth weight, and unemployment of the father. It follows that the most effective interventions are those that are non-stigmatising and avoid labelling problem families. Elsewhere New Labour's first 'poverty report' does acknowledge that "not all children born into low income families fare badly in later life" and that "parental attitudes and interest in education have a significant effect on educational attainment" (DSS, 1999, p 44, 45). It goes on, however, to argue that governments cannot expect to stimulate a higher level of parental interest without first tackling the broader and more deep rooted 'poverty of ambition' which characterizes such communities. This in turn will require the provision of more effective schools and far greater opportunities for employment.

At the same time those experiencing exclusion are expected to take advantage of the opportunities that New Labour is creating, and they will be compelled to do so if necessary. Moreover, the growth of poverty in the past is explained at least in part by the failure of previous governments to provide the requisite encouragement and pressure. Another recent government document, for example, argues that the "passive administration of Invalidity Benefit is likely to have exacerbated" the increase in inactivity among older men. This is because its "more generous level encouraged people to define themselves as incapacitated rather than unemployed", and because there was "inadequate scrutiny of claims to benefits" (DSS, 2000, p 34).

In terms of the literature, then, New Labour's analysis draws upon two conflicting interpretations of the relationship between behaviour and social pathology. Without doubt it is closest to William Julius Wilson's argument that what he terms ghetto-related behaviours and cultures should be understood as adaptations to the levels of worklessness experienced by poor communities. It shares Wilson's belief that if public policy succeeds in improving the economic prospects of such communities, then those behaviours "no longer sustained and nourished by persistent joblessness, will gradually fade" (Wilson, 1996, p 238). At the same time there are clear echoes of Lawrence Mead's understanding of a culture of poverty as one that condones the failure of the poor to meet their obligations and to conform to agreed social norms. For Mead the task of public policy is to close "the gap between the norm and the welfare recipient's lifestyle" by a combination of "help and hassle" (Mead, 1997, p 64). This authoritarian approach, so dominant in the implementation of PRWORA, is becoming increasingly evident in the rhetoric of some New Labour ministers.

What is most significant, however, is the way in which New Labour has integrated these perspectives. It views social exclusion as both structural – because people are excluded by deprivations that are transmitted across generations – and individual – because if people do not take advantage of their opportunities they will have excluded themselves. In policy terms, this produces a combination of measures, some of which are designed to level the playing field and some of which are designed to activate the players. The Green Paper, for example, set out three ways in which New Labour's welfare reform would change behaviour. The New Deals would stimulate and cajole people into doing more to find a job, the new tax credits would encourage them to work harder and longer, and a better-designed and more rigorously policed system would deter fraud. None of those measures, however, should be seen in isolation from the commitment to reduce child poverty and the very significant increases that have been made to the rates of benefits for children.[4]

## Conclusion

The argument of this chapter is that policy makers in Britain and the US do indeed operate in very different cultural, political and institutional contexts, but that they are seeking to achieve similar objectives and draw upon a similar range of policy instruments in order to do so. It is this similarity of approach that creates the potential for policy transfer between the two countries – in both directions. Americans do not need lessons from Britain – or anywhere else – about the need to enforce work or to emphasise the obligations of claimants. Nevertheless, the approach adopted by New Labour raises an important question for policy makers and commentators in the US. If it is the case that, as Besharov and Germanis put it, welfare reform is "ultimately" the means and that the end is "reducing poverty" and "producing better outcomes for children" (Besharov and Germanis, 2001, p 79), then why not make this objective explicit? Why not accept a commitment to reduce poverty and view the enforcement of work and the promotion of effective and responsible parenting as the primary means of attaining this goal? It is in this sense that the rhetoric of the third way is still valid. Tackling dependency and eliminating poverty requires a combination of policies drawn from both sides of the political aisle and from both sides of the Atlantic.

## Acknowledgement

The author would like to thank Pat Fairfoot, Larry Mead and the editors of this book for helpful comments on an earlier version of this chapter.

## Notes

[1] There has been an extraordinary shift in attitudes towards fraud and abuse in recent years. For much of the post-war period academics and politicians on the centre-left dismissed popular fears of widespread fraud. These fears were portrayed as a moral panic that was fuelled by the lurid exaggerations of the tabloid press and conservative backwoodsmen. The consensus was that fraud was a minor problem, especially in comparison to that of tax evasion. Moreover the fraud that did occur was thought to be due more to the inadequacy of benefits and the complexity of the rules regarding part-time and occasional work than it was to the dishonesty of claimants. Attempts to clamp down on fraud were fiercely resisted. Not only were they unnecessary, went the argument, but they impeded the more important task of improving the take up of benefits. The stance adopted by New Labour could hardly be more different. First in opposition and then in government it has claimed that it will be possible to save large sums of money by the early detection and prevention of abuse. New Labour now argues that far from undermining the proper administration of benefits, such measures are essential if public confidence in the integrity of the system is to be restored.

[2] This approach is very different from that of earlier social democratic governments, and is one that has caused considerable dismay on the left. Robert Page, for example, argues that New Labour's abandonment of the "ideal of caring for strangers ... amounts to nothing less than a seismic break from the past" (Page, 2000, p 617).

[3] These quotations are taken from the accompanying press release. The report was published eleven days after Blair's announcement of the poverty target.

[4] By April 2000, for example, the level of the universal child benefit had risen by 26% in real terms since New Labour took office, and that of the income support (welfare) benefits for children under 11 by 72% (HM Treasury, 2000, p 10). The major constraint upon still bigger increases in benefits for children is New Labour's reluctance to redistribute incomes, or at least to do so openly. In the words of a leading conservative politician, David Willetts, it is pursuing a "social policy which dare not speak its name" (Willetts, 2000, p 28). This is not just the view of the government critics. Indeed New Labour's approach is captured perfectly in the comment of the Prime Minister's advisor on education, Andrew Adonis, that "while New Labour wants to help the poor as a matter of principle, it refuses to hit the rich as a matter of principle". It is this, Adonis added, "which separates Old Left from New Left" (quoted in Page, 2000, p 618). The continued viability of this approach was emerging as a crucial issue as New Labour began its second term in government.

# References

Besharov, D. and Germanis, P. (2001) 'Welfare reform: four years later', in D. Besharov, P. Germains, J. Hein, D. Jones and A. Sherman (eds) *Ending dependency: Lessons from welfare reform in the USA*, London: Civitas, pp 60-81.

Blair, T. (1995) 'The rights we enjoy reflect the duties we owe', *The Spectator lecture*, London: Labour Party, 22 March.

Blair, T. (1996) Speech to Commonwealth Prime Ministers Conference, Cape Town, 14 October.

Blair, T. (1997) 'The 21st century welfare state', Speech to Social Policy and Economic Performance Conference, Amsterdam, 24 January.

Blair, T. (1998a) 'Building a modern welfare state', Speech at Dudley Town Hall, 15 January.

Blair, T. (1998b) *The Third Way: New politics for the new century*, London: Fabian Society.

Blair, T. (1999) 'Beveridge revisited: a welfare state for the 21st century', in R. Walker (ed) *Ending child poverty: Popular welfare for the 21st century?*, Bristol: The Policy Press, pp 7-18.

Blank, R. and Haskins, R. (ed) (2001) *The new world of welfare*, Washington, DC: Brookings Institution Press.

Borrie Commission (1994) *Social justice: Strategies for national renewal*, London: Vintage.

Brown, G. (1999) 'Equality – then and now', in D. Leonard (ed) *Crosland and New Labour*, London: Fabian Society, pp 35-48.

Bryner, G. (1998) *Politics and public morality*, London: Norton.

Deacon, A. (2000) 'Learning from the USA? The influence of American ideas on New Labour thinking on welfare reform', *Policy & Politics*, vol 28, no 1, pp 5-18.

Deacon, A. (2002) *Perspectives on welfare: Ideas, ideologies and policy debates open*, Buckingham: Open University Press.

DSS (Department of Social Security) (1998) *A new contract for welfare: New ambitions for our country*, Cm 3805, London: The Stationery Office.

DSS (1999) *Opportunity for all*, Cm 4445, London: The Stationery Office.

DSS (2000) *The changing welfare state: Social security spending*, London: DSS.

Driver, S. and Martell, L. (2000) 'Left, right and the Third Way', *Policy & Politics*, vol 28, no 2, pp 147-61.

Dwyer, P. (1998) 'Conditional citizens? Welfare rights and responsibilities in the late 1990s', *Critical social policy*, vol 18, no 4, pp 493-517.

Dwyer, P. and Heron, E. (1999) 'Doing the right thing: Labour and welfare reform: a new moral order?', *Social policy and administration*, vol 33, no 1, pp 91-104.

Ellwood, D. (1988) *Poor support: Poverty in the American family*, New York, NY: Basic Books.

Ellwood, D. (1996) 'Welfare reform as I knew it: When bad things happen to good policies', *The American Prospect*, vol 7, no 26, pp 22-9 (www.prospect.org, retrieved 11 September 2002).

Giddens, A. (1998) *The Third Way: The renewal of social democracy*, Cambridge: Polity Press.

Giddens, A. (2000) *The Third Way and its critics*, Cambridge: Polity Press.

Hills, J. (1998) *Income and wealth: The latest evidence*, York: Joseph Rowntree Foundation.

HM Treasury (1998) *The working families tax credit and work incentives: The modernization of Britain's tax and benefit system*, no 3, London: The Stationery Office.

HM Treasury (1999) *Tackling poverty and extending opportunity: The modernization of Britain's tax and benefit system*, no 4, London: HM Treasury.

HM Treasury (2000) *Tackling poverty and making work pay: Tax credits for the 21st century: The modernization of Britain's tax and benefit system*, no 6, London: HM Treasury.

Horn, W. and Sawhill, I. (2001) 'Fathers, marriage and welfare reform', in R. Blank and R. Haskins (eds) *The new world of welfare*, Washington, DC: Brookings Institution Press, pp 421-41.

Jenkins, S. (1998) 'Income dynamics', in J. Hills (ed) *Persistent poverty and lifetime inequality: The evidence*, HM Treasury Occasional Paper, no 10, London: The Stationery Office, pp 5-10.

King, D. and Wickham-Jones, M. (1999) 'Bridging the Atlantic: the Democratic (Party) origins of Welfare-to-Work', in M. Powell (ed) *New Labour new welfare state? The 'Third Way' in British social policy*, Bristol: The Policy Press, pp 257-80.

Klein, R. and Rafferty, A.M. (1999) 'Rorschach politics', *The American Prospect*, vol 10, no 45, pp 44-50.

Leisering, L. and Walker, R. (1998) *The dynamics of modern society: Poverty, policy and welfare*, Bristol: The Policy Press.

Mandelson, P. (1997) *Labour's next steps: Tackling social exclusion*, London: Fabian Society.

Marquand, D. (1996) 'Moralists and hedonists', in D. Marquand and A. Seldon (eds) *The ideas that shaped post-war Britain*, London: Fontana Press, pp 5-28.

Mead, L. (1997) 'Welfare employment', in L. Mead (ed) *The new paternalism*, Washington, DC: Brookings Institute, pp 39-88.

Naughtie, J. (2001) *The rivals*, London: Fourth Estate.

Page, R. (2000) 'For richer, for poorer? New Labour and the welfare state', *Social policy and administration*, vol 34, no 5, pp 614-19.

Price, D. (2000) *Office of hope: A history of the Employment Service*, London: Policy Studies Institute.

Rainwater, L. and Yancey, W. (1967) *The Moynihan report and the politics of controversy*, Cambridge, MA: MIT Press.

Teles, S. (1996) *Whose welfare? AFDC and elite politics*, Kansas: University Press of Kansas.

Teles, S. (1997) 'Can New Labour dance the Clinton?', *The American prospect,* vol 8, no 31, pp 49-56.

Theodore, N. and Peck, J. (1998) 'The limits of policy transfer: Innovation and emulation in welfare-to-work', Paper presented to APPAM Twentieth Research Conference. New York, October.

Walker, R. (1998) 'The Americanisation of British welfare: a case-study of policy transfer', *Focus*, vol 19, no 3, pp 32-40.

Weaver, K. (1998) 'Ending welfare as we know it', in M. Weir, (ed) *The social divide: Political parties and the future of activist government*, Washington DC: Brookings Institute, pp 361-416.

Weaver, K. (2000) *Ending welfare as we know it*, Washington, DC: Brookings Institute.

White House (2002) *Working toward independence*, Washington, DC: The White House.

White, M. (1998) 'What's new, what's old in the New Deal for the unemployed', Paper presented to APPAM Twentieth Research Conference, New York, October.

Willetts, D. (1999) *Browned-off: What's wrong with Gordon Brown's social policy*, London: Politeia.

Wilson, W.J. (1987) *The truly disadvantaged: The inner city, the underclass and public policy*, Chicago, IL: University of Chicago Press.

Wilson, W.J. (1996) *When work disappears*, New York, NY: Knopf.

# FOUR

# Eradicating child poverty in Britain: welfare reform and children since 1997

*Mike Brewer and Paul Gregg*

"Our historic aim will be for ours to be the first generation to end child poverty". (Tony Blair, Beveridge Lecture, 1999)

Perhaps the most ambitious commitment made by the current Labour government in the UK is its stated intention to eliminate child poverty within a generation – defined as 20 years. In this chapter the government's motivation for this initiative, what the government means when it talks about child poverty, and the welfare reform strategy developed to achieve it is discussed. What the reform package has accomplished so far is then discussed and followed with a look at future developments the government has announced or proposed but not yet implemented. The chapter concludes with a short discussion of what are seen as the strengths and weaknesses of the Labour programme.

## Motivation

Chapters One and Three have already previewed the factors leading up to and influencing Labour's child poverty initiative. The economic and social evidence on which the government bases its commitment is concentrated on here. This evidence falls into three parts: how the changing British economy has affected the ability of working-age adults to secure incomes above poverty levels, the particularly stark deterioration in the circumstances of Britain's children relative to other groups, and the mounting evidence that deprivation in childhood adversely affects a person's long-term outlook. The importance attached to this evidence is apparent in a number of Treasury publications, in particular analyses of developments in the labour market (HM Treasury, 1997), the problems of inactive workers (HM Treasury, 2001), and poverty dynamics and life-chances (HM Treasury, 1999b).

## The changing economy

Of the many changes in the British social economy over the past two decades that have affected the ability of working-age adults to secure incomes above poverty levels, four are particularly important: (1) growth in workless households, (2) increased earnings inequality, (3) reduced earnings mobility, and (4) an increased wage loss from spells of unemployment.

*Growth in workless households:* Britain has one of the highest employment rates among developed nations, with 75% of working-age adults in work (a fraction below that in the US). Although this aggregate employment rate has been pretty stable, the share of households with at least one working-age adult but no one employed has grown sharply, from 8% in 1979 to 17% in 2000 (Gregg and Wadsworth, 1996, 2002a). The latter compares with around 10% in the US (Gregg et al, 2002). Over the same period, the number of UK households where all adults are in work has increased. About a quarter of this rising gap is due to a relative increase in single adult households, with the rest due to a polarization of work that produces both more workless and more fully employed households (Gregg and Wadsworth, 2002a).

*Increased earnings inequality:* Among developed nations over the period 1979 to 1995, the UK was second only to the US in its absolute increase in the ratio of the 90th earning percentile to the 10th (OECD, 1996). Male wage inequality continued to grow in the UK between 1990 and 1996, but at a slower rate than in the 1980s. Since 1996, wage inequality has changed little (Tables A28/A33, Office of National Statistics, 2000; for more detail and interpretation, see Machin, 1999; or Gosling et al, 2000).

*Reduced earnings mobility:* The extent of mobility up and down the UK earnings distribution has fallen sharply since the late 1970s. For example, 29% of men in the second lowest earnings decile in 1979 were still there a year later. By 1988, this measure of earnings persistence had risen to 37% (Dickens, 1999, p 218), and it has been broadly stable since.

*Increased wage loss:* On average, men who lose jobs and take up unemployment-related benefits return to work on, and remain at, lower wages than in their previous jobs. The past two decades in the UK have seen this wage loss grow (Nickell et al, 1999; Gregg and Wadsworth, 2000a). What is more, job loss is not evenly distributed across the labour force. For example, the lowest paid tenth of men are twice as likely not to be earning a year after a job loss as are those in the middle of the earnings distribution (Dickens, 1999).

Taken together, these four trends suggest that lifetime earnings inequality may have risen even faster than the inequality evident in conventional cross-sectional measures. In addition, reductions in income tax rates and a failure to increase welfare benefits in line with average real incomes have further increased after-tax income inequality (Johnson and Webb, 1993; Clark and Leicester, 2002). These developments have contributed to a general increase in poverty in the UK, with growth in poverty among children especially marked.

## Income poverty and worklessness in households with children

Over the last twenty years, children have replaced pensioners as the poorest group in UK society. While average incomes among elderly households, even among the poorest fifth, have risen in real terms, the poorest fifth of children in 1996/97 were in households with real incomes no higher than those of the corresponding group in 1979 (Gregg et al, 1999). Poverty during childhood – defined, following traditional UK practice, as household income less than 50% of the national mean – is now almost evenly split between in-work poverty (an earner in the household) and workless poverty (no working adult present).[1] In 1996/97, nearly 20% of UK children lived in households where no adult worked, up from 7% in 1979 and 4% in 1968. Ninety per cent of these children were in poor households, creating a large spike in the income distribution substantially below the poverty line.

The UK, at 20%, has a substantially higher share of children living in workless households compared with other developed nations. The country with the next worst record in 1996 was Ireland, at 15%. In all other European countries the share of children in workless households in 1996 was 11% or less (OECD, 1998, p 12). Even before the current emphasis on getting people off welfare, only 10% of US children lived in a household where no adult worked (OECD, 1998; Dickens and Ellwood, 2001).

The increase in the proportion of UK children in workless households is driven by more lone parents being workless (due partly to a small decline in lone parents' employment rates, but also to an increasing propensity for lone parents not to live with other relatives), a rise in the number of lone-parent households, and an increase in the proportion of workless couples.

The increase in child poverty over past decades, on the other hand, is due to an increase in the incidence of poverty for all family types combined with an increased proportion of children in lone-parent families, who have much higher poverty rates than do couples with children. For example, one quarter of all children living with two parents were in poverty in 1996/97, up from one tenth in 1979 (Gregg et al, 1999). Over the same period, poverty rates among children of lone parents rose from one in two to two in three, while the proportion of all children living with a lone parent rose from around one in ten to a little more than one in five.

Comparative studies suggest that the US has higher child poverty levels on a within-country relative income measure, but lower levels on an absolute measure – such as the US official poverty line – because US living standards are higher across the distribution. For example, on the same relative poverty definition (50% of mean income before taxes and housing costs, adjusted for family size) the US whole-population poverty rate rose from 25% in 1979 to 32% in 1999 (Dickens and Ellwood, 2001), while in the UK it rose from 11% to 26%. But 29% of UK children were living on incomes below the US poverty line in 1995 (Bradbury and Jantti, 1999) compared with 21% of US children (Dalaker, 2001).

## The impact of deprivation on life chances

Growing acceptance among UK policy makers that childhood deprivation has longer-term consequences was probably the most crucial factor in assembling the political will to address childhood poverty. That children growing up in deprived households and communities do less well in terms of life chances has long been documented in cross-sectional correlations, but these cannot establish causal links. More recently, a literature has emerged that suggests that financial deprivation has an identifiable impact on educational attainment, wages, employment rates and other social outcomes in adulthood – even after controlling for child ability and family background (Gregg and Machin, 2000, 2001).

The UK literature relies mainly on the birth cohorts of the National Child Development Survey of 1958 and the British Cohort Study of 1970. These surveys follow children from birth through to adulthood, giving a wider range of individual child and family characteristics than is common in other available evidence. These data reveal an increased intergenerational income correlation as income inequality rises and evidence that children growing up in financially deprived households underachieved in terms of education, were more likely to have had contact with the police and probation services, and experienced higher unemployment and lower wages in adulthood. Since these studies can control for a wealth of aspects of child and family background but not for residual unobserved family or child differences, they may somewhat overestimate the impact of financial deprivation. A more important limitation is that they cannot say conclusively, since some of the studies relate to childhoods in the 1960s, whether the effects identified are associated with relative or absolute deprivation. These limitations are not true of the US evidence that child-based interventions can make a difference to child outcomes for a range of deprived children, which was perhaps equally influential in the debate. In particular, evidence that the Head Start programme (Currie and Thomas, 1995) or the Abercedarian Project (Ramey and Ramey, 1998) made substantive differences to child development for children from low-income families suggests that, whatever the causal origin, educational disadvantage among deprived children is malleable by policy intervention.

## Measuring and defining child poverty

Prime Minister Tony Blair's pledge to end child poverty is a dramatic one, and appears to be deeply felt. The government has been slow to translate this formally into a specific and measurable target, however, for both institutional and intellectual reasons. First, the UK has never had an official poverty definition: welfare programmes do not have an income cut-off such as (say) 150% of the poverty line, as is common in the US.

The closest equivalent – which is often used by academics, commentators, and, indeed, the Labour government on occasion – is a relative definition of poverty, counting a household as poor when its income is below some point in the income distribution. The most common definition used since 1999 has been 60% of median household income (adjusted for household size, and after subtracting housing costs). This is similar to the European Union's preferred indicator of poverty, which also uses 60% of the median before housing costs but different adjustment scales for household composition.[2] Measuring incomes after housing costs results in 4.4 million UK children (34%) living in relative poverty in 1996/97 (the year before Labour came to power), compared with 1.7 million (14%) when Labour last held office in 1979. This is the single statistic most commonly used by the government to describe its 'inheritance'. The 1996/97 relative poverty line corresponds (in 1996/97 prices) to annual disposable incomes after deducting housing costs of £8,013 and £9,458 for a couple with (respectively) one and two children; before deducting housing costs, the numbers are £9,225 and £10,889. In 1996, the official US poverty standards for the equivalent families were £8,344 ($12,516) and £10,691 ($16,036) (see Bureau of Census, 2000).

Using this definition, the government set itself a short-term target to reduce child poverty by a quarter of its 1998 level by 2004 (DWP, 2001b). But use of a poverty measure based on relative income has disadvantages that are well recognized by the government. One is that rising living standards and rising poverty rates can occur simultaneously, as indeed was the case in Ireland in the latter half of the 1990s. Although these two events are mathematically completely consistent, they may well not accord with the politicians' or the populace's view of what poverty is, which may undermine the credibility of an anti-poverty campaign. Another significant problem, which is true of both relative and absolute measures defined in terms of income, is that an income-based poverty line will show the effects of income transfer programmes almost immediately, while programmes to reduce long-term disadvantage or the damaging effects of living in a low-income household will barely register. This is particularly important, given that UK policymakers tend to think about child poverty not simply in terms of relative (or absolute) low incomes, but also in terms of childhoods that can be damaging due to a sustained lack of financial resources in a household. This anti-poverty agenda is, thus, part of a wider 'opportunity agenda' (HM Treasury, 1999b), which aims to reduce the incidence and severity of circumstances that have long-term adverse repercussions for individuals.

Partly to address these issues, the government has produced a range of 'poverty' indicators since 1999 that cover relative incomes and absolute incomes – as well as education, health, crime, and labour market outcome incidences. Thirteen of these are directly related to children (DWP, 2002). But a multitude of indicators gives no clear standard by which to judge when child poverty has been 'abolished'. The government, therefore, is currently debating openly how to "[measure] poverty in a way that helps to target effective policies and enables the government to be held to account for progress" (DWP, 2002c). The debate is looking at four options: (1) maintaining the multi-dimensional indicators,

(2) aggregating some subset of these into a single index, (3) focusing only on income-based measures, and (4) measuring relative low incomes and material deprivation simultaneously – as does the official poverty measure now adopted by the Irish government (see Nolan and Whelan, 1996 – for the theory; Callan et al, 1999 – for the practice).

The material deprivation measure is increasingly common in the European literature on poverty. It counts people as poor if they lack socially perceived necessities, which might include adequate food consumption, clothing, and other basic commodities. There have been a number of such studies in the UK, none of which, unfortunately, are directly comparable. The most recent is the Poverty and Social Exclusion Survey (Gordon et al, 2000).

## The strategy

The policy response to child poverty and its consequences has three main components: (1) raising direct financial support to families with children; (2) reducing worklessness in households with children; and (3) ameliorating the long-term consequences of child poverty.

### 1. Raise direct financial support for families with children, targeted on – but not exclusive to – low-income families

The most immediate and obvious response to observed low incomes in many families with children is to increase the net transfers available through the tax and benefit system. Between 1997/8 and 2002/3, spending on the four main programmes that provide financial support for families with children is predicted to increase by 58% (or £7.8 billion a year, around £1,100 for each family with children in the UK[3]). Around a third of this increased expenditure for children has the sole goal of reducing the relatively low incomes experienced by the poorest children. This child-specific support has been buttressed by increased general support for low earners. A National Minimum Wage (NMW) – the first in the UK – was established in 1999. Reforms to the National Insurance scheme (roughly equivalent to the Old Age, Survivors, and Disability Insurance programmes in the US) lowered costs for low-wage workers and their employers. The starting rate of income tax was lowered from 20% to 10% to further increase take-home earnings in low-skilled entry-level jobs.

The new child-specific resources have been delivered through both expanded tax credits and cash transfers. The tax credits include the Working Families' Tax Credit (WFTC), the associated Childcare Tax Credit, and the Children's Tax Credit. Increased cash payments have come in Income Support benefit rates for children (mainly paid to workless families) and in the universal Child Benefit. Although the WFTC has received more press and analytical attention than any of the other reforms aimed at increasing the generosity of support for families with children, this emphasis is misleading. The changes since 1997 should be considered together, because they combine to form a systematic overhaul of the structure of financial transfers to the 7 million families and the 13 million children in the UK. Their interrelationship is made clear in the government's announced plan (discussed later under Future Directions) to merge all the major parts of financial support for children into a new Child Tax Credit in 2003 (Inland Revenue, 2001; HM Treasury, 2002).

Here is how the child-specific reform package differs from the programmes that went before. Before the 1998 budget, support for children came from four sources: a universal per child transfer (Child Benefit) normally paid to mothers; extra payments in means-tested benefits for those not working (Income Support or Jobseeker's Allowance) normally paid to the family head; a refundable tax credit for working families (Family Credit) paid to the mother; and one of two related non-refundable tax credits available to one taxpaying earner per family (normally the father). Starting with the March 1998 budget, the government has increased the generosity of all four of these, and all but the Child Benefit have undergone structural change.[4]

### Increased generosity of Child Benefit

The 1998 and 1999 Budgets together raised the real level of Child Benefit by 27% for the eldest child, with inflation-only increases for younger siblings.[5] The increases in support for children in means-tested benefits have been focused on younger children: between April 1997 and 2002, in real terms weekly payments for children aged 0-4 rose by £15 a week – an 82% real increase – and those for children aged 11-15 rose by £6.50. The result is that financial support for children up to age 15 has been equalised – older children had previously received more generous support. This reform partly reflects recognition by the government that poverty rates were higher among families with younger children and partly facilitates the proposed move to a Child Tax Credit, with its emphasis on simplicity and transparency.

As in the US, Britain increasingly uses the tax administration service to target transfers to families with children. The UK has an individual system of income tax with an exact withholding system. Credits and allowances appear in a person's tax schedule, which employers then use to assess and deduct income tax directly from wage or salary payments. Allowances are typically less generous than in the US, so people start paying income tax at lower annual incomes (see Gale, 1997 and Brewer, 2001, for more comparisons of the US and UK tax systems).

### Children's Tax Credit

This credit (which will only exist between April 2001 and April 2003, when it will be merged into the proposed new Child Tax Credit) is a non-refundable tax credit that replaces two mutually exclusive and equal-valued tax credits: the Married Couple's Allowance (MCA) and the Additional Person's Allowance

(APA). The overall impact is that, since 1999, married couples without children have lost a tax break, and families with children, regardless of their marital status, have seen a tax break more than double in value. The MCA and APA were available to all taxpayers, but the Children's Tax Credit is withdrawn at 6.7% from people paying higher rates of income tax (over £34,515 from April 2002), similar to the Child Tax Credit in the US. It is doubled in value for families who have a child under 1 year old.

### Working Families' Tax Credit

The WFTC is an evolutionary reform to the existing in-work benefit, Family Credit. Announced in the Labour Government's first full budget in spring 1998 and available to claimants from October 1999, it is available to families with children where any adult member is working 16 hours a week or more. It consists of a per-family element – the same for couples and lone parents – and per-child elements. There is a very short flat zone where the maximum award is paid, and the credit is phased out beyond earnings of £94.50 a week at a rate of 55% of after-tax income. For a person on the basic rate of income tax and paying National Insurance contributions (like payroll tax), this adds up to a total effective marginal tax rate of 69%, a rapid rate of withdrawal compared with the combined phase-out faced by Earned Income Tax Credit (EITC) claimants in the US.[6]

The WFTC is more generous than its predecessor, as both the family and the child elements have been increased. For a family with one child, the WFTC is worth a maximum of £86.45 a week – or around $6,700 a year, substantially more than the EITC in the US. Each additional child raises the maximum credit by £26.45 a week. But most of this increased generosity in the maximum value of the WFTC has been matched in the level of out-of-work support, and so has by itself made little difference in the financial gain from moving from welfare-to-work. In addition, families can earn more before support is withdrawn, and the withdrawal rate has been lowered. These changes have increased support for those in full-time or better-paid part-time work (i.e. earning more than £94.50 a week in 2002 prices) and extended eligibility for in-work support to a large number of families.

### Childcare Tax Credit

This new refundable credit pays parents up to 70% of formal, registered childcare costs up to a (generous) maximum of £135 a week for 1 child (£200 for more than 1 child). The Childcare Tax Credit entitlement is a supplement added to the credits in WFTC and is treated in the same way as WFTC in all respects. It is, however, restricted to households where all parents are in paid work, although lone parents have been the prime beneficiaries to date. This represents a substantial increase in generosity of support for childcare costs compared to that provided under Family Credit, which offered only a childcare cost disregard rather than a direct cash payment.

## 2. Reduce the number of children living in workless households

The second part of the strategy is to reduce the numbers of workless families with children. This part of the strategy contains elements designed to improve the financial returns to employment, a reform of welfare administration to develop work-oriented case management of the welfare dependent population, and improvements in childcare opportunities.

### Reform of tax and benefits structure

This reform, described above as increasing the direct financial support to families, is not neutral in its impact on the financial attractiveness of employment. The package was deliberately slanted towards increasing the net gains from employment, or, in the jargon, to 'making work pay'. There are two specific work incentive features. First, the maximum weekly earnings level at which withdrawal started under the old Family Credit system was £77.15. This has increased by £13.70 in real terms. Thus, earners can keep 100% of what they earn up to a higher earning level than before. Second, the withdrawal rate was lowered from 70% to 55% of net-of-tax income, implying that less is taken out of each additional pound earned above the level at which withdrawal starts.

These reforms generally increased support for full-time or better-paid part-time work. For lower-paid, part-time lone parents, the improved incentives come mainly through the increased support for childcare costs in the Childcare Tax Credit.

### Case management

The New Deal employment strategy also involves development of a case management approach to promoting work by welfare recipients. This was already partially developed for those claiming unemployment-related benefits in the UK, but has been extended substantially under the New Deal framework. Nearly all welfare participants are now contacted by a Personal Adviser to establish if they want to work or participate in a programme to improve job-readiness. The New Deal for Lone Parents and the New Deal for Partners are particularly relevant for families with children – groups that had previously been ignored in strategies to encourage employment. (Chapters Five and Six discuss these New Deals in detail.)

### National childcare strategy

This strategy aims to create childcare opportunities for all those wishing to use them. Out-of-work parents, and especially out-of-work lone parents, identify the absence of available and affordable childcare as a major barrier to increasing employment (Shaw et al, 1996; Finlayson and Marsh, 1998). The essential problem appears to be that, given wages available to mothers, the supply price of formal childcare is too high to create demand in low- and even middle-income areas. The government strategy here is both to reduce the effective cost to parents and to stimulate supply. The Childcare Tax Credit described earlier affects the demand side by directly helping parents afford paid childcare places. The supply side of the strategy consists of a guaranteed half-day place in a pre-school for 4 year olds (run by state schools that provide full-time schooling for 5 to 7 year olds, and soon to be extended to 3 year olds), Early Excellence Centres, and Neighbourhood Childcare Centres, which provide subsidized childcare in some of the poorest communities and encouragement for schools or Local Authorities to run After School Clubs and holiday play schemes.

### 3. Reduce incidence and severity of scarring factors from childhood and early adulthood

The third major arm of the strategy is to try to reduce the impact of deprivation on educational attainment, and to limit the carry-over of social problems to adulthood. There is a diverse range of initiatives targeted at key life-stages or events, generally originating from the Social Exclusion Unit attached to the Prime Minister's Cabinet Office (Social Exclusion Unit, 1998). These cover teen pregnancy, children leaving social care, and homelessness among the young. In addition, a failure to connect to stable employment during the teenage years has been identified as causally linked to higher unemployment and lower wages in adulthood (Arulampalam, 2000; Gregg, 2001). The New Deal for Young People aims to eliminate long-term youth unemployment, and to improve matching with sustained employment among youth. Chapter Six provides details on this aspect of reducing long-term disadvantage. Those parts of the strategy directed at low educational attainment are focused on here.

On international assessments of comparable reading and maths abilities among adults, the UK – along with the US – has a high variation in standards and a large number of adults with low levels of literacy and numeracy (Layard et al, 2000). Schools with high levels of child poverty among their pupils underachieve on school-leaving exams and generally have fewer pupils staying in education after the minimum leaving age of 16. To what extent this underachievement is due to teaching quality or the attendant problems the children bring with them remains controversial. Since income itself can only be partially responsible for this low achievement, it makes sense not only to improve incomes but also to address the education deficit directly. Sure Start, school attainment in poor areas, and Educational Maintenance Allowances (EMAs) tackle this deficit from birth through to the end of the teenage years.

### Sure Start

Sure Start is perhaps the most important of these initiatives so far. Its design was loosely motivated by the US Head Start programme (Currie and Thomas, 1995), but there are large differences in the details. Sure Start is targeted on children aged 0 to 4 living in the most disadvantaged communities in the country. It aims to promote physical, social, and emotional development of children, and hence to make them more ready to learn by the time they enter into school. So far, Sure Start programmes operate in some 200 poor communities, but there are well-developed plans for expansion. These do not always overlap with the childcare centres mentioned above, but overlap and co-ordination is increasing as both expand.

### Raising educational qualifications on leaving school

Successive governments have developed an extensive series of tests to assess child development through the education system. These are undertaken at ages 7, 11 and 14. Final examinations on leaving secondary school (always referred to as GCSEs, which stands for General Certificates of Secondary Education) are undertaken at 16. These tests are increasingly used to assess the value-added made by a school, and to highlight underperformance. Schools have regular inspections by government-appointed inspection teams, and failing schools may be closed or have their senior teaching staff replaced. Local Authorities are also assessed for the support structures they supply. Again, failing areas may lose local control and be replaced by private-sector management consortia. One of the key aims of this near-continuous assessment regime is to raise standards of achievement among poorly performing pupils and schools. This is being supported by extra financial resources directed at children with greater learning needs, rather than explicitly focused on poverty. There has been no attempt, however, to break with nationwide pay scales for teachers (which allow only for a small 'London bonus') to make teaching in schools serving more deprived areas more attractive to high-quality teachers.

### Educational Maintenance Allowance

Compulsory full-time education ends at age 16, and the one third of young adults who cease full-time education at this point are those, unsurprisingly, with fewer qualifications and from less well-off families. Educational Maintenance Allowances (EMAs) – means-tested cash payments to young adults who continue in post-compulsory full-time education – are being piloted in a number of disadvantaged areas, and will be available nationally from 2004. They are designed to raise educational participation, retention, and achievement after age 16. Four variants are being piloted, with the maximum weekly payment ranging from £30 to £40 per week subject to full school attendance, plus retention bonuses each semester, and a final achievement bonus. As well as the financial amounts, the variants are also testing whether it matters to whom in the household the payments are made.

The evaluation strategy is to compare outcomes of young adults in areas where the EMA is available with outcomes of young adults in similar areas where the EMA is not available. A matching approach based on propensity scores is used to control for differences in young people's characteristics that might influence their educational outcomes. So far, the evaluation has focused on whether EMAs have affected participation. Results indicate that they increased it. Among young people eligible for the full allowance – approximately one third of young people in the pilot areas, with gross family incomes under £13,000 – participation increased by around 7 percentage points. Since the increase in participation was lower for those eligible for less than the full amount of EMA, the average effect over all young people eligible for some payment was an increase of around 5 percentage points (Ashworth et al, 2001). As data emerges, the evaluation will go on to assess impacts on attendance and course completion.

## What the reform package has accomplished so far

The reform package aims to reduce child poverty – not only through increases in child-specific financial support, but also through reductions in the numbers of children in workless households, particularly lone-parent households. The latter goal is to be achieved through reductions in marginal deduction rates and increases in the overall returns to work. This section looks, in turn, at what the reform package has done to: (1) numbers of children in poverty; (2) overall financial support for families with children; and (3) marginal deduction rates and overall returns to work, and whether the incentives embodied in the reforms are, in fact, changing behaviour – ie, increasing employment among lone parents.

### 1. Numbers of children below the poverty line

As of April 2002, there are two ways to analyse the impact of the reforms on incomes, and on child poverty. Micro-simulation models can predict the first-round changes in incomes that should arise through the reforms, compared with a base system of no real changes to taxes and transfers. The use of relatively high phase-out rates for in-work and means-tested benefits means that the beneficiaries from the extra money directed towards families with children since 1997 are heavily concentrated in the poorest households (Figure 4.1). Households with children in the second and third income deciles see disposable incomes rise by over 6%, whereas families in the top three deciles gain by less than 1%. Of course, the general focus on children in successive budgets means that all these households are gaining relative to households without children.[7]

Micro-simulations can also estimate the impact these reforms would have on child poverty. A number of different studies of the impact of the reforms between April 1997 and April 2001 (a slightly different period from that used in the rest of

**Figure 4.1 Estimated income gains for families with children from increases to child support, 1997-2002**

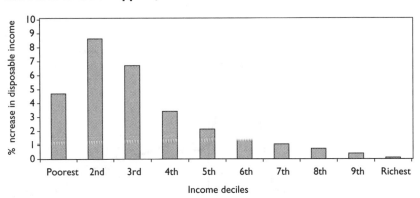

*Notes:* Income deciles are derived by dividing all families (with and without children) into 10 equally sized groups according to income adjusted for family size using the McClements equivalence scale. This graph shows the effect on families with children only. For example, the reforms will increase incomes of working-age families with children in the poorest tenth of the population by 4.7 percent. Assumes full participation in all income-related transfer programmes.

*Source:* The IFS tax and benefit model, TAXBEN, based on 1999/00 Family Resources Survey.

this chapter, but one that corresponds to the Labour government's first term in office) all suggest around 1.2 million children would be lifted out of relative poverty, assuming nothing changed between April 1997 and April 2002 except taxes and benefits (HM Treasury, 2001; Piachaud and Sutherland, 2001; Brewer et al, 2002). This assumption is, of course, unrealistic. It is also potentially misleading, given that the UK government has explicitly accepted that its notion of child poverty is a relative one and real incomes are generally rising. A better way, then, to assess the impact of the reforms on child poverty is to use actual data on the changing distribution of incomes. The latest official data cover the 2000/01 financial year, and show that the number of children in poverty had fallen by 0.5 million since 1996/97.[8] Between 1996/97 and 2000/01, the poverty line grew by some 10% in real terms: if we disregard this, and merely count the number of children in 2000/01 in households below the 1996/97 poverty line (fixed in real terms like the US Census Bureau's poverty thresholds are), then child poverty would have fallen by 1.3 million, or 30%, in just four years.

The changing shape of the income distribution for children is shown in Figure 4.2. As can be seen, the increased generosity of the package is helping to raise incomes of the poorest families with children in real terms. It is also moving the large spike in the income distribution of children closer towards the relative poverty line, although it has so far pushed only a small minority of children across this line. This shows how hard large reductions in relative poverty are to achieve. On a more encouraging note, real incomes of the poorest fifth of children are rising rapidly for the first time in twenty years. If the spike continues to move to the right faster than the poverty line, the impact on relative poverty will be greater.

**Figure 4.2: The changing real income distribution for children in low-income households**

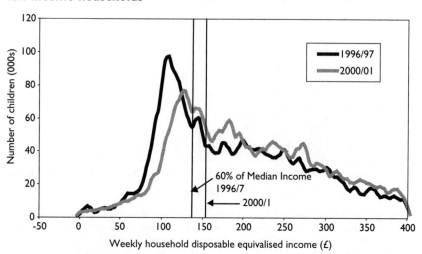

Note: Figure shows estimated distribution of equivalised weekly disposable household income after deducting housing costs for children in households below £400/wk (in 2000/1 prices). The proportion of children living in such households was respectively 88% and 84% in 1996/7 and 2000/1; 60 percent of median income on this definition was, respectively, £139 and £153 in 1996/7 and 2000/1. Deducting housing costs from disposable income is consistent with the poverty measures used by the government (and discussed in "Measuring and Defining Child Poverty"), and leads to a small proportion of households with children having negative incomes.

*Source:* from Brewer et al, 2002, and calculated using data from Family Resources Survey.

## 2. Increased financial support to low-income families with children

### *Policy impact*

As noted earlier, the reform package includes four major programmes designed to increase the disposable incomes of families with children: the Children's Tax Credit; the WFTC; a higher level of Income Support; and a more generous Child Benefit. The effect of these changes is compared with the situation before reform in Figure 4.3. Panel A of the figure shows the total cash support available for a live-alone parent with two children under 11 under the pre-reform (1997) support package. Panel B shows the total support available to the same stylised family post-reform (as of April 2002). (A figure for couples with children would be identical except for the income support payments, which would be higher in both cases.) The figures do not show the impact of the generous Childcare Tax Credit, because it is difficult to choose a single value of childcare costs that is plausible throughout the indicated income range: this omission makes the reformed system appear less generous than it is to those working but on a low income and with some formal childcare costs. The real world impact is always more complicated than these sorts of charts

**Figure 4.3: Total financial support by gross income, before and after reform**

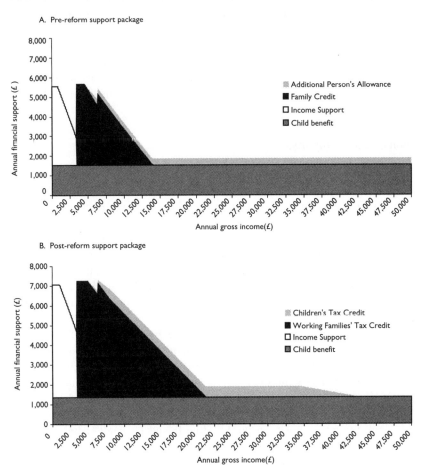

A. Pre-reform support package

B. Post-reform support package

*Note:* Assumes live-alone lone parent, 2 children under 11, no housing costs or childcare costs. Entitlement for WFTC reached at £3,400, or 16 hours work/week at the minimum wage. Values uprated to April 2002 prices.

imply. In particular, Figure 4.3 does not capture all the potential interactions between welfare programmes and tax credits. The two programmes of concern are Housing Benefit (HB), which supports low-income households with rental costs (owner-occupiers normally get no housing support), and rebates against local taxes, known as Council Tax Benefit (CTB). Both of these benefits are withdrawn as income rises, but crucially – unlike the EITC in the US – WFTC awards count as income when calculating awards of these benefits. There are two implications for families with children with relatively high rents or local taxes. First, the extra generosity of WFTC awards over Family Credit may be largely offset in smaller HB and CTB awards. Second, such families will also be on multiple benefit withdrawals with effective marginal tax rates of over 70%. In fact, the introduction of the WFTC has substantially reduced the number of households who are in work but facing effective marginal tax rates over 70% (as shown in Table 4.1 in the next subsection). The large number of families with children where no adult works are much more likely to be claiming Housing Benefit than those currently in work, and hence the impact of the WFTC on the incentive to work 16 or more hours remains muted by its interaction with Housing Benefit.

## Transatlantic comparisons

How does this situation compare with its US counterpart, the EITC? This question is particularly appropriate given Chancellor Gordon Brown's assertion, when the UK government first announced that it was interested in reforming in-work support, that it would examine "the advantages of introducing a new in-work tax credit for low-paid workers ... [and] would draw upon the successful experience of the American earned income tax credit, which helps reduce in-work poverty" (Hansard, 2 July 1997). Even now, there is a strong political resonance between the WFTC and the EITC: in the words of the respective political leaders in the late 1990s, both support "hard-working families" and "reduce child poverty".

A direct financial comparison between the WFTC and the EITC (Brewer, 2001) suggests that the UK system is substantially more generous. But this comparison can be misleading, because the WFTC reduces entitlements to other benefits whereas the EITC represents truly additional income. What is less often realized is that the structure and administrative details of the WFTC (following its predecessor, Family Credit) are also quite different from the EITC. Although the tax authority in the UK (the Inland Revenue) administers the system, the WFTC has little direct connection to the rest of the tax system, unlike the EITC, and does not operate as an annual tax rebate. Instead, it is paid either directly through the wage packet, or fortnightly, if it is paid to a non-working individual whose partner satisfies the work condition. For new jobs, the size of the award is assessed on expected weekly earnings. For claimants with stable jobs, it is calculated by looking at the past four pay cheques (seven if paid weekly) and then paid at the same rate for six months, regardless of changes in income.

This desire to get money to claimants quickly – rather than waiting for the end of the tax year – is primarily motivated by two concerns. First, most taxpayers in the UK have their income tax correctly withheld by employers, and only the rich, the self-employed, and those with complex tax affairs file a tax return. Second, people entering work on low wages would be worse off in work without the WFTC, because of the relatively high level of out-of-work benefits compared to the US. This means that the 'real-time' work incentives of the WFTC are stronger than those provided by the EITC (Walker and Wiseman, 1997).

Of course, the WFTC and the EITC are not the only ways that the UK and US governments support families with children. In both countries, children are recognized in the benefit system by in-work refundable credits and by non-refundable tax credits or extra tax deductions or allowances. However, the vagaries of perception and political economy mean that these support systems are often presented from very different perspectives, making them difficult to compare.

In Figure 4.4 the two systems are summarized by comparing the full annual budget constraint – the relationship between gross income and income of taxes and benefits and welfare payments – for a live-alone lone parent with children in the UK in 1997 and 2002 with that in the US in 2001. The UK's system of financial support for children was broadly in line with that in the US at lower incomes prior to the current reforms, but the reforms have made it substantially more generous. It is also more redistributive among families with children, with higher net tax rates at higher incomes than the US. The US system has been necessarily simplified: these figures do not include state taxes, state EITCs or Medicaid; we include Food Stamps; and we have assumed the TANF system operating in Florida, a relatively low-benefit state (Committee on Ways and Means, 2000, p 384). Housing support and help with childcare costs are ignored in both countries.

Figure 4.4 gives a representation of the total budget. Figure 4.5 shows the supports specifically dependent on children, by calculating the cash difference in the budget constraints of a single person and a live-alone lone parent with 2 children.[9] In the UK (Panel B), financial support for children falls in cash

**Figure 4.4: Disposable income after welfare and tax payments, by gross income, UK before and after reform, and US in 2001**

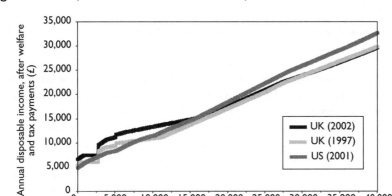

*Note:* Assumes live-alone lone parent, 2 children under 11. Does not include housing or childcare support or costs.

**Figure 4.5: Financial support for children, by gross income, UK and US**

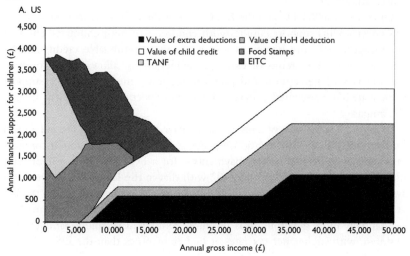

A. US

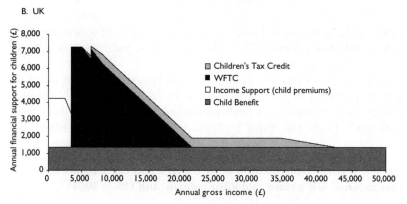

B. UK

*Note:* Assumes live-alone lone parent, 2 children under 11. Entitlement for WFTC reached at £3,400, or 16 hours work/week at the minimum wage. Values uprated to April 2002 prices.

terms as income rises, apart from the short phasing in of the non-refundable Children's Tax Credit. This is not true in the US. First, the phase-in of the EITC gives a range where support increases with income at the lowest incomes. Second, after the EITC has been phased out, the value of the child exemptions and the head of household filing status increase with income. A striking feature of the US system is the trough after the EITC has been withdrawn and before the tax allowances and deductions increase in value (from around $50,000), discussed more in Ellwood and Liebman (2000).

## 3. Marginal deduction rates and overall incentives to work

Marginal deduction rates for working families have changed as a result of the WFTC reform. The reduction in the headline phase-out rate from 70% to 55% and the fall in the number of families entitled to rent support have reduced the number of families on very high marginal deduction rates. But the increased generosity of WFTC has increased the number of families on some form of benefit phase-out. Before the WFTC was introduced, around 750,000 households had marginal deduction rates of over 70%, and 130,000 had rates over 90%. (Table 4.1 shows these as 8.4% and 3.7%, respectively of all employees with children.) The WFTC reduced these numbers to 250,000 (4.3%) and 30,000 (1.4%), respectively, but the numbers on marginal deduction rates of 60% or more rose by nearly 200,000, to just under a million. This may be an acceptable trade-off. However, if the WFTC continues to expand further up the income distribution, the terms of the trade-off will rapidly deteriorate.[10]

The rates in Table 4.1 are above those typically found in the US because of the higher phase-out rates used in the UK. But work incentives are not universally worse in the UK, because a large discontinuity in the budget constraint in the UK makes families become eligible for WFTC at 16 hours work a week. In fact, both countries seem to have good financial incentives for lone parents to do some work – assuming full take-up of all entitled benefits

### Table 4.1: Distribution of marginal deduction rates faced by employees with children before and after the reforms

| Marginal deduction rate | % of employees with children | |
|---|---|---|
| | 1997/98 | 2002/03 |
| more than 100% | 0.1 | 0.0 |
| more than 90% | 3.7 | 1.4 |
| more than 80% | 4.7 | 3.9 |
| more than 70% | 8.4 | 4.3 |
| more than 60% | 8.9 | 15.4 |
| more than 50% | 8.9 | 19.1 |
| more than 40% | 27.3 | 30.9 |
| more than 30% | 73.2 | 80.4 |
| more than 20% | 91.6 | 89.7 |
| more than 10% | 94.0 | 92.2 |
| more than 0% | 94.4 | 92.4 |
| All | 100.0 | 100.0 |

*Notes:* A marginal deduction rate is the percentage of the marginal pound of earnings that is lost in taxes and withdrawn benefits or tax credits. Calculations are performed on employees only, assuming full participation in all means-tested benefits and tax credits. 1997/98 values calculated using FRS 1997/98 and the tax and benefit system as of April 1997; 2002/03 figures estimated using FRS 1999/00 with earnings adjusted for two years of average growth, and the tax and benefit system as of April 2002. There were around 7.5 million employees with children in both years.

– but poorer incentives for lone parents to increase earnings beyond part-time or minimum-wage jobs (Brewer, 2001).

With respect to improving incentives to work more generally, the WFTC (including the Childcare Tax Credit) and the Children's Tax Credit combine to increase the financial returns to working rather than being on welfare. The intention is to induce entry into work, and so further reduce child poverty. This is because a reduction in the number of children wholly or nearly-wholly supported by the state is probably vital if the numbers in child poverty – given the use of a relative definition – are to be reduced. First the gain to taking a job is looked at and then the effect of increasing earnings once in work.

Table 4.2 shows how the reforms have altered the financial gain to work – the difference in zero-income position on benefits and in-work income after taxes and benefits – for some benchmark families. (These calculations ignore in-work costs, but here the focus on *change* in the gain to work minimises the impact of this omission.) The reforms have slightly improved the financial gain to work at 16 hours a week, but have had more of an impact on the incentive to do full-time work, particularly for lone parents (first row). The reverse is true for the first earner in a couple working at the minimum wage

**Table 4.2: The effect of the reforms on the financial gain to work for parents with children**

| | Gain to work (£) | | | |
| | 16 hours | | 35 hours | |
| | 1997 | 2001 | 1997 | 2001 |
| --- | --- | --- | --- | --- |
| *Not on HB:* | | | | |
| Lone parent | 63 | 71 | 107 | 130 |
| Primary earner in a couple with children | 26 | 50 | 79 | 99 |
| Single person, no children | 13 | 13 | 72 | 79 |
| *With HB:* | | | | |
| Lone parent | 43 | 43 | 65 | 80 |
| Primary earner in a couple with children | 20 | 21 | 42 | 49 |
| Single person, no children | 2 | 8 | 2 | 31 |
| Lone parent with childcare of £50/week when in work | 13 | 56 | 92 | 115 |
| Second earner in a couple with children, no childcare costs, first earner on £300 a week | 67 | 30 | 127 | 93 |

*Notes:* Table measures difference between zero-income benefit income and income after taxes and benefits in work. Assumes 2 children under 11 and full take-up of all entitled benefits, hourly wage of £4.20, rent of £50 a week where indicated, in-work childcare costs of £50 a week where indicated (slightly more than the average of those lone parents currently claiming the Childcare Tax Credit). All values expressed in 2002 prices.

*Source:* Authors' calculations based on the TAXBEN model.

(second row). The values for a single person (third row) show that the reform package has had very little impact on those without children.

The other rows show variations on this theme. Because it is withdrawn as income rises, Housing Benefit typically dulls the financial incentive to work, and it also reduces the increase in the cash gain to work brought about by the WFTC (compare rows 4 with 1; 5 with 2; and 6 with 3). Working in the other direction, though, the Childcare Tax Credit produces a large improvement in the (net of childcare costs) gain from moving to work for a lone parent paying £50 a week for childcare (seventh row of table; £50 a week childcare costs is slightly higher than the average of those currently claiming the Childcare Tax Credit). The negative aspect of the reforms is that entry into work by a second adult in a family where the primary worker earns £300 a week (the last row in the table) has seen a sharp drop in the financial incentive. Such a person had the highest return to full- or part-time employment in 1997, but in the 2001 scenario has some of the lowest financial gains to employment (the first wage in this stylised two-earner family is sufficient to get the family off Housing Benefit, so housing tenure makes no substantial impact here).

There has been a debate in the UK as to whether these changes in financial incentives will cause people to change their behaviour. Blundell et al (2000), simulate the impact of the introduction of the WFTC (so they compared the WFTC system of October 1999 to the system in April 1999) using a structural labour supply model. They predict that the WFTC will reduce workless households with children by just under 60,000 (affecting around 100,000 children). They also suggest that there will be some offsetting reduction of labour supply by women with working husbands.[11] The UK government's estimates are that the total package of reforms will encourage around 80,000 extra parents to enter work, a little more than twice the estimate in Blundell et al (2000) for the WFTC alone (HM Treasury, 2000b). These estimates use elasticities derived from data on labour market transitions using the methodology laid out in Gregg et al (1999). Comparisons for the WFTC alone suggest the two methodologies give very similar results (Blundell and Reed, 2000).

## Lone parents' employment change: Early evidence

The WFTC has been in operation for thirty months now, and the first evidence of its impact is beginning to emerge. As of November 2001, there were 1.3 million claims for WFTC – 430,000 more than for its predecessor in summer 1999 – while the numbers of children covered by these claims rose by 870,000 (see Table 4.3). The numbers of children of lone parents supported by the WFTC was 1.1 million in November 2001, over 400,000 more than under the previous regime. So, by November 2001 the numbers supported through in-work tax credits was almost equal to those supported by out-of-work welfare payments. However, the number of children for whom support through in-work tax credits was claimed was also rising prior to 1999, especially among single parents. Moreover, the number of children for whom out-of-work

**Table 4.3: Numbers of children for whom payments are made by type of welfare benefit and tax credit, 1995-2001**

| | Number of children (thousands) | | | | | | | |
|---|---|---|---|---|---|---|---|---|
| | Nov 1995 | Nov 1996 | Nov 1997 | Nov 1998 | Aug 1999 | Nov 1999 | Nov 2000 | Nov 2001 |
| *Welfare benefits for workless families* | | | | | | | | |
| Unemployed | 633 | 510 | 382 | 341 | 325 | 298 | 251 | 201 |
| Sick and disabled | 628 | 633 | 656 | 646 | 658 | 649 | 666 | 671 |
| Lone parents | 1,884 | 1,853 | 1,795 | 1,718 | 1,731 | 1,704 | 1,643 | 1,593 |
| Other | 111 | 93 | 90 | 83 | 77 | 78 | 66 | 61 |
| Total | 3,256 | 3,089 | 2,923 | 2,788 | 2,797 | 2,729 | 2,626 | 2,526 |

*Tax credits for working families*

| | Family Credit | | | | | | WFTC | |
|---|---|---|---|---|---|---|---|---|
| | Nov 1995 | Nov 1996 | Nov 1997 | Nov 1998 | Aug 1999 | Nov 1999 | Nov 2000 | Nov 2001 |
| Couple | 788 | 882 | 901 | 885 | 871 | 1000 | 1208 | 1330 |
| Single | 450 | 520 | 580 | 647 | 663 | 761 | 935 | 1071 |
| Total | 1238 | 1402 | 1481 | 1532 | 1534 | 1761 | 2143 | 2401 |

*Note:* The Working Families' Tax Credit replaced Family Credit in October 1999.

*Source:* Office for National Statistics (2001)

welfare payments are claimed has itself fallen, by around 730,000 since the peak at the end of 1995, with children of lone parents accounting for nearly half of this fall (290,000).

So, there has been a sustained decline in the number of children supported by welfare payments and this was well established prior to the advent of WFTC. Among lone parents, though, the rate of decline has been faster since August 1999 (the last date prior to the advent of the WFTC) than before, and faster than the decline in the number of children in all families claiming out-of-work benefits since the summer of 1999 (DWP, 2002a; and earlier editions). These differences are encouraging, but since they are modest and take no account of changing population demographics or the state of the economic cycle, they yield no clear conclusion about the impact of the WFTC.

In search of a more definitive conclusion, Table 4.4 explores the evidence for lone parents more formally, using a simple difference in difference methodology. Lone parents in the UK have long had very low employment rates. From the mid-1980s to the early 1990s, employment rates for lone mothers were broadly stable at just above 40%, even though over the same period, employment among mothers with working husbands rose sharply (Desai et al, 1999; Blundell and Hoynes, 2001). But in 1993 the employment of lone parents started to rise. Table 4.4 compares the annual changes in this rate for 1996-99 (before the advent of WFTC) and 1999-2001 (after its introduction). Splitting the data in this way (see the raw annual changes in column 2 of Table 4.4) supports the suggestion in the administrative caseload data of Table 4.3 of a modest increase

## Table 4.4: Annual changes in employment rates among live-alone lone parents, 1996-99 and 1999-2001

| Period | Raw annual changes | Adjusted to control for parenthood and age of youngest child |
|---|---|---|
| 1996-99 | 1.82 | 0.16 |
| 1999-2001 | 2.40 | 1.20 |
| Difference | 0.58 | 1.04 |

*Note:* Column 3 is the difference in employment growth rates between comparable lone parents and single adults within the two periods. They have been estimated from probit equations of employment status controlling for year, age 18-24, 25-34, 35-44 (45+ as the base), qualifications of degree level or equivalent, a level but below degree, O level or equivalent and below O level (the base). Gender and age, qualification interactions and interactions of gender, age and qualifications with time are also included. As are dummies for age of youngest child being 0-1, 2-4, 5-10 and 11+ (5-10 as the base) which are not interacted with time. The marginal effects reported are the transformed coefficients on a year/lone parent interaction for the two periods.

*Source:* Labour Force Survey.

in the rate of growth of lone parent employment post-1999, although the difference between the two periods is not statistically significant.

In any case, raw differences do not take account of the strong employment recovery over the last few years in the UK, which slowed after 1999 and stopped entirely in 2001. To account for the state of the economic cycle and the differing performance of different age and skill groups in the recovery, we compared the raw changes in column 2 of Table 4.4 with those of single (live-alone) adults without children of similar age and education – a natural comparison group as they were unaffected by the policy shift and have similar household circumstances apart from the presence of children. We also adjusted for differences in age of the children of the lone parents. The results are shown in column 3 of Table 4.4.

The difference between the pre- and post-reform periods is more marked, and on the borderline of statistical significance. These results suggest that the buoyant labour market drove the bulk of the improving employment rates of lone parents between 1996 and 1999. They also suggest, however, that since 1999 there has been an acceleration in employment growth for lone parents that is higher than employment growth among childless individuals with similar characteristics. Hence, it tentatively appears that lone parents have had an exceptional increase in employment rates over this period, which could reflect a behavioural response to the financial incentives and other aspects of welfare reform since 1999.

## Future directions

All three of the main areas of policy development described earlier – raising direct financial support for families with children, reducing the numbers of workless households, and mitigating the scarring factors of childhood deprivation – are continuing to develop. Two current policy proposals in particular – for expanded case management and greater system integration – would profoundly change the picture of the UK welfare system.

### Jobcentre Plus, and the expansion of case management in the welfare system

Jobcentre Plus is a tag used by the government to describe the unification of administration systems for different out-of-work working-age benefits. In practice, this means that, over time, all benefit claimants will get regular contact with a personal advisor (case manager), with the frequency of the contact depending on the specific benefit. Under the New Deal programmes this has been compulsory for the unemployed but voluntary for disabled workers and lone parents. This is in the process of changing. In the future all claimants will have a compulsory 'work-focused interview' at regular intervals, with a personal advisor asking about a person's desire to work and the inhibiting factors. Claimant groups will have different job-search requirements, but similar support systems will be available to all, whatever benefit they are on, if they want them.

This reform places work at the heart of the welfare administration process for all groups, whereas in the past the unemployed were clearly given a higher priority for job placement efforts. It also means that benefit advisors will not have implicit incentives to push people onto other benefits. All groups will have readily available job-search support systems. The case management will not just help with job search, but will cover issues of transition in the benefit system and access to care services for dependants as well.

This development follows from the New Deal framework of contacting a wide range of benefit groups to discuss, promote, and support a transition into employment (see Chapter Six for discussion). The main difference is that it will be embedded routinely in the benefit administration and attending the 'work focused interview' will be compulsory. It falls a long way short, though, of compulsory job search or time limits on welfare receipt.

### Integration of child support payments

The integration of all child support payments is another unifying reform, but one affecting the tax and benefit system rather than the administration regime. The aim is to pull together all the financial support for children (outlined in Figure 4.5 earlier in the chapter) that is currently paid through welfare payments, in-work benefits and tax credits into a single instrument, with the same rules and administration. This new Child Tax Credit has many more similarities with the Canadian Child Tax Benefit than with the US system. It will remain nominally distinct from the universal Child Benefit, but in most practical terms – such as who receives the payment, and how it is paid – the two will be identical. Payments in respect of adults in Income Support and the WFTC will remain outside this system. And, at the same time as the switch to the Child Tax Credit, in-work support will be extended to adults without children (with restrictions to full-time employment and a minimum age of 25) in something called the Working Tax Credit.

There will be few immediate changes in family incomes as a result of the Child Tax Credit: the emphasis is on a structural change to how payments to families with children are delivered, rather than how much is paid.[12] The new features are as follows. First, all payments in respect of children will be paid to the mother or the main caregiver. Under the current system, who gets the payment depends on which benefit is being paid and even how the payment is being made. Second, income uncertainty at the time of transitions into and out of work will be reduced. This is because there will be a stable platform of financial support for children across the welfare-to-work divide, rather than the uncertainty (and possible delay) of moving from out-of-work benefits to in-work benefits. Third, as almost all families will be able to receive some support, take-up rates for the Child Tax Credit may be substantially higher than for the WFTC. Fourth, payments will be assessed against family income throughout. This represents the most significant step towards joint assessment for families with children since income tax became individualized in 1990.

Although the new tax credits will notionally depend upon annual income, they will not be a retrospective annual system like the EITC. The aim is to operate an annual system (and so minimise hassle for families whose circumstances are stable) but also to provide some protection for families whose income falls. In practice, this means that awards will depend upon either the previous fiscal year's annual income or expected annual income in the current fiscal year. A novel feature is that a year-on-year income rise of under £2,500 will be ignored by the tax credit system. The impact of this, which will lower the short-run effective marginal tax rates for some families with children, is hard to predict (see Inland Revenue, 2001; HM Treasury, 2002, for the development of official policy; see Brewer et al, 2001, for more details of the background to the reform).

## Conclusion and assessment

While the UK government's strategy contains many of the main elements of the US welfare-to-work agenda – such as increased financial incentives and case management of the welfare caseload to support transition into work – it also has substantial differences. The most striking factors that are different in the UK are:

* Levels of welfare support for those not in work – as well as those in work – are rising substantially.
* There is no time limiting of welfare support or requirement to seek work for lone mothers. Sanctions only apply to those claiming unemployment benefits

who do not meet their responsibilities to look for work and accept appropriate job offers.
- There is a strong emphasis on tackling poverty and its consequences for children.

The objectives which underlie welfare development in the UK are primarily the economic circumstances for families with children and the outcomes achieved by the poorest of those children. Reducing welfare rolls and reducing expenditure are clearly secondary priorities. Hence, from a British perspective, welfare-to-work is a policy success if and only if it results in reduced deprivation for the child. It is also clear that the reform process is far from over. The second round of reform currently underway has been more about the structures of welfare systems and caseload management than payment generosity, although support levels are still rising. This reflects in part the difficulty of quick implementation of fundamental reform to institutions.

While the objective in general is clear, the more specific target is not. At some stage the government will have to declare its position on what it means by elimination of child poverty. Elimination of poverty on a high relative income measure is almost impossible. The most successful European Union countries (Sweden, Denmark and Norway) have child poverty rates (on a 50% of mean income before housing costs basis) of a little under 5% (Bradbury and Jantti, 1999). Measurement error and lumpiness of income over the short windows commonly used to assess income in the UK data will always leave some people below such a benchmark. The longer-term financial position may be a better guide to the financial situation that actually matters to children's well-being and development.

The government has a number of sensible ways forward. It could assert that such imprecise data means that an estimated child relative poverty rate of 5% – or higher – is consistent with its intention to eliminate child poverty. Alternatively it could focus on the measurement of material deprivation or some combination of a relative income and material deprivation measure, as used by the Irish government. A reliance on relative income will require large resources to be committed to supporting children, and child support systems to rise in line with median incomes thereafter. This is difficult but not impossible. Indeed one crucial new announcement in the April 2002 Budget was that the per child payments in the new Child Tax Credit will be automatically linked to earnings rather than prices, ensuring the relative value of these payments. It is clear from government publications, however, that the intended target is larger than a simple financial measure. As a result, it is likely that the measures ultimately adopted to assess success will include some indicators of material and perhaps even psychological well-being.

The strategy is clear, however, even if the target is not. The government has substantially raised financial support for families with children. Increased payments have been focused on low-income families, whether or not they are working, but all families with children have gained something under the government's package of reforms. Work incentives have risen, especially for full-time work, and those lifted out of poverty to date are much more likely to be working. Increasing the financial rewards for work at low wages is part of a wider strategy to reduce the number of children living in workless households. This part of the strategy would appear vital if the costs of eliminating childhood poverty are not to prove prohibitive. Here there are some early signs of improvement, with the number of children in workless households down from 19.4% in 1996 to 15.3% in spring 2001. There have also been substantial reforms to the way welfare is administered to support transitions into work. The most important is the development of a case management approach, with all claimants having a personal advisor. The final part of the strategy is to reduce the extent to which children from the poorest households and communities underachieve in terms of development and education. This involves a mixture of extra resources and focusing the machinery of government and service delivery on out-turns among the poorest children. All elements of this strategy are evolving, and further steps have already been announced or proposed.

The intention is commendable, and the strategy coherent, but the scale of the task so large that many argue it is unachievable. Some cynics even suggest the government has little intention of achieving it. The central problem is maintaining political and public support for the large financial transfers required to reduce poverty on a relative income basis, especially if recent reductions in worklessness do not continue. The increased work incentives are certainly not substantial enough alone to drastically reduce the numbers in such workless households; hence the strategy relies heavily on the reforms to welfare administration and increased childcare availability to facilitate moves back to work. Increased generosity of support in and out of work may actually reduce the desire for work, as life without work may become more tolerable at these higher-income levels. Increased generosity of support will also mean that the high withdrawal rates cover an ever-expanding section of the population. This could be reduced by greater use of the universal, or near universal, parts of the child support system, but at a large extra cost.

In addition, there are problems in establishing exactly what the impacts of financial resources are on child development outcomes, and even more problems in designing and implementing successful interventions. In mainstream policy areas, Britain has not developed as strong an experimental and evaluation culture as the US. Nor has it developed systematic mechanisms by which evidence can influence policy delivery on the ground. This becomes all the more difficult where policy allows for significant local inputs and choices. On a more up-beat note, if interventions and reduced financial distress lead to fewer people with very low levels of literacy, for example, then fewer parents in the next generation will suffer as acute problems earning and supporting their families. This intergenerational transmission aspect of deprivation is very important in government thinking.

The ambition of this programme will perhaps be a surprise to American readers, and it seems unlikely to us that such ambition would be ever attempted in the US. It is interesting, however, to think about whether it should be and what form supporting federal and state policy might take.

## Acknowledgement

This work forms part of the research programme of the ESRC-funded Centre for the Microeconomic Analysis of Public Policy at the Institute for Fiscal Studies and the Centre for Market and Public Organisation at the University of Bristol. The authors are grateful to Tom Clark for comments and advice. Labour Force Survey data was made available by the Office for National Statistics through the ESRC Data Archive, and is used with permission of the Controller of Her Majesty's Stationery Office; Family Resources Survey data was used with permission of the Department of Work and Pensions. Neither of those institutions bear responsibility for the results presented here.

## Notes

[1] Income is adjusted for household composition using the McClements scale: this uses a couple with no children as a reference household, and adjusts incomes of households with different compositions. There is no agreement on what the right equivalence scale should be, but the UK government and academics have used this one for over 20 years. As is the case for the US poverty line, the main advantage of the McClements scale is consistency (these issues are explored further in Banks and Johnson, 1993). Income is also calculated after subtracting housing costs; this helps regional comparisons and problems comparing expenses for homeowners and renters. The definition used by the current UK government is discussed later in this chapter.

[2] The main difference is that younger children are given a higher weight than in the UK McClements scales. This places the child poverty rate for the UK on the EU basis half way between the before housing cost measure and the after housing cost measure, at about 28% in 1998.

[3] This estimate, in 2002 prices, is from a micro-simulation model, and includes only the cost of the changes to child benefit, family credit/WFTC, income support for families with children, and the children's tax credit compared with a world where child support was unchanged in real terms between 1997 and 2002. It does not count the saving from abolishing the married couples' and related allowances. Families with children will also have been affected by budgetary reforms affecting all families: These overall impacts are summarized in Figure 4.1 in Brewer et al, 2002.

[4] There was one cut: lone parent benefit, a small addition to child benefit for lone parents, was abolished for new claimants in 1998. The cost estimates presented here do not account for the consequential saving, but the figures later on do.

[5] Rates correct as of April 2002. Real-terms comparisons for Child Benefit use the RPI index, other benefits use the ROSSI index (which is the RPI index less housing costs) (see DWP, 2003 for more on this).

[6] In other words, for most WFTC claimants, the WFTC withdrawal adds 38 percentage points to the effective marginal tax rate. This rate measures what proportion of an extra pound of income is lost to income tax and National Insurance payments, as well as withdrawn welfare benefits and tax credits. The higher the effective marginal tax rate, the lower the incentive to work for any additional earnings.

[7] These calculations do not analyse changes in the personal taxes and benefits that affect all families: this is shown in Brewer et al (2002). The effect of Labour's first-term in office on family incomes overall is analysed in Clark et al (2002). None of these simulations allows for behavioural changes from the reforms.

[8] Analysis of data covering the last 6 months of 2000/01 – which fully captures the large increase in children's allowances in means-tested benefits in October 2000 – shows a fall of 650,000 children since 1996/97: see Brewer et al (2002); the official source is DWP (2002b).

[9] So, for example, it does not show the full award of food stamps for a 3-person household, but the difference between a 1-person and 3-person household. The same applies for the UK. This is the approach used by Ellwood and Liebman (2000), who look at the tax treatment of US families with children, and in Battle and Mendelson (2001), who compare systems of support in the UK, US, Australia and Canada.

[10] Table 4.1 assumes full participation in all income-related transfer programmes. This is a fair assumption for Income Support, where participation rates among eligibles is over 95%, but not for Family Credit and WFTC, where participation rates are lower (72% and 62%, respectively, measured, respectively, in summer 1999 and summer 2000). Sources: WFTC take-up rates from McKay (2002), FC take-up rates from Marsh et al (2001). Take-up rates of other means-tested benefits from Department of Work and Pensions (2001a).

[11] The authors have benchmarked this model against labor supply estimates derived from past reforms to in-work benefits in the UK (Blundell, 2000, reviews this evidence) and believe it to be consistent.

[12] Writing some time before the final details had been announced, some authors noted that a unified and integrated Child Tax Credit would require either benefit increases for families on out-of-work benefits or benefit cuts for those on in-work benefits (see Brewer, Myck and Reed, 2001). In the end, the government chose the former and phased these in gradually in the years leading up to the new tax credits so that most families with children will see almost no change in incomes in April 2003. The main exceptions are better-off families with children, some of whom will qualify for the Child Tax Credit but not the Children's Tax Credit, and some the other way round).

# References

Arulampalan, W. (2001) 'Is unemployment really scarring? Effects of unemployment experience on wages', *Economic Journal*, vol 111, no 475, pp 585-606.

Ashworth, K., Hardman, J., Woon-Chia, L., Maguire, S., Middleton, S., Dearden, L., Emmerson, C., Frayne, C., Goodman, A. and Meghir, C. (2001) *Education maintenance allowance: The first year*, London: DfEE.

Banks, J. and Johnson, P. (1993) *Children and household living standards*, London: Institute for Fiscal Studies.

Battle, K., Mendelson, M., Meyer, D., Millar, J. and Whiteford, P. (2001) *Benefits for children: A four country study*, Ottawa/York: Caledon Institute Joseph Rowntree Foundation.

Blair, T. (1999) 'Beveridge revisted: a welfare state for the 21st century', in R. Walker (ed) *Ending child poverty: Popular welfare for the 21st century?* Bristol: The Policy Press, pp 7-18.

Blundell, R. (2000) 'Work incentives and in-work benefit reforms: A review', *Oxford review of Economic policy*, vol 16, no 1, pp 27-44.

Blundell, R., Duncan, A., McCrae, J. and Meghir, C. (2000) '"The labor market impact of the working families" tax credit', *Fiscal Studies,* vol 21, no 1, pp 75-104.

Blundell, R. and Hoynes, H. (2001) 'Has in-work benefit reform helped the labor market?', National Bureau of Economics Research Working Paper 8546, in R. Blundell, D. Card and R.B. Freeman (eds) *Seeking a premier league economy*, Chicago, IL: University of Chicago Press

Blundell, R. and Reed, H. (2000) '"The employment effects of the working families" tax credit', Institute for Fiscal Studies Briefing Note 6 (www.ifs.org.uk/labmarket/wftc_bn.pdf; accessed 27 February 2003).

Bradbury, B. and Jantti, M. (1999) 'Child poverty across industrialized nations', Florence: UNICEF Occasional Papers Economic and Social Policy Series EPS 71.

Brewer, M. (2001) 'Comparing in-work benefits and the reward to work for families with children in the US and the UK', *Fiscal Studies*, vol 22, no 1, pp 41-77.

Brewer, M., Myck, M. and Reed, H. (2001) *Financial support to families with children: Options for the new integrated child credit*, Commentary 82, London: Institute for Fiscal Studies.

Bureau of Census (2000) 'Poverty thresholds, 1996' (www.census.gov/hhes/poverty/threshold/thresh96.htm; accessed 27 February 2003).

Callan, T., Layte, R., Nolan, B., Watson, D., Whelan, C.T., Williams, J. and Maitre, B. (1999) *Monitoring trends in poverty: Data from the 1997 Living in Ireland survey conducted by the ESRI for the National Anti-Poverty Strategy*, Dublin: Department of Social, Community and Family Affairs.

Clark, T. and Leicester, A. (2002) 'Twenty years of UK tax and benefit reforms and inequality?', Paper presented at the International Association for Research in Income and Wealth Conference, Summer 2002, and forthcoming in *Fiscal Studies*.

Clark, T., Dilnot, A., Goodman, A. and Myck, M. (2002) 'Taxes and transfers 1997 2001', *Oxford Review of Economic Policy*, vol 18, no 2, pp 187-201.

Committee on Ways and Means (2000) *2000 Green book: Background material and data on programmes within the jurisdiction of the Committee on Ways and Means*, Washington, DC: United States House of Representatives.

Cowell, F., Jenkins, S. and Litchfield, J. (1996) 'The changing shape of the UK income distribution: Kernel density estimates', in J. Hills (ed) *New inequalities*, Cambridge: Cambridge University Press, pp 49-75.

Currie, J. and Thomas, D. (1995) 'Does Head Start make a difference?', *American economic review*, vol 85, no 3, pp 341-64.

Dalaker, J. (2001) 'Poverty in the United States: 2000', Current Population Reports 60-214, Washington, DC: US Census Bureau.

DSS (Department of Social Security) (2000) *Households below average income 1994/5-1998/9*, London: Corporate Document Services.

DWP (Department for Work and Pensions) (2001a) 'Income related benefits: estimates of take-up in 1999-2000' (www.dwp.gov.uk/asd/irb.html; accessed 27 February 2003).

DWP (2001b) *Public service agreement, 2001–2004* (www.dwp.gov.uk/publications/dss/2001/dwp_psa/psa.pdf; accessed 27 February 2003).

DWP (2002a) *Client group analysis: Quarterly bulletin on families with children on key benefits, August 2001*, London: DWP.

DPW (2002b) *Households below average income 1994/5-2000/1*, London: Corporate Document Services.

DWP (2002c) *Measuring child poverty: A consultation document*, London: DWP.

DWP (2002d) *Opportunity for all – Fourth annual report*, London: The Stationery Office.

DWP (2003) *The abstract of statistics: 2001 edition*, London: DWP (www.dwp.gov.uk/asa/asd1/abstract/Abstract2002.pdf).

Desai, T., Gregg, P., Steer, J. and Wadsworth, J. (1999) 'Gender and the labor market', in P. Gregg. and J. Wadsworth (eds) *The state of working Britain*, Manchester: Manchester University Press, pp 168-84.

Dickens, R. (1999) 'Wage mobility in Britain', in P. Gregg and J. Wadsworth (eds) *The state of working Britain*, Manchester: Manchester University Press, pp 206-24.

Dickens, R. and Ellwood, D. (2001) 'Whither poverty in Great Britain and the United States? The determinants of changing poverty and whether work will work', National Bureau of Economic Research Working Paper 8253, in R. Blundell, D. Card and R.B. Freeman (eds) *Seeking a premier league economy*, Chicago, IL: University of Chicago Press.

Eissa, N. and Hoynes, H.W. (1998) 'The Earned Income Tax Credit and the labor supply of married couples', NBER Working Paper 6856.

Eissa, N. and Liebman, J. (1996) 'Labor supply response to the Earned Income Tax Credit', *Quarterly journal of economics*, vol 111, pp 605-37.

Ellwood, D. and Liebman, J. (2000) 'The middle class parent penalty: child benefits in the US tax code', NBER WP 8031.

Finlayson, L. and Marsh, A. (1998) *Lone parents on the margins of work*, DSS Research Report 80, London: Corporate Document Services.

Gale, W. (1997) 'What can America learn from the British tax system?', *Fiscal Studies*, vol 18, no 4, pp 341-70.

Gordon, D., Adelman, L., Ashworth, K., Bradshaw, J., Levitas, R., Middleton, S., Pantazis, C., Patsios, D., Payne, S., Townsend, P. and Williams, J. (2000) *Poverty and social exclusion in Britain*, York: Joseph Rowntree Foundation.

Gosling, A., Machin, S. and Meghir, C. (2000) 'The changing distribution of male wages in the UK', *Review of economic studies*, vol 67, pp 635-66.

Gregg, P. (2001) 'The impact of youth unemployment on adult unemployment in the NCDS', *Economic journal*, vol 111, no 475, pp 626-53.

Gregg, P., Harkness, S. and Machin, S. (1999). 'Poor kids: Trends in child poverty in Britain, 1968-1996', *Fiscal studies,* vol 20, no 2, pp 163-88.

Gregg, P., Johnson, P. and Reed, H. (1999) *Entering work and the British tax and benefit system*, London: Institute for Fiscal Studies.

Gregg, P. and Machin, S. (2000a) 'Childhood disadvantage and success in the young adult labour market', in D. Blanchflower and R. Freeman (eds) *Youth employment and joblessness in advanced countries*, NBER Comparative Labor Market Series, Chicago, IL: University of Chicago Press, pp 247-89.

Gregg, P. and Machin, S. (2000b) 'Childhood experiences: educational attainment and adult labour market performance', in K. Vleminckx, and T. Smeeding (eds) *Child well-being, child poverty and child policy in modern nations: What do we know?*, Bristol: The Policy Press, pp 129-50.

Gregg, P., Scutella, R. and Wadsworth, J. (2002) 'Why we should (also) measure joblessness at the household level: the polarisation of work across households in OECD counties', Centre for Economic Performance, LSE working paper, no 1168.

Gregg, P. and Wadsworth, J. (1996) 'More work in fewer households', in J. Hills (ed) *New inequalities*, Cambridge: Cambridge University Press, pp 181-207.

Gregg, P. and Wadsworth, J. (2000) 'Mind the gap, please: the changing nature of entry jobs in Britain', *Economica*, vol 67, no 268, pp 499-524.

Gregg, P. and Wadsworth, J. (2002) 'Everything you wanted to know about workless households but were afraid to ask', *Oxford bulletin of economics and statistics*, forthcoming.

Hansard (2 July 1997) vol 297, col 311, London: The Stationery Office.

Hills, J. (ed) (1999) *Persistent poverty and lifetime inequality: The evidence*, CASE Report no 5, London: Centre for Analysis of Social Exclusion, London School of Economics and Political Science.

HM Treasury (1997) *Employment opportunity in a changing labour market: The modernization of Britain's tax and benefit system*, no 1, London: HM Treasury.

HM Treasury (1999a) *Supporting children through the tax and benefit system: The modernization of Britain's tax and benefit system*, no 5, London: HM Treasury.

HM Treasury (1999b) *Tackling poverty and extending opportunity: The modernisation of Britain's tax and benefit system*, no 4, London: HM Treasury.

HM Treasury (2000a) *Budget 2000 prudent for a purpose: Working for a stronger and fairer Britain*, HC 346, London: The Stationery Office.

HM Treasury (2000b) *Tackling poverty and making work pay: Tax credits for the 21st century: The modernization of Britain's tax and benefit system*, no 6, London: HM Treasury.

HM Treasury (2002) *The child and working tax credits: The modernisation of Britain's tax and benefit system*, no 10, London: HM Treasury.

Hobcraft, J. (1999) 'Intergenerational and life-course transmission of social exclusion: influences of childhood poverty, family disruption and contact with the police', CASE paper 15, Centre for Analysis of Social Exclusion, London School of Economics and Political Science.

Inland Revenue (2001) *New tax credits: Supporting families, making work pay and tackling poverty*, London: Inland Revenue.

Jenkins, S., Schluter, C. and Wagner, G. (2000) 'The dynamics of child poverty: Britain and Germany compared', University of Essex, mimeo.

Johnson, P. and Webb, S. (1993) 'Explaining the growth in income inequality', *Economic journal*, vol 103, pp 429-35.

Layard, R., McIntosh, S. and Vignoles, A. (2000) 'Britain's record on skills', Centre for Economic Performance, LSE mimeo.

Machin, S. (1999) 'Wage inequality in the 1970s, 1980s and 1990s', in P. Gregg and J. Wadsworth (eds) *The state of working Britain*, Manchester: Manchester University Press, pp 185-205.

Marsh, A., McKay, S., Smith, A. and Stephenson, A. (2001) *Low-income families in Britain*, DSS Research Report no 138, Leeds: Corporate Document Services.

McKay, S. (2002) *Low/moderate income families in Britain: Work, WFTC and childcare in 2000*, DSS Research Report no 161, Leeds: Corporate Document Services.

Micklewright, J. and Stewart, K. (2000) *The welfare of Europe's children: Are EU member states converging?*, Bristol: The Policy Press.

Nickell, S., Jones, T. and Quintini, G. (1999) *A picture of job insecurity facing British men: The labor market consequences of structural change*, Discussion Paper no 42 Centre for Economic Performance, London School of Economics and Political Science.

Nolan, B. and Whelan, C.T. (1996) *Resources, deprivation and poverty*, Oxford: Clarendon Press.

OECD (Organisation for Economic Co-operation and Development) (1996, July) 'Earnings inequality and mobility', *Employment outlook*, pp 59-108.

OECD (1998, June) 'Patterns of employment and joblessness: a household perspective', *Employment outlook*, pp 7-21.

ONS (Office of National Statistical Studies) (2000) 'New earnings survey, 2000. Part A: Streamlined analysis', London: The Stationery Office.

Piachaud, D. and Sutherland, H. (2001) 'How effective is the British government's attempt to reduce child poverty?', *Economic Journal*, vol. 111, pp F85–F101.

Ramey, C. and Ramey, S. (1998) 'Early intervention and early experience', *American psychologist*, vol 53, pp 109-20.

Shaw, A., Walker, R., Ashworth, K., Jenkins, S. and Middleton, S. (1996) *Moving off income support: Barriers and bridges*, DSS Research Report no 53, London: Corporate Document Services.

SEU (Social Exclusion Unit) (1998) *Bringing Britain together: A national strategy for neighbourhood renewal*, Cm 4045, London: The Stationery Office.

Walker, R. and Wiseman, M. (1997) 'The possibility of a British Earned Income Tax Credit', *Fiscal Studies*, vol 18, no 4, pp 401-25.

# FIVE

# The art of persuasion? The British New Deal for Lone Parents

*Jane Millar*

A lone parent should be able to decide whether to stay at home or to work part time or full time without due hardship or difficulty resulting from the decision. (Cmnd 5629, the Finer Report, 1974, para 7.11)

We set ... a new challenging objective for lone parent employment – that, by the end of the decade, we reach 70% of lone parents in employment. (Gordon Brown, Chancellor of the Exchequer, Speech at 10 Downing Street, 30 November 2000)

Almost thirty years separate these two statements about lone parents and employment. When the official Finer commission reported in the early 1970s, there were about half a million lone-parent families (8% of all families with children) in Britain, and concern was growing about the high levels of poverty they faced. The commission's proposals were never fully implemented, but the principle – that lone parents should be able to choose between paid employment and staying at home to care for their children – became the guiding precept for UK policy for the next three decades. Lone parents receiving social assistance are still not required to be available for employment if they have a child less than 16 years old, the minimum school-leaving age.

The social, economic, and political world has changed radically since the 1970s. The number of lone-parent families has more than tripled, their employment rate has fallen, their receipt of benefits has risen, and their poverty rate has increased dramatically. But even the politically secure and strongly neo-liberal Conservative governments of the 1980s and early 1990s did not directly challenge this non-employment-based model, despite concerns about the rising rates of benefit receipt among lone parents. However, as Chancellor of the Exchequer Gordon Brown's statement indicates, the current Labour government has initiated a significant policy shift, one that begins to reconceptualise lone parents as workers as well as parents and that, for the first time, sets an employment target for policy.

One justification for setting this target comes from cross-national comparisons. In an earlier speech, Gordon Brown pointed out that "the UK still lags behind other countries in the 'league table' of international comparisons of the numbers of lone parents in work" (Gordon Brown, October 2000a). He quoted figures to show that lone mothers in the UK have much lower employment rates, especially for full-time employment, than those in France, Germany, Sweden and the US. But it is the US, rather than any European country, that has been most influential in British policy debates about lone parenthood. In the 1980s and early 1990s, the 'underclass' view of lone parents prevailed in both countries, and the growth in lone parenthood was interpreted as a sign of declining moral standards. This is very much in contrast to the debates in many European countries, where there has been much less moral concern over changing family patterns (Lewis, 1997). However, shared rhetoric does not necessarily translate into similar policies, then or now, and the extent to which the UK and the US are actually following the same policy path with respect to lone parents and employment is open to debate.

Since poor children in the UK live disproportionately in lone-parent households, the discussion in Chapter Four of the New Labour policies regarding elimination of child poverty in 20 years pays considerable attention to the whole array of policies that influence the incomes and earnings of lone parents in Britain. The aim of this chapter is to focus on lone parents rather than their children, concentrating particularly on the New Deal for Lone Parents, but also considering other policies directed towards the employment of lone parents. The chapter outlines these policies, explores the outcomes so far, and discusses future policy directions. It starts by setting the stage for these developments in the context of the lone-parenthood situation and policy debate in Britain.

## Lone parenthood in Britain

The standard British definition of lone parenthood is a person living without a cohabiting partner and with one or more dependent children, defined as children aged under 16 or under 19 if still in full-time education. This definition excludes cohabiting couples but includes lone parents living with their parents (or other adults) in the same household.

In 1976 there were estimated to be 0.75 million lone-parent families, with 1.3 million children, constituting 8-9% of all families with children (Figure 5.1). By 1996 there were 1.6 million lone-parent families, with 2.8 million children, comprising 22% of all families with children (Haskey, 1998). The 2001 census will provide a more up-to-date figure, but the most recent estimates, for 2000, are that there are about 1.75 million lone-parent families with about 2.9 million dependent children (Haskey, 2002). This is almost one in four children in the country.

The antecedents to lone parenthood changed markedly between the 1970s and 1990s. Those who were widows declined from about 22% in 1976 to about 5% in 1996, while those who were single, divorced, or separated all increased markedly. By the mid-1990s, 48% of lone parents (excluding widows and widowers) were separated from marriage and 28% from cohabitation. The remainder were single, never-married women (Marsh, 2001). The vast majority – over nine in ten – of lone parents are women. They have similar sized families to partnered women (mean of 1.7 children compared with 1.8 for married/cohabiting women) but are less likely to have a youngest child under school-age (38% compared with 41% of married/cohabiting mothers) (Walker et al, 2002). They are also less likely to have any educational qualifications, with 28% of lone mothers having no qualifications compared with 17% of married mothers (Holtermann et al, 1999). About 11% of lone mothers come from ethnic minorities (compared with about 7% of married mothers), and there is substantial variation in the rates of lone parenthood across different ethnic groups. Almost half (49%) of black families are headed by a lone mother, compared with 21% of white, 8% of Indian, and 15% of Pakistani and Bangladeshi families, and 29% of mixed race or other ethnic groups (ONS, 1999).

The gap between lone and married mothers' employment rates has widened steadily over these years, as Figure 5.1 shows. In the mid-1970s, 47% of lone mothers were employed compared with 52% of married mothers. By the mid-1990s, the proportion of lone mothers employed had fallen to 42% while the corresponding figure for married mothers had risen to 66%. These falling employment rates have meant that lone mothers have become increasingly reliant upon social security benefits, notably Income Support (a national means-tested benefit providing a basic minimum benefit for those with no, or very little, income from other sources). The proportion of lone parents receiving Income Support rose from about 43% in the mid-1970s to about 65% by the mid-1990s. In 1996 (just before the Labour government took office) just over one million lone-parent families were receiving Income Support (DSS, 1999). Of these, about two thirds had been in receipt for two years or more.

Lower employment rates have meant more poverty among lone parents, since benefit levels are below poverty thresholds. In 1979 about 19% of lone parents had incomes of less than half the contemporary mean (after meeting housing costs and taking account of family size) and this rose to about 60% by 1994/95 (DSS, 2000a).[1] Indeed, living in a lone-parent family has become one of the main factors associated with child poverty. Of the 4 million children living in poor households (defined as above) in 1994/95, about 1.5 million were in lone-parent families. Lone parents also tend to stay poor for longer periods than any other working-age households, and often only escape poverty if they repartner (Jenkins, 2000).

These trends put lone parenthood firmly onto the UK policy agenda, particularly from the late 1980s onwards (Duncan and Edwards, 1997, 1999; Kiernan et al, 1998; Lister, 2002). However, while lone parents occupy a significant and distinctive place in British political and policy discourse, the politics of lone parenthood are, in important ways, very different in Britain than in the US. This applies both to current Labour and past Conservative policy. First, the key policy issue in Britain has, until very recently, been (male) unemployment rather than (female) lone parenthood. The growth in male

**Figure 5.1: Lone parents in Britain: mid-1970s to mid-1990s**

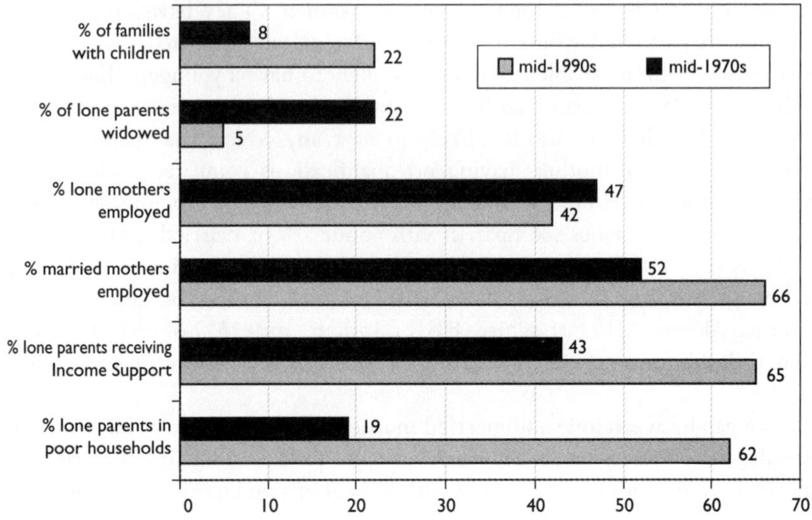

| | mid-1990s | mid-1970s |
| --- | --- | --- |
| % of families with children | 22 | 8 |
| % of lone parents widowed | 5 | 22 |
| % lone mothers employed | 42 | 47 |
| % married mothers employed | 66 | 52 |
| % lone parents receiving Income Support | 65 | 43 |
| % lone parents in poor households | 62 | 19 |

*Sources:* Haskey, 1998; DSS, 2000a; ONS, 1999

unemployment, from 5.1% to 9.4% of the active workforce over the period 1977 to 1991 (McLaughlin, 1994), was a major factor in increased public expenditure. Throughout the 1980s and into the 1990s, high rates of unemployment, especially long-term unemployment in the areas of declining manufacturing industry, had a very strong political resonance. In the late 1990s, the New Labour government began focusing on 'worklessness', rather than just unemployment. While this brought in groups not previously targeted in labour market policy, including lone parents as well as disabled people, the main policy focus was and remains male unemployment, especially among young people (Land, 1999). One of the five key policy pledges made by the Labour Party in their 1997 election manifesto was to reduce youth unemployment by 250,000. Thus young people, not lone parents, were the major target of attention in welfare-to-work policies for Prime Minister Blair's first government. Plans for the future continue to focus on worklessness, with the greatest resources still targeted on youth and long-term unemployment (Cm 5084; 2001). Lone parents are very important in British welfare policy, but they do not occupy the central place that they do in the US.

Second, there is no consensus in Britain that lone mothers should be expected to take employment and only limited support for policies that would require, or compel, paid work. While the proportion of mothers in employment has increased steadily over the past decades, as noted above, most mothers work part time, and the view that paid work should take second place to motherhood remains strong, reinforced by politicians and the media and apparent in the attitudes of women themselves. The public generally agrees that women should work full-time before they have children and after children leave school. But six in ten adults believe that a mother with a pre-school child should not work outside the home at all, 30% that she should work part time, and only 2% that she ought to be employed full-time (Bryson et al, 1998). Although 81% agree that mothers of school-age children should be in employment, only 11% believe this should be full time. Similarly half of people (echoing the Finer Commission) think that lone mothers should be able to choose for themselves whether to go out to work or not (Hills and Lelkes, 1999). Indeed, 24% believe that a lone mother with a pre-school child "has a duty to stay at home and look after the child" and only 17% that "she has a duty to work" (Hills and Lelkes, 1999, p 16). If her children are of school age, 44% agree she should go out to work, and 4% that she should stay at home. Clearly, public attitudes towards mothers' employment in the UK are contingent upon circumstances, and there is no agreement that paid work is always the best option. Orloff (2002) argues that, in the US, increased employment among women was one of the key factors that made the 1996 welfare reform acceptable across a wide range of opinion. This contrasts with the UK, where there is much stronger support – again across a range of political opinion – for the view that lone mothers should not necessarily be expected to engage with paid work.

The issue of lone mother's employment was especially problematic for Conservative governments in the 1980s and 1990s, because it highlighted a particular tension within the party at that time. As Lister notes, the Conservative "government was torn between the continued power of traditional thinking, which accorded primacy to mothers' place in the home, and its espousal of the strand in neo-liberal policy which prioritized reducing 'welfare dependency'" (Lister, 2002, p 122). The former proved to be stronger and was also more in tune with public opinion. As a result, there was only limited support within government for policies that would require lone mothers to seek employment, although (as discussed below) there were some moves to improve financial incentives to work.

Failure to agree on an employment-based strategy is also part of the explanation as to why child support came to the fore as a policy issue in Britain when, and in the way that, it did (Millar, 1994). Instead of work requirements for lone mothers, policy attention focused on child support requirements for separated fathers for whom, it was assumed, there would be clearer consensus about the goals of policy. The child support reforms in the UK in the early 1990s were driven both by ideology (separated parents have an obligation to contribute towards the costs of their children and the state has a duty to enforce this) and economic considerations (pursuing the separated parents for child support should lead to reduced benefit expenditure on lone parents). The experience of other countries in implementing more stringent child support regimes was also important, and the 1991 Child Support Act was clearly influenced by policy in both the US and Australia (Millar and Whiteford, 1993; Barnes et al, 1999; Dolowitz and Marsh, 2000).

This legislation introduced a standard formula for the calculation of child support liabilities and a new agency to determine these and to collect and distribute payments. Lone parents receiving benefits were *required* to cooperate with the agency. But any child support paid by former partners was deducted directly from Income Support, leaving the lone-parent family no better off. These measures were deeply unpopular and controversial, both in respect of the policy itself and its implementation. There was no consensus around the principle that all separated biological fathers owed an unconditional obligation of support to their children; the formula was generally seen as too rigid; and the implementation was very heavy-handed in the early stages (House of Commons Select Committee, 1993, 1994; Lister, 1994; Land, 1995; Millar, 1996). The men affected proved to be a very effective pressure group who resisted the policy by both individual non-compliance and collective lobbying. In response, changes were made to the scheme almost every year between 1993 and 1997, when the Conservatives lost the election.

This very public failure of the child support legislation led policy attention back to the employment issue. By the 1990s, the Conservatives were starting to introduce measures to increase the work incentives, both for unemployed families and for lone parents (see Table 5.1). The most significant of these was the 1992 reduction in the weekly hours of work needed to qualify for the in-work, means-tested Family Credit from 24 to 16. Possibly as a result of this change, the number of lone parents receiving Family Credit rose by about one third between 1992 and 1994. There was also a small pilot study of the use of caseworkers to advise lone parents about employment opportunities (Vincent et al, 1996). Thus, by the mid-1990s, British policy towards lone parents and employment was steadily moving away from the neutral model favoured by

**Table 5.1: Lone parents and employment: Conservative government policy measures, 1988 to 1997**

| Year | Measure |
|------|---------|
| 1988 | Income Support replaces Supplementary Benefit, earnings disregard of £15 per week for lone parents. |
|      | Family Credit introduced, for low-waged families with children. Parent must be working at least 24 hours per week. |
| 1992 | Child Support disregard of £10 per week for Family Credit calculation. |
|      | Family Credit qualifying hours for lone parents reduced to 16 per week. |
| 1994 | Childcare disregard of £40 per week for Family Credit calculation. |
| 1995 | Family Credit bonus for those employed 30 hours per week plus. |
|      | Pilot of caseworker support for lone parents – advice and information about employment. |
| 1996 | Childcare disregard on Family Credit raised to £60 per week. |
|      | Back to Work Bonus introduced for lone parents leaving part-time employment and Income Support for full-time employment. |
| 1997 | Child Support Bonus introduced for lone parents leaving Income Support for full-time employment. |

the Finer Committee. Even so, it was still far from being an employment-based model.

A third difference between the UK and the US is that the moral or ideological agenda has played out in different ways in the two countries. This is particularly true in respect of race, which has not been an issue in UK debates about lone parenthood. Nor is lone parenthood viewed as a 'ghetto' problem in the UK, although levels of lone parenthood are often used as markers of disadvantaged neighbourhoods. However, and as in the US, it has been argued by some advocacy groups in the UK that governments should seek to encourage marriage and discourage lone parenthood. For example, throughout the 1980s, the Institute of Economic Affairs (a right-of-centre London think-tank) published a series of papers and reports arguing that social policy had had the effect of undermining the family and that government policy should be reformed in order to encourage marriage and "traditional" two-parent families (for example, Davies, 1993; Morgan, 1995).

In the early 1990s, the Conservative government appeared to be moving closer to such a stance, at least in rhetoric. In his closing speech to the 1993 Conservative Party conference, the then Prime Minister, John Major, argued that the country needed to go "back to basics" in moral values and that governments should take the lead in changing expectations regarding family responsibilities. But there was little public resonance for this view of government as a moral leader, and these ideas were not pursued further (see Lister, 1996 for a detailed analysis of family policy and politics at this time). Negative constructions of lone parenthood were common in much of the media and political representation of lone parenthood at this time, and lone parents were often depicted as a 'social threat' to the values of society (Duncan and Edwards, 1997). But in practice there has been little support for the view that government should use welfare policy to directly influence family behaviour.[2]

Finally (as discussed in Chapters One and Three), 'welfare' does not have the same negative connotations in Britain as it does in the US. The 1980s were probably the decade in which popular support for the welfare state was at its lowest level in Britain, but even then there was much opposition to cuts in benefits and other welfare provisions (Taylor-Gooby, 1991). Moreover, based on social attitudes survey data, support for redistributive policies has strengthened in recent years (Hills and Lelkes, 1999; Jarvis et al, 2000).

In the US welfare reform has focused upon lone parents, has been based on a broad consensus that the goal should be paid work for all lone parents, and has included a strong family values dimension – an emphasis that has grown since the 2000 election. None of this is the case in the UK, where lone parents are one among several groups of policy interest, where attitudes towards employment for mothers are more ambivalent, and where family values rhetoric has not been translated directly into welfare policy. Moreover, given bedrock popular support for welfare, reform in the direction of compulsion to work outside the home risks electoral unpopularity.

## Labour's policy for lone parents

Table 5.2 summarizes the main measures affecting lone parents' employment as they have developed since 1997.[3]

The New Deal for Lone Parents is the first of the Labour policies affecting lone-parent families, and it remains the policy component uniquely associated with this group. This programme is essentially an advice and information service, with voluntary participation. The objectives of the programme are "for lone parents to be offered advice by the Employment Service to develop a package of job search, training and after-school care to help them off benefits and into work" (DWP, 2002a). Those who take part in the New Deal are allocated to a New Deal Personal Adviser, a caseworker who provides advice and support concerning job search, training opportunities, childcare services, and in-work taxes and benefits.[4] The New Deal Advisers can also offer in-work support and mentoring for those lone parents who find jobs. The programme was introduced in three phases, the first, in July 1997, being a prototype in eight areas of the country. The second, from April 1998, extended the scheme nationally to lone parents making new or repeat claims for Income Support. The third, from October 1998, brought in existing Income Support recipients to the national scheme. In addition there have been a number of 'pilots' of alternative 'innovative' models of delivery, for example, through private sector and non-profit organisations.

As Table 5.2 shows, a number of changes have been made in the way the New Deal for Lone Parents programme operates since it was originally introduced. These have included a progressive widening of the target group,[5] initially from lone parents with children aged over five years and three months, then to those with children over three years, and finally to all lone parents. In addition, although participation in the New Deal remains voluntary, lone parents in receipt of Income Support are now required to attend a (rather confusingly termed) 'personal adviser' interview as part of their benefit claim. At this interview they are given information about the New Deal programme and invited to join. These compulsory personal adviser interviews were introduced in April 2001 for all lone parents making a new or repeat claim for Income Support, and are being phased in nationally over two years from April 2002 for existing recipients.

Other employment-based policies include replacement of Family Credit with the more generous Working Families' Tax Credit (part of the wider 'making work pay' strategy discussed in detail in Chapter Four) and the introduction of state support for childcare provisions and costs. The National Child Care Strategy, which began in May 1998 with a start-up budget of £470 million, aims to "ensure good quality, affordable childcare for children aged up to 14, and up to 16 for those with special needs, in every neighbourhood" (DfEE, 1998, p E-3). Nursery school places are guaranteed for all four-year-olds and up to 80% of three-year-olds. The strategy is being pursued through partnerships between local authorities, the voluntary sector and employers. The annual

## Table 5.2: Lone parents and employment: Labour government policy measures, 1997 onwards

| | |
|---|---|
| July 1997 | Phase 1 New Deal for Lone Parents in 8 'prototype' areas – voluntary interviews, target group of those with youngest child aged 5 years and 3 months. |
| April 1998 | Phase 2 New Deal for Lone Parents, national for new and repeat Income Support claimants. |
| October 1998 | Phase 3 New Deal for Lone Parents, national for all claimants. |
| April 1999 | Ten 'innovative' pilots of variations within the New Deal run for 12 months. |
| June 1999 | ONE Service pilots in 4 areas – voluntary work-focused interviews for claimants of various benefits including lone parents. |
| October 1999 | Introduction of Working Families' Tax Credit to replace Family Credit, includes childcare tax credit. |
| | Benefits 'run-on' for lone parents who have been on Income Support for at least 12 months, benefits payments to continue for first 2 weeks of a job of 16 hours plus. |
| | Ten 'innovative' pilots of variations within the New Deal to run for 12 months. |
| November 1999 | ONE Service pilots extended to a further 8 areas. |
| April 2000 | ONE work-focused interviews compulsory for new claimants in the pilot areas. |
| May 2000 | Target group for voluntary interviews extended to lone parents with youngest child aged 3 years plus. |
| | In-Work Training Grant pilots in 40 areas. Lone parents finding jobs can receive up to £750 which can be used to access further education or other training. |
| October 2000 | Compulsory work-focussed interviews for lone parents with youngest child aged 5 years and 3 months in 3 'pathfinder' areas. |
| | Pilot of provisions for lone parents receiving Income Support – £15 per week Training Premium, £20 per week earnings disregard, help with childcare costs for first year in employment (less than 16 hours per week). |
| March 2001 | 'Innovation Fund' – 12 projects to run for 12 months to develop local services via public, voluntary and private sector partnerships with the aim of increasing sustainable employment, including among lone parents from ethnic minorities and those with disabilities. |
| April 2001 | Compulsory 'personal adviser' interviews for all new and repeat lone-parent Income Support claimants with youngest child aged 5 years and 3 months. Interviews to be phased in over 3 years for existing claimants, starting with those with children aged 13-15 years. |
| | National implementation of Oct 2000 pilot measures for lone parents receiving Income Support. |
| | Launch of the 'Outreach Service', aimed at lone parents and partners living in isolated communities. |
| | Extension of Work-Based Learning for Adults to lone parents aged 18-24. |
| November 2001 | Lone parents not on Income Support eligible for the New Deal. |
| April 2002 | Compulsory 'personal adviser' interviews extended to all lone parents on Income Support, including those with children aged under 5. Personal adviser interviews to take place at 6-monthly intervals. These measures to be phased in over two years. |
| | Jobcentre Plus introduced nationally |
| | £10 disregard of Child Support payments for Income Support recipients. |
| April 2003 | Child Tax Credit and Working Tax Credit introduced. |

budget for childcare in England (Scotland, Wales, and Northern Ireland have their own programmes) is to increase from £66 million in 2000/01 to over £200 million by 2003/04, and a campaign to recruit 80,000 new child care workers has been launched (DfEE, 2000). A Childcare Tax Credit can be claimed as part of the Working Families' Tax Credit and pays up to 70% of the costs of registered childcare, up to a maximum of £135 per week for one child and £200 for more than one child.

One of the goals of the National Childcare Strategy is that lone parents living in disadvantaged areas and taking up employment will be guaranteed a childcare place. However, these policies are not only for lone parents, or even for poor two-parent families, but are intended in general to help parents reconcile work and family life. Other 'family-friendly' measures include improvements in maternity rights and pay and the introduction for the first time of statutory parental leave,[6] and extensions of these are proposed in a policy document recently published by the Department of Trade and Industry (DTI, 2001). These provisions represent a significant policy break with the past, with the acceptance of a role for government in the provision of childcare and in helping working parents to care for their children replacing the assumption that childcare was essentially a private matter (Randall, 2001).

## The New Deal for Lone Parents: Evidence on participation, outcomes, and process

There is a substantial ongoing programme of evaluation for all the New Deal Schemes, an example of what the Labour government has come to term 'evidence-based policy making' (Davies et al, 2000). The evaluation of the New Deal for Lone Parents is based on three main sources of data. The New Deal Statistical Database consists of administrative data for all participants since the national programme started in October 1998. These data are the basis for regular (previously monthly, now quarterly) statistical reports (for example, DWP, 2002a)[7] and provide a picture of overall participation, of the range of activities undertaken, and of the first destinations of leavers. The second is a quasi-experimental evaluation of the prototype programme that ran from July 1997 to October 1998 (Finch et al, 1999; Hales et al, 2000a, 2000b; Hasluck et al, 2000). The third is a set of initial evaluation studies of the national scheme, including surveys of client satisfaction, in-depth interviews with participants and advisers, and a large national postal survey of lone parents within the scope of the programme (Dawson et al, 2000; Hamblin, 2000; Lewis et al, 2001; GHK, 2001; Lessof et al, 2001, 2003). There is also an overall synthesis report from the Employment Service (Evans et al, 2002), bringing together data from a range of sources.

Understanding the impact of Labour's New Deal for Lone Parents and its attendant programmes, as of all social programmes, requires that we consider three main issues. The first is participation and take-up. Since the New Deal for Lone Parents is a voluntary programme in which all participants have elected to take part, it is important to know how many people have elected to participate and what proportion of the eligible population this represents (that is, the take-up rate). This gives an indication of the success of the scheme at reaching the target population. The reasons for non-take-up may also provide pointers to the sort of measures that would be necessary to increase participation.

The second issue is outcomes, what effect the programme has on the factors it was designed to change. Since the main objective of the New Deal for Lone Parents is to help them enter work, the number entering work as a consequence of programme participation is the main outcome measure of interest. However, the government has also put forward various other objectives, including reducing Income Support receipt among lone parents, helping non-working lone parents to become more 'work ready', and helping working lone parents to stay in work. In addition, there is also a government pledge to eliminate child poverty, and so levels of in-work poverty among lone parents who find jobs are also relevant.

The final issue is process: how well various parts of the programme work on the ground. This includes understanding which parts of the programme are most effective at increasing employment and which are not, comparing the effectiveness of different models of delivery, and identifying any gaps and problems in the programme's organisation.

Information on all these would provide a very comprehensive picture of the impact of the New Deal for Lone Parents. In practice this is only partly available, however. The national scheme was introduced before the full evaluation of the prototype was completed and, as discussed above, there have been a number of changes to the programme since it started (Millar, 2000). Getting an accurate picture of outcomes in the context of ever-changing policy is difficult, if not impossible. In addition, the priority of the evaluation strategy was to examine process rather than outcomes. This was in order to 'learn lessons' from each stage of implementation. Thus there is a great deal of qualitative data on the way in which the programme operates but rather less quantitative data on wider outcomes. Here is what the evidence so far indicates.

## Participation and take-up

Almost 320,000 lone parents had participated in the national New Deal for Lone Parents by the end of January 2002 (DWP, 2002a). In August 1998, just before the programme started, there were about 935,000 lone parents in receipt of Income Support, suggesting that the programme has reached around one third of the initial population of lone parents receiving benefits. But this is not an accurate measure of take-up, because it is not based on the total number of lone parents potentially eligible for the programme over that time period. In the evaluation of the prototype programme, it was estimated that about 24% of those in the target group were participating (Hales et al, 2000a). In the first two years of the national programme, about 20% of those in the target group responded to the invitation to participate (DfEE, 2001). This is a low participation rate but, at the same time, many participants were coming forward from outside the target group. The New Deal database shows that, in the first two years, about two fifths of participants came from outside the target group (i.e. were lone parents with children under school age) and a further fifth came from within the target group but had put themselves forward before being invited for interview. Extending the programme to all lone parents thus reflects the actual pattern of participation.

The introduction of compulsory personal adviser interviews was intended to improve participation. The national statistics show that the vast majority (80% to 90%) of lone parents who attended an initial interview did go on to take part in the programme. This suggests that many people are willing to join the programme once they have learned about it from an initial interview. The qualitative data from the evaluations also suggest that the vast majority of participants responded very positively to the programme, even if they had been reluctant or concerned beforehand (see further discussion later). The ONE pilots, which were carried out in 12 areas between June and November 1999 as an antecedent to Jobcentre Plus (discussed in Chapter Four), therefore included lone parents in the trial of work-focused interviews. Early results from these pilots were encouraging, and seemed to suggest that compulsory interviews increased participation in the New Deal programme and also led to increased employment outcomes, although later evidence did not confirm these results in respect of employment (Evans et al, 2002). The pilot for the compulsory personal adviser meetings did show, however, that lone parents were generally positive in their responses (Pettigrew et al, 2001) and the introduction of compulsory interviews does seem to have improved participation in the New Deal programme. Evans et al (2002) estimate that the percentage of all lone parents on Income Support joining the New Deal programme has risen since the introduction of compulsory personal adviser interviews but, as they point out, 'the majority of lone parents still do not participate' (Evans et al, 2002, p 93).

There have also been some changes in the characteristics of participants over time. There are now more older lone parents, the average age of their children is slightly older, and there is a higher proportion with longer spells in receipt of Income Support. These changes in the characteristics of lone parents receiving Income Support over the past five or six years suggest that participants are increasingly including the 'harder to help' lone parents, those who lack recent work experience (Evans et al, 2002).

## Outcomes

The numbers of lone parents who have participated in the national New Deal programme since October 1998, and their destinations after programme participation, are shown in Table 5.3. About two thirds (66%) of the participants had left the programme by the end of January 2002. About one third (36%) of the participants had entered employment, representing just over half (54%) of all who had left the programme. About a quarter of the participants (38% of all exits) had returned to Income Support.

Men are less likely to have left the programme for work than women (49% compared with 55%), as are lone parents with a youngest child aged under two (50%), those from ethnic minority groups (41% ), and those with disabilities (46%). There is also substantial regional variation in exits to employment, which range from about 44% in London and the South-East to about 63% in Yorkshire and Humberside (Evans et al, 2002).

However, these national statistics give no indication of the impact of the New Deal in comparison with what would have happened it there had been no programme. There is some evidence available from both the evaluation of the prototype and from the evaluation of the national programme. As noted above, the prototype was designed to be an implementation trial and to provide a basis for impact assessment for national implementation. Its quasi-experimental design (a) introduced the programme in eight prototype areas, chosen to represent areas with low, medium, and high unemployment, and (b) included six comparison areas matched to the prototype sites in unemployment, industrial mix, and geographical location. Data were collected from administrative records, from large-scale surveys, and from in-depth interviews. In the prototype areas the interview data covered both participating and non-participating lone parents, New Deal Personal Advisers, and local managers. In the comparison areas it included lone parents in the range of eligibility for the prototype programme (that is, with children aged five and over).

In addition, advantage was taken of a natural experiment arising from the fact that invitations to participants were issued according to National Insurance numbers, in effect creating an individualized random allocation design within prototype areas. The prototype ran for about eight months before the national scheme was implemented.

The main outcome results from the prototype are reported by Hasluck et al (2000) and also summarised by Hales et al (2000a). The most marked difference

**Table 5.3: New Deal for Lone Parents: exits and destinations, October 1998 to January 2002**

|  | Number | % of participants | % of leavers |
|---|---|---|---|
| Participants | 318,990 | 100 |  |
| Left New Deal | 211,350 | 66 | 100 |
| • Into employment | 115,060 | 36 | 54 |
| • Withdrew, still on Income Support | 80,870 | 25 | 38 |
| • Unknown destination | 8,970 | 3 | 4 |
| • No longer eligible | 4,480 | 1 | 2 |
| • Other benefits | 1,970 | 1 | 1 |

*Source:* New Deal Evaluation Database, Statistical First Release, March 2002

between the participant and control groups, as defined in the natural experiment, occurred six months into the project – when the odds of long-term recipients leaving benefit were 12% higher for participants. This differential declined with time and averaged about 5% over 18 months. Models based on comparisons across the prototype and comparison areas also showed small but positive effects. These indicated that the programme led to statistically significant reductions in the number of Income Support claimants of about 1.54% after six months and about 3.28% after 18 months.

Survey data revealed that not all participants left Income Support for employment (Hales et al, 2000a). The same data also indicated that, at least over the period October 1998 to January 1999, there was no significant difference between prototype and comparison areas in the proportion of lone parents who secured jobs on leaving Income Support (17% and 18% respectively), nor in the types of jobs secured, the hours worked, or the pay received. However, those lone parents who found jobs were more likely to report that they were better-off financially in work if they had participated in the programme than if they had not (66% compared with 46%), perhaps suggesting that participants were able to make better job matches and/or more often accessed in-work benefit support. In their synthesis of the evaluation as whole, Hales et al conclude that the programme had a "small but appreciable effect" (Hales et al, 2000a, p 9) at a modest net cost. However, there are important limits in the extent to which we can extrapolate from the prototype findings to the national programme. The prototype was small, staffed by people who were highly committed to the programme, and was generally well resourced, although there were few complementary services in place at the time. The Working Families' Tax Credit had not been introduced nor had the National Childcare Strategy. In addition, as noted above, there have been some important changes to the programme itself since 1998, and the characteristics of participants have also changed. The content of the programme is also, as Evans et al put it, "intangible. [It] offers a personalised service to lone parents that is responsive to individual lone parent's needs and circumstances.... It is an information resource, a type of mentoring service and a problem resolution centre" (Evans et al, 2002, p 87).

The national programme was evaluated over a period of seven months from late 2000 to 2001 by means of a matched comparison quasi-experimental design. This involved a postal survey of about 7,000 lone parents from whom matched pairs of participants and non-participants were identified. The impact of the programme was estimated by comparing the outcomes of these two groups. After six months, about 43% of participants had entered full-time or part-time work compared with with about 19% of matched participants. This suggests an additional effect of participation of about 24% (Lessof et al, 2003). Thus, it appears that employment outcomes in the national programme may be better than those achieved in the prototype.

## Process

The New Deal for Lone Parents is, as noted earlier, essentially an advice and information service, with some opportunities for referrals to training. The National Database shows that most participants are 'receiving advice and guidance'. This accounted for 66% of participants at January 2002, with a further 29% receiving 'in-work support' from a New Deal Personal Adviser, and 5% in education or training (DWP, 2002a).[8] When the prototype was introduced, many lone parents were a little anxious when first invited to participate – not surprisingly, since they had not been included in labour market programmes in the past (Hales et al, 2000b). Those who attended usually said they did so because they were interested in work or training, wanted to know what help they might get, and were interested in the possible financial implications of working. However, almost half of participants in the prototype thought they had no choice, and about a quarter thought they might lose benefit if they did not attend the interview (there were no significant differences in the outcomes of those who entered the programme thinking it was compulsory and those who did not). Most lone parents who did not take part after receiving an invitation letter said that this was either because they felt they could find jobs by themselves without additional support or because they did not want to seek work, at least not immediately. But for two fifths of the non-participants, taking part 'just did not happen': some faced particular circumstances at the time (such as illness in the family, school holidays); others were waiting for further information. Very few of these non-attenders were contacted again, but this evidence led to various changes in the way lone parents were contacted and followed up in the national programme (for example, more use of telephone follow-ups to the initial letter).

Those who did take part usually said they had found the process helpful. Most participants had just one interview, usually lasting an hour or less which was generally considered to be 'about right'. Only one fifth of participants said they would have liked more contact. The main topics discussed in interviews were job search, benefits, and childcare. Very few participants were referred to other services or offered access to education or training. Most felt the discussion to be helpful, but some were disappointed that there was such limited follow-up help available. About half of those who found work said they had been encouraged and helped by the advice on job seeking; about 34% said the programme had directly aided them in finding work.

Lone parents' assessment of the programme was closely linked to their perceptions of their Personal Advisers, which fell into two quite different categories. The majority (eight in ten participants) were very positive about the manner and approach of Advisers (they were seen as friendly, helpful, supportive) and were also positive in their overall responses, even if they had not received much concrete help. But about one fifth found their Advisers patronizing, unclear, and unhelpful. Most participants felt that they would have liked more information, especially about jobs and childcare.

The evaluations of the national programme tend to confirm this picture from the prototype (Dawson et al, 2000; Hamblin, 2000; Lewis et al, 2000; GHK, 2001; Lessof et al, 2001, 2003). These studies also found that lone parents had a variety of motivations for taking part in the programme – including curiosity, a wish for further information or guidance, a motivation to work and a search for specific help, and a belief that participation was compulsory (Lewis et al, 2000). Some participants had very high expectations about what the programme might offer and were disappointed with the limited help available. Help with job search and the limited type and level of training on offer were seen as the weakest elements.

Information about the financial aspects of working was highly valued and most participants were very positive about the New Deal Personal Advisers, as participants in the prototypes had been. Many reported that their confidence had improved and that they were encouraged to start looking for work. The New Deal Personal Advisers themselves also reported that they were very satisfied with the work and very positive about the programme (GHK, 2001). There was some evidence from the qualitative studies that participants were highly motivated and the large postal survey (which included 42,000 lone parents) found that participants tended to be more work-ready than non-participants (Lessof et al, 2001). However, the matched pairs analysis, discussed above, did find an additional impact of the programme and also confirmed the positive responses to the programme, especially from the Personal Advisers, found in the prototype (Lessof et al, 2003).

## A New Deal success

The latest figures show rising employment among lone parents, as noted in Chapter Four, up to just over 50% in 2001 (HM Treasury, 2001) and to just under 54% in 2002 (DWP, 2002b). Similarly, trends in benefit receipt among lone parents show that, since about 1996 but accelerating after 1998, receipt of Income Support has been falling. In May 1997 there were 1,014,000 lone parents receiving Income Support; by November 2001 this had fallen to 867,000. The decline in benefit receipt in fact started before the New Deal was introduced and, although the programme has had a positive outcome in terms of additional employment, the aggregate impact on lone employment cannot be very substantial because participation rates have not been high. Thus, the impact of the programme cannot, by itself, account for the emerging trends. And, although just over half of all those who leave the New Deal programme do so because they enter work, we do not have any robust measures of how far this represents additional employment.

However, the New Deal for Lone Parents should be judged for what it is – the first British labour market policy that has been targeted at lone parents, mainly providing advice and information to support job search, with a relatively modest budget (of £220 million between 1997 and 2002 compared with the allocated budget of £1,480 million for the New Deal for Young People over the same period). The national statistics show a small but steady number of lone parents (between two and five thousand) moving into employment from the New Deal each month. The evaluation evidence is limited in many ways, but tends to confirm what has also been found by other studies of similar programmes elsewhere (particularly Australia and the US) – that voluntary, work-focused, information- and advice-oriented services can help individuals find work, particularly those who are most ready for work (Millar, 2001b; Whiteford, 2001).

The evaluation evidence also confirms the findings from previous research that lone parents often face very substantial barriers to work (Bradshaw and Millar, 1991; McKay and Marsh, 1994, Marsh et al, 1997; Millar and Ridge, 2001, provide a summary). These include barriers arising from personal attributes (health, work experience, and skills) and from location (the lack of suitable jobs in the vicinity, transport). But the barriers most often mentioned in the evaluation studies relate to the financial risks and consequences of working and to difficulties of finding and managing childcare. Lone parents were concerned about the transition to work, about access to in-work benefits, about how to make ends meet, and about what would happen if they had to return to Income Support. They also identified the problems of finding affordable, convenient, reliable childcare, of high quality and appropriate to the needs of their children. Finally, they reflected UK attitudes generally in expressing some ambivalence about the impact of working on children and a feeling that employment would have to wait if it was not seen to be in the best interests of the children. Since the New Deal programme by itself cannot tackle many of these barriers nor the problem of low labour demand in particular geographical areas (Webster, 2000), it is almost certainly the whole policy bundle – the New Deal, the National Childcare Strategy, the make work pay measures, alongside a favourable economic climate – that has contributed to rising employment rates among lone parents over the past three to four years. Disentangling the relative contributions of the different components is complex and perhaps impossible. The limited descriptive information that currently exists on the impact of the other measures, which have not yet been subject to detailed evaluation, indicates the following.

The National Childcare Strategy has led to a net increase of 74,000 childcare places in England (DSS, 2000b), but there is still a long way to go in meeting the childcare gap (Land, 2002). The National Minimum Wage has benefited women in particular, with over three quarters of a million women workers receiving higher pay as a result (Low Pay Commission, 2000). And as Chapter Four indicates, making work pay policies are known to be benefiting lone parents. For example, the number of lone parents receiving in-work financial support increased sharply, from 335,600 receiving Family Credit in November 1996 to 632,400 receiving Working Families' Tax Credit in August 2001. Over the same period, the average payment rose from about £56 per week to about £86 per week. The number of lone parents receiving help with childcare costs alongside Working Families' Tax Credit also increased substantially, from 28,300 in November 1996 to 134,900 in August 2001. And the average amount received per week rose from about £20 to about £37 (Inland Revenue, 2001).

Among the employed lone parents interviewed for the 2000 *Families and Children Survey* (a panel study of lone parents and low-income two-parent families), 56% were receiving Working Families' Tax credit, giving a take-up rate of about 78%. About a third (34%) said that receiving this support had enabled them to take, or stay in, work and 62% said they could not manage in work without it (McKay, 2002). More lone-parent families who leave Income Support for employment are moving onto Working Families' Tax Credit than used to be the case for Family Credit, which suggests that Working Families' Tax Credit is encouraging more lone parents to move into work (DSS, 2000b, p 32). Brewer and Gregg (2001) estimate that Working Families' Tax Credit has led to a net rise in lone-parent employment of about 25,000 above that which would be predicted on the basis of labour market trends and the personal characteristics of the parents.

## Policy moving on

Policy and practice have been moving quickly and, as shown in Table 5.2 earlier, a number of additional measures are currently being implemented, in particular the phased introduction of compulsory personal adviser interviews for all lone parents receiving Income Support. There have also been various operational changes to the way the New Deal is delivered – for example, more use of telephone contacts and home visits and the introduction of an Innovation Fund to encourage new initiatives by local Jobcentre Plus offices (Hasluck et al, 2000). In addition, greater emphasis has been placed on education and training, with lone parents who take up training able to access, and get financial support for, a wider range of training opportunities and also to access help with childcare costs while training. Benefit rules have also been changed to make it easier for lone parents to work part-time (under 16 hours per week) or to undertake training while receiving Income Support. A much simpler formula is to be introduced into the child support system in 2003 to reduce liabilities for absent parents, while lone parents on Income Support will in future gain financial benefit from child support payments due to the provision of a £10 per week disregard (Cm 4349, 1999).[9] As explained in Chapter Four, from 2003 a new Child Tax Credit will bring together the children's benefits in Income Support and Working Families' Tax Credit, so that parents moving into work will not need to make a new benefit claim for their children (HM Treasury, 2000).

Two of the new elements warrant special attention: the introduction of compulsory personal adviser interviews as part of the process of claiming benefits and the measures to encourage part-time work.

The element of compulsion is mild by US standards. It does not compel lone parents to join the New Deal, which will remain voluntary. Nor does it change the rules regarding availability to work: lone parents will continue to be eligible for benefits without any work requirements as long as they have a youngest child under 16. But it is the first time that such requirements have been placed upon lone parents in the modern British welfare state.

The additional support for part-time employment is intended to make it possible for lone parents to construct an 'income package' from part-time wages, benefits, and child support. Once the Child Tax Credit is introduced, the benefits element of the package will be divided into benefits for children (which will be payable at the same rate across a wide range of earnings) and benefits for adults (Income Support for those in part-time work and a new Working Tax Credit for those in full-time – 16 hours plus – work).

The overall contours of the Labour government's approach to lone parents and employment have thus become much clearer. This is an approach that supports employment but also recognizes that lone parents cannot always be available for work. Lone parents will be required to attend interviews where they will be given regular information about employment and training options, but they will not be compelled to act upon these. There are financial measures intended to make work pay and in-kind measures designed to make work possible. The financial support is typically income-tested and mainly delivered through the tax rather than the benefits system, with additional spending aimed particularly at benefits for children. Child support is integrated into the income package and, if paid, always benefits the lone parent. Childcare is the most important in-kind support, and here there is reliance upon a mixed economy of public, private, and voluntary provision.

How far is this a coherent package? And how far does it derive from the US model? In terms of coherence the UK system is still very complex, with income-tested support creating a long 'poverty trap', where increases in earnings do not necessarily translate into increases in disposable income. Access to education and training has improved but remains very limited, failing to provide lone parents with the skills they would need to get better-paying jobs, and little attention has so far been given to issues of work retention and progression. It will take a long time before the childcare provision matches demand, and the childcare credit only meets part of the costs of childcare. Nevertheless there is a developing coherence in both goals and policies, and the sharp work/welfare dichotomy is being replaced by a continuum, with different possible combinations of sources of income.

References to US policy and, in particular, US research findings are frequent in UK welfare to work policy debates. Nevertheless, as this discussion of policies for lone parents has shown, there are significant differences in both objectives and implementation. Glennerster (1999, p 6) has argued that the UK welfare-to-work policies are "not a carbon copy of the 1996 welfare reforms in the US", but that "they do look like the set of proposals put forward by liberal academics like David Ellwood".[10] This British lone-parent package does include policies intended to make it easier for lone parents to combine income from wages, child support, and tax-based wage supplements, as Ellwood advocated in his 1998 book. However, the UK package more closely resembles the proposals of the Finer report in 1974, which also proposed wage supplements, a formula-based child support system, and subsidized childcare services. Arguably, current policy comes closer to giving lone parents more 'choice' about whether or not to take paid work than ever before, because no previous British government has established positive measures to support employment. Lone parents often could not choose employment, even if they wanted to, because they could not get childcare nor survive on low wages. Perhaps the UK is finally implementing Finer, rather than copying US models.

A substantial gap still exists between the 54% currently in employment and the 70% target, however. What more could be done to increase employment rates? Marsh (2001, p 30) suggests that one option would be to "wait and see", to give the current policies a chance to settle down, to become accepted, and to reach more lone parents. He argues that the current policies are going in the right direction but could be strengthened by further investment in childcare, by measures aimed at improving health and reducing hardship, and by increasing the flow of child support payments. Another option would be to follow the US route more closely and introduce further elements of compulsion into the system, for example by making participation in the New Deal programme a condition of benefit receipt. The US evidence about the impact of compulsion is not unequivocal, but Freedman et al (2000), conclude that, while high compulsion does not necessarily mean high outcomes, low compulsion does produce low results. They conclude:

> It thus appears that a minimum level of enforcement by program staff is required to produce at least moderate earnings and welfare impacts, presumably because this extra 'push' is needed in order to engage in program activities those who normally would not participate on their own initiative. (Freedman et el, 2000, p 6)

The compulsory interviews being implemented for lone parents under Jobcentre Plus in the UK are intended to provide this extra push and, as noted earlier, they do seem to have been successful at increasing participation in the New Deal programme under the ONE pilots. However, there is no hard evidence that they have changed either attitudes or work behaviour (Evans et al, 2002). If compulsion were to be extended to include participation in the New Deal it would certainly change the nature of the programme, leading to higher caseloads and probably less motivated participants. But it is not clear that it would lead to higher employment outcomes.

Another alternative would be to introduce work requirements for lone parents, making benefit receipt conditional upon job search, employment, or employment-related activities. Currently, as noted above, lone parents in the UK are not required to be available for work as long as they have a youngest child under 16. The Conservative Party spokesperson for Social Security has suggested that work requirements should be compulsory for all lone parents with children over 11 (Willetts and Hillman, 2000). In many countries lone parents are expected to do some paid work once their children reach school age (Millar, 2001b). Changes in employment patterns for women in general may be leading inevitably towards a situation in which full-time care is seen as appropriate only for mothers of very young children. Orloff compares the US and UK welfare reforms and argues that mothers' full-time care giving remains "legitimate and politically defensible in Britain, in a context where mothers generally are more likely to stay at home full-time or work part-time" (Orloff, 2002, p 100). Whether this continues to be the case is likely to depend both on what happens to British women's employment rates in general and on whether current policy is successful or not.

However, the employment target set in Britain does not necessarily imply that 70% of lone parents should be in *full-time* work and, as discussed above, policy is increasingly focused upon measures that would allow lone parents to combine 'work and welfare'. This shift – away from tax and social security systems that sharply distinguish between workers and non-workers towards more integrated systems that recognize more varied patterns of employment, both contemporaneously and over time, and that are based on providing wage supplements rather than wage replacements – may be one of the most significant developments in UK policy. Such an approach may be better adapted to current labour market and family patterns, although it runs the risk of institutionalising a large low-paid sector of employment, particularly for women.

## Notes

[1] These figures are derived from the government's regular statistical series on "Households Below Average Income". More recent editions report the numbers below 60% of the median, although earlier reports do not. In the mid-1994/95, about 55% of lone parents had income of below 60% of the median.

[2] However this is a topic now under active debate, with a proposal from a former Labour government minister (Frank Field) for legislation to allow Housing Benefit to be withheld from 'anti-social' tenants, and a suggestion from the Prime Minister that Child Benefit should be withheld from parents whose children truant from school (Wintour and Smithers, 2002).

[3] The table (and discussion) focuses on employment related measures and does not summarize all the changes to taxes and benefits. In particular it does not show the increases in benefits for children, although these have obviously affected lone-parent families. That aspect of policy is covered in detail in Chapter Four. See also Millar (2001a).

[4] The New Deal Personal Advisers have mainly been drawn from existing staff of either the Benefits Agency (the government agency responsible for paying benefits) or the Employment Service (the agency responsible for job placement and labour market programmes). Since 2002 these have been merged into a single body, called Jobcentre Plus.

[5] This is not the same as the eligible group, which has always included all lone parents receiving Income Support (and since November 2001 non-Income Support recipients), who could choose to come forward at any time.

[6] Summaries of all these measures, and others, can be found in the government's third poverty audit (DWP, 2001), which reports on their progress from various baseline measures established in the previous years (Cm 4445, 1999; DSS, 2000a).

[7] These are available on the Department for Work and Pensions website (www.dwp.gov.uk)

[8] Overall, since the national programme started about 9% of participants have taken part in education or training.

[9] This was to have been introduced from April 2002, but operational difficulties have lead to a postponement and it is not yet known precisely when these measures will be implemented.

[10] See also Glennerster, 2002, p 97-98, in which he argues that "if we take the main recommendations in Ellwood's book, or the proposals he made to President Bill Clinton for welfare reform, we find every one of them either was implemented by the Blair government between 1997 and 1999 or was already a part of British social policy".

## References

Barnes, H., Day, P. and Cronin, N. (1999) *Trial and error: A review of UK child support policy*, London: Family Policy Studies Centre.

Bradshaw, J. and Millar, J. (1991) *Lone parent families in the UK*, London: HMSO.

Brewer, M. and Gregg, P. (2001) 'Lone parents, the working families tax credit and employment in households with children', in R. Dickens, J. Wadsworth and P. Gregg (eds) *The state of working Britain: Update 2001*, London: Centre for Economic Policy, pp 8-13.

Brown, G. (2000a) Pre-budget consultation launch, 9 October (www.hm-treasury.gov.uk).

Brown, G. (2000b) Speech, no 10 Downing Street, 30 November (www.hm-treasury.gov.uk).

Bryson, C., Budd, T., Lewis, J. and Elam, G. (1998) *Women's attitudes to combining paid work and family life*, London: Central Office of Information for the Cabinet Office.

Cm 5629 (1974) *Report of the committee on One-Parent Families*, (The Finer Report), London: HMSO.

Cm 4349 (1999) *A new contract for welfare: Children's rights and parents' responsibilities*, London: The Stationery Office.

Cm 4445 (1999) *Opportunity for all: Tackling poverty and social exclusion*, London: The Stationery Office.

Cm 5084 (2001) *Towards full employment in a modern society*, London: The Stationery Office.

Davies, I I.T.O., Nutley, S. M. and Smith, P.C. (2000) (eds) *What works? Evidence-based policy and practice in public services*, Bristol: The Policy Press.

Davies, J. (1993) *The family – is it just another lifestyle choice?*, London: Institute of Economic Affairs.

Dawson, T., Dickens, S. and Finer, S. (2000) *New Deal for lone parents: Report on qualitative studies with individuals*, Sheffield: Employment Service, ESR55.

DfEE (Department for Education and Employment) (1988) *Meeting the childcare challenge: A framework and consultation document*, London: DfEE.

DfEE (2000) 'New places for 1.6 million children', Press Release 10 September, London: DfEE.

DfEE (2001) *Personal adviser meetings and the New Deal for lone parents: A guide to policy and practice*, London: DfEE.

DSS (Department of Social Security) (1999) *Social security statistics, 1997*, Leeds: Corporate Document Services.

DSS (2000a) *Households below average income 1994/5-1998/9*, London: Corporate Document Services.

DSS (2000b) *Opportunity for all – One year on: Making a difference*, London: The Stationery Office.

DTI (Department of Trade and Industry) (2001) *Work and parents: Competitiveness and choice*, London: The Stationery Office.

DWP (Department for Work and Pensions) (2001) *Opportunity for all: The third annual report*, London: The Stationery Office.

DWP (2002a) *New Deal for lone parents and personal adviser meetings: Statistics to January 2002*, London: ONS, March.

DWP (2002b) *Opportunity for all – Fourth annual report*, London: The Stationery Office.

Dolowitz, D.P. and Marsh, D. (2000) 'Learning from abroad: the role of policy transfer in contemporary policy-making', *Governance: An international journal of policy and administration*, vol 13, no 1, pp 5-32.

Duncan, S. and Edwards, R. (1997) *Single mothers in international context: Mothers or workers?*, London: UCL Press.

Duncan, S. and Edwards, R. (1999) *Lone mothers, paid work and gendered moral rationalities*, Basingstoke: Macmillan.

Ellwood, D. (1988) *Poor support: Poverty in the American family*, New York, NY: Basic Books.

Evans, M., McKnight, A. and Namazie, C. (2002) *Evaluating the New Deal for lone parents: A synthesis of the evidence*, Sheffield: The Employment Service.

Finch, H., O'Connor, W. with Millar, J., Hales, J., Shaw, A. and Roth, W. (1999) *New Deal for lone parents: Learning from the prototype areas*, Social Security Report, no 92, London: Corporate Document Services.

Freedman, S., Friedlander, D., Hamilton, G., Rock, J., Mitchell, M., Nudelman, J., Schweder, A. and Storto, L. (2000) *National evaluation of welfare-to-work strategies: Evaluating alternative welfare-to-work approaches: Two-year impacts for eleven programs*, New York, NY: Manpower Demonstration Research Corporation.

GHK (Griswold, Heckel & Kelly Associates, Inc.) (2001) *New Deal for lone parents: Case studies on delivery*, Sheffield: Employment Service, ESR85.

Glennerster, H. (1999) 'Which welfare states are most likely to survive?', *International Journal of social welfare*, vol 8, pp 2-13.

Glennerster, H. (2002) 'United States poverty studies and poverty measurement: the past 25 years', *Social service review*, March, pp 83-107.

Hales, J., Lessof, C., Roth, W., Gloyer, M., Shaw, A., Millar, J., Barnes, M., Elias, P., Hasluck, C., McKnight, A. and Green, A. (2000a) *Evaluation of the New Deal for lone parents: Early lessons from the phase one prototype – synthesis report*, London: DSS Research Report, no 108.

Hales, J., Roth, W., Barnes, M., Millar, J., Lessof, C., Gloyer, M. and Shaw, A. (2000b) *Evaluation of the New Deal for lone parents: Early lessons from the phase one prototype – findings of surveys*, London: DSS Research Report 109.

Hamblin, M. (2000) *A report on lone parents client satisfaction survey: Part of the evaluation of the NDLP Phase 3*, Sheffield: Employment Service, ESR39.

Haskey, J. (1998) 'One-parent families and their dependent children in the UK', in R. Ford and J. Millar (eds) *Private lives and public responses: Lone parenthood and future policy in the UK*, London: Policy Studies Institute, pp 22-41.

Haskey, J. (2002) 'One parent families and their dependent children living with them in Great Britain', *Population Trends*, no 109, pp 46-57.

Hasluck, C. (2000) *The New Deal for lone parents: A review of the evaluation evidence*, ESR51, Sheffield: Employment Service.

Hasluck, C., McKnight, A. and Elias, P. (2000) *Evaluation of the New Deal for lone parents: Early lessons from the phase one prototype – cost-benefit and econometric analyses*, London: DSS Research Report 110.

HC (House of Commons Social Security Select Committee) (1993) *The operation of the Child Support Act, first report*, HC 69, London: HMSO.

HC (1994) *The operation of the Child Support Act, second report*, HC 50, London: HMSO.

Hills, J. and Lelkes, O. (1999) 'Social security, selective universalism and patchwork redistribution', in R. Jowell, J. Curtice, A. Park and K. Thomson (eds) *British social attitudes, the 16th report: Who shares New Labour values?*, Aldershot: Ashgate, pp 1-22.

HM Treasury (2000) *Tackling poverty and making work pay: Tax credits for the 21st century: The modernization of Britain's tax and benefit system*, no 6, London: HM Treasury.

HM Treasury (2001) *Pre-budget report New Deal for lone parents*, London: HM Treasury.

Holtermann, S., Brannen, J., Moss, P. and Owen, C. (1999) *Lone parents and the labour market: Results from the 1997 Labour Force survey and review of research*, Sheffield: Employment Service, ESR23.

Inland Revenue (2001) *Working families tax credit statistics, quarterly enquiry*, London: National Statistics Office.

Jarvis, L., Hinds, K., Bryson, C. and Park, A. (2000) *Women's social attitudes: 1983 to 1998*, London: Central Office of Information for the Cabinet Office.

Jenkins, S. (2000) 'Dynamics of household incomes', in R. Berthoud and J. Gershuny (eds) *Seven years in the lives of British families: Evidence on the dynamics of social change from the British household panel survey*, Bristol: The Policy Press, pp 107-32.

Kiernan, K., Land, H. and Lewis, J. (1998) *Lone motherhood in twentieth century Britain*, Oxford: Oxford University Press.

Land, H. (1995) 'Reversing the inadvertent nationalisation of fatherhood: the British Child Support Act and its consequences for men, women and children', *International social security review*, vol 47, no 4, pp 91-100.

Land, H. (1999) 'New Labour, new families?', in H. Dean and R. Woods (eds) *Social Policy Review*, vol 11, Luton: Social Policy Association, pp 127-44.

Land, H. (2002) *Meeting the child poverty challenge: Why universal childcare is key to ending poverty*, London: The Daycare Trust.

Lessof, C., Hales, J., Phillips, M., Pickering, K., Purdon, S. and Miller, M. (2001) *New Deal for lone parents evaluation: A quantitative survey of lone parents on income support*, Sheffield: Employment Service, ESR101.

Lessof, C., Miller, M., Phillips, M., Pickering, K., Purdon, S. and Hales, J. (2003) *New Deal for Lone Parents Evaluation: Findings from the quantitative survey*, Sheffield: Employment Service, WAE147.

Lewis, J. (1997) *Lone mothers in European welfare regimes*, London: Jessica Kingsley.

Lewis, J., Mitchell, L., Sanderson, T., O'Connor, W. and Clayden, M. (2000) *Lone parents and personal advisers: Roles and relationships*, DSS Research Report 122, Leeds: Corporate Document Services.

Lister, R. (1994) 'The Child Support Act: shifting financial obligations in the UK', *Social Politics*, vol 1, no 2, pp 211-22.

Lister, R. (1996) 'Back to the family: family policies and politics under the major government', in H. Jones and J. Millar (eds) *The politics of the family*, Aldershot: Avebury, pp 11-31.

Lister, R. (2002) 'The responsible citizen: creating a new welfare contract', in C. Kingfisher (ed) *Western welfare in decline: Globalization and women's poverty*, Philadelphia: University of Pennsylvania Press, pp 111-127.

Low Pay Commission (2000) *Second annual report*, London: Low Pay Commission.

Marsh, A. (2001) 'Helping British lone parents get and keep paid work', in J. Millar and K. Rowlingson (eds) *Lone parents employment and social policy: Cross-national comparisons*, Bristol: The Policy Press.

Marsh, A., Ford, R. and Finlayson, L. (1997) *Lone parents, work and benefits*, DSS, Research Report no 61, London: The Stationery Office.

McKay, S. (2002) *Low/moderate income families in Britain: Work, WFTC and childcare in 2000*, DSS Research Report no 161, Leeds: Corporate Document Services.

McKay, S. and Marsh, A. (1994) *Lone parents and work*, London: HMSO.

McLaughlin, E. (1994) 'Flexibility or polarisation?', in M. White (ed) *Unemployment and public policy in a changing labour market*, London: Policy Studies Institute, pp 7-28.

Millar, J. (1994) 'State, family and personal responsibility: the changing balance for lone mothers in the UK', *Feminist review*, no 48, pp 24-40.

Millar, J. (1996) 'Family obligations and social policy: the case of child support', *Policy Studies*, vol 17, no 3, pp 181-93.

Millar, J. (2000) 'Lone parents and the New Deal', *Policy studies*, vol 21, no 4, pp 333-45.

Millar, J. (2001a) 'Benefits for children in the UK', in K. Battle and M. Mendelson (eds) *Benefits for children: A four country study*, Ottawa: Caledon Institute, pp 187-256.

Millar, J. (2001b) 'Work-related activity requirements and labour market programmes for lone parents', in J. Millar and K. Rowlingson (eds) *Lone parents, employment and social policy: Cross-national comparisons*, Bristol: The Policy Press, pp 189-211.

Millar, J. and Ridge, T. (2001) *Families, poverty, work and care: A review of the literature on lone parents and low-income couples with children*, DWP Research Report no 153, Leeds: Corporate Document Services.

Millar, J. and Whiteford, P. (1993) 'Child support in lone-parent families: policies in Australia and the UK', *Policy & Politics*, vol 21, no 1, pp 59-72.

Morgan, P. (1995) *Farewell to the family: Public policy and family breakdown in Britain and the US*, London: Institute for Economic Affairs.

ONS (Office of National Statistics) (1999) *Social trends 1999*, London: The Stationery Office.

Orloff, A.S. (2002) 'Explaining US welfare reform: power, gender, race and the US policy legacy', *Critical social policy*, vol 22, no 1, pp 97-112.

Pettigrew, N., Garland, C., BMRB (British Market Research Bureau) and Irving, P. (2001) *An evaluation of the lone parent Personal adviser meetings*, Sheffield: Employment Service, ESR90.

Randall, V. (2001) *The politics of child daycare in Britain*, Oxford, England: Oxford University Press.

Taylor-Gooby, P. (1991) 'Attachment to the welfare state', in R. Jowell, L. Brook and B. Taylor (eds) *British social attitudes: The 8th report*, Aldershot: Dartmouth Publishing, pp 23-42.

Vincent, J., Walker, R., Dobson, B., Stafford, B., Barnes, M. and Bottomley, D. (1996) *Lone parent caseworker pilots evaluation*, Final Report, Working Paper 263, Loughborough: Centre for Research in Social Policy, University of Loughborough.

Walker, A., Maher, J., Coulthard, M., Goddard, E. and Thomas, M. (2002) *Living in Britain: Results from the 2000/01 General household survey*, London: The Stationery Office.

Webster, D. (2000) 'The geographical concentration of labour market disadvantage', *Oxford Review of economic policy*, vol 16, no 1, pp 114-28.

Whiteford, P. (2001) 'Lone parents and employment in Australia', in J. Millar and K. Rowlingson (eds) *Lone parents, employment and social policy: Cross-national comparisons*, Bristol: The Policy Press, pp 61-86.

Willetts, D. and Hillman, N. (2000) *A raw deal for lone parents*, London: Centre for Policy Studies.

Wintour, P. and Smithers, R. (2002) 'New benefit crackdown: Blair backs bill to dock housing allowance for antisocial behaviour', *The Guardian*, Tuesday 30 April (www.society.guardian.co.uk).

# SIX

# Beyond lone parents: extending welfare-to-work to disabled people and the young unemployed

*Bruce Stafford*

## Introduction

Despite the generality of its title, the Temporary Assistance for Needy Families (TANF) in the US primarily addresses single parents with children. In the UK this client group is targeted by the New Deal for Lone Parents (see Chapter Five), which is one of a family of New Deal programmes that are central to New Labour's strategy for moving people from welfare-to-work and modernizing the welfare state. The New Deals are active labour market policies that differ in client group, by whether participation is mandatory or voluntary, and according to the nature of the intervention. Many of the key features of these New Deals, such as case working, will be familiar to an American audience, but the UK government has applied these policies to client groups not currently covered by welfare-to-work policies in the US. This chapter, therefore, looks beyond lone parents to consider the Labour government's application of a welfare-to-work model to two quite different target groups, young people and people of working age with disabilities. The intent is to show how, in the UK, the generic model has been modified, both in light of the characteristics of the particular target groups and in response to prevailing norms and expectations as well as political objectives.

Both New Deals discussed here encompass recipients not just of means-tested, cash benefits but also of contributory, social insurance benefits. New Labour has therefore moved beyond welfare as reflected in TANF and addressed groups that in the US would at least potentially be recipients of unemployment insurance payments. The welfare-to-work model has also been applied in the UK to people claiming benefits on the grounds of incapacity for work – who have, therefore, in both the US and Britain, traditionally been considered exempt from the expectation that they should obtain paid work. Being assessed as incapable of work in Britain does not prohibit all forms of work, and claimants performing certain tasks – such as caring, domestic work, voluntary work, and therapeutic work[1] – can retain incapacity benefit entitlement. Nevertheless, until the New Deal for Disabled People, the government did not systematically endeavour to help those on incapacity-related benefits into paid employment.

## The programmes in brief

### The New Deal for Young People

The New Deal for Young People was established as a national programme in April 1998 and is targeted at 18- to 24-year-olds who generally have been unemployed for six or more months. (Certain groups, including young disabled people, lone parents, ex-offenders, and people with problems with basic skills may gain early entry to the programme.) Unlike in the US, in Britain almost all young unemployed people over age 17 are entitled to a cash benefit, Jobseeker's Allowance, even if they have never worked. Most will receive this benefit following a means test, but some will have acquired the right to benefit on the basis of insurance contributions made while working. Jobseeker's Allowance paid on the basis of social insurance contributions is only paid for up to the first 26 weeks of a spell of unemployment, after which the individual is eligible for means-tested Jobseeker's Allowance. Claimants of contribution-based Jobseeker's Allowance with a partner or children often claim means-tested Jobseeker's Allowance from the beginning of their spell of unemployment as their household circumstances mean that they often meet the requirements of the means test. To be eligible for the New Deal for Young People, participants must be claiming Jobseeker's Allowance, either means tested or contribution-based.

Under New Deal for Young People, the activity sequence begins with a four-month Gateway. The Gateway aims to get young people into work through providing intensive help with job search, and all participants are allocated a personal adviser (or caseworker). For those who fail to find unsubsidised employment, the Gateway is followed by a choice of one of four activity options (subsidised work, voluntary work, the Environmental Task Force, or full-time education or training). Once the chosen activity is completed, participants who have not obtained unsubsidised employment move to a Follow Through phase of additional intensive job search.

Each of the Options generally lasts for up to six months and provides vocational training of at least a day a week leading to accreditation. Participation is mandatory; the sanction for refusal to participate is a time-limited withdrawal of Jobseeker's Allowance. Sanctions can be imposed for a variety of reasons and for different lengths of time. Young people face two sanction regimes depending upon their stage in the New Deal process. While in the Gateway they are subject to the same sanction regime as all Jobseeker's Allowance claimants. For example, if they fail to look for work or are a full-time student their claim to benefit is terminated; if they refuse an offer of an unsubsidised job without good cause their benefit can be suspended for up to 26 weeks; if they refuse to take up one of the Options (or any other government programme or course) benefit is stopped for two weeks, or four weeks if previously sanctioned. At the Options stage, the sanctions regime changes. Failure to attend an Option, leaving early, or being dismissed without good cause can lead to an initial two-week benefit suspension that rises to four weeks, then to 26 weeks for subsequent breaches. The Personal Adviser does not impose benefit sanctions, rather the case is referred to an Adjudication Officer for a decision on whether a penalty should be imposed.

## The New Deal for Disabled People

In contrast to the New Deal for Young People, participation in the New Deal for Disabled People is voluntary. It was introduced in 1998, initially as a two-year pilot, because the government recognized the particular difficulties the client group encountered in obtaining employment and considered that a period of experimentation was needed to identify best practice (HC, 1999). Two versions of the New Deal for Disabled People were piloted – the Innovative Schemes and the Personal Adviser Service. The Innovative Schemes comprised 24 pilots, evaluating different approaches to engaging and supporting people into work. The Personal Adviser Service was piloted in 12 areas. A government agency, the Employment Service, ran six. The remainder were operated by partnerships of public, private (for-profit), and voluntary sector (not-for-profit) organisations. Because the Personal Adviser Service more closely follows the generic New Deal model, when the New Deal for Disabled People pilot is referred to, it is this pilot that will be discussed.[2]

The New Deal for Disabled People targeted people claiming incapacity-related benefits who have been incapacitated for 28 weeks or more. Benefit regulations mean that it is not possible to be in receipt of both Jobseeker's Allowance and an incapacity-related benefit, although the benefit for disabled people on Jobseeker's Allowance does include a disability premium payment. The different qualifying benefits for the two New Deals meant that unemployed young people with a disability living in the New Deal for Disabled People pilot areas would not be eligible for that pilot but only for the New Deal for Young People. Nationally, 13% of New Deal for Young People participants were disabled (that is, their Jobseeker's Allowance included a disability premium payment) in May 1999 (HC, 1999). Young people in receipt of an incapacity-related benefit and resident in a pilot area, however, were eligible for the New Deal for Disabled People.

The rest of this chapter considers the context of the New Deal for Disabled People and New Deal for Young People. This is followed by a detailed comparison and assessments of the two programmes. The chapter concludes by highlighting policy issues that arise from the comparison.

## Context

### Policy

The New Deals form part of the New Labour government's modernization of the welfare state. The consultation paper, *New ambitions for our country: A new contract for welfare* (Cm3805, 1998c) outlined the government's principles and vision for reform.[3] The broad policy intent is to tackle poverty (especially childhood poverty) and social exclusion through helping people find paid work and assisting them to stay and progress in employment, to improve labour market efficiency, and to make the UK economy more internationally competitive (HM Treasury, 2000a). There is also a desire to change the nature of the contract between the individual and the state, whereby the right of individuals to get support from the government when looking for work is balanced by the responsibility to seek training and work where able to do so (Blunkett, 2000). These are ambitious goals, some of which extend beyond social security and welfare objectives as traditionally conceived in both Britain and the US (see Sainsbury, 1999).

As such, the New Deals for disabled and young people are products of a common policy paradigm comprising the following elements:

- a belief that paid work is the surest route out of poverty and social exclusion and the best means of securing independence (Cm3805, 1998c; HM Treasury, 2000a);
- an expectation that increasing the supply of labour will increase the pool of (skilled) labour available to employers which, in turn, will increase production and productivity (Blunkett, 2000; HM Treasury, 2000a);
- a presumption that movements into work can be assisted by:
    - delivering a proactive benefit system founded on a flexible, integrated, personalised (or caseworker) service backed by investment in information and communication technology (Cm4102, 1998b); and
    - providing enabling services and support that tackle people's barriers to work and improve their employability;
- a stress on the rights and responsibilities of individuals as well as those of the state (Blair, 1997; Blunkett, 2000; Cm3805, 1998c); and
- a commitment to government working in partnership with the voluntary and private sectors to deliver benefit and employment services.

As explained in Chapters One and Four, the New Deals operate within a wider policy framework of work incentives, tax changes, and employment service initiatives and schemes aimed at specific client groups and geographical areas (Gardiner, 1997; Cm3805, 1998c; Millar, 2000).

## Background to the New Deal for Young People

New Labour was elected in 1997 with a well-publicised manifesto commitment to move 250,000 young people from benefit into work. The New Deal for Young People is the mechanism by which this objective is mainly to be achieved; hence, as well as being a central element in the government's labour market policy, it has a high political and policy profile (HC, 2000).

The commitment to tackling unemployment among young people resulted from a number of interrelated economic, social, and ideological factors. Perhaps most important was concern about the adverse consequences of youth unemployment. The strong presumption was that unemployment among young people leads to benefit dependency, social exclusion, dysfunctional and anti-social behaviour, low self-esteem, and even the emergence of an underclass (see Blair, 1997). Papers accompanying the first full Labour budget emphasised the link between youth unemployment and crime, citing US evidence (HM Treasury, 1997). Paid work, on the other hand, was perceived as providing a route to independence and 'mainstream' society: "For young people, entering the labour market is a critical rite of passage to adulthood" (Cm3805, 1998c, para. 9).

Such beliefs – discussed in more detail in Chapter Three – were formed against a backcloth of substantial change in the UK youth labour market (Hasluck, 1999). Youth unemployment rose following the 'oil crisis' of the 1970s and recessions in the 1980s, peaking in 1993 at 21.3% for males and 13.6% for females aged between 18 and 24 (International Labor Organisation [ILO] definition,[4] ONS, 2000). Since then, the trend has been downwards – unemployment had fallen to 13.5% and 10.3% for young men and young women, respectively, by the time the New Deal for Young People was introduced. Nevertheless, the risk of experiencing unemployment before the age of 25 has increased with successive cohorts of young men. Forty per cent of the 1967 to 1971 birth cohort had been unemployed by the age of 25 compared with just 8% of those born between 1942 and 1946 (Stafford et al, 1999). Also, higher proportions of young people, men in particular, enter the labour market after a prolonged spell of unemployment.

Education is compulsory in the UK between ages 5 and 16. Many students complete their final year of compulsory education having been accredited, on the basis of examination performance, with a General Certificate of Secondary Education (GCSE) for each of their curricula studies. Some then leave school for the labour market or economic inactivity, but many 16 year olds (71% in 1998; DfEE, 1999) stay on in education for a further two years to gain, through examinations, additional qualifications that will help them secure employment or a place at university.

Since the 1980s more young people have stayed on in full-time education after reaching the age when schooling is no longer compulsory (Robinson, 1999), causing the number entering the labour market to decline. Rates of participation in education have risen dramatically, mainly due to the replacement of the previous system of qualifications with GCSEs in 1988. This, in turn, has led to expansion of the higher education sector: 30% of young people now enter universities and other higher education institutions (Dearing, 1997).

For those young people leaving school between the ages of 16 and 17, the transition from school to (unsubsidised) employment has become increasingly problematic (Maguire, 2000). There has been a decline in the number of jobs requiring no or few qualifications, coupled with a growth in employment in the service sector demanding academic and vocational qualifications (SEU, 1999). Consequently there are fewer job opportunities than in the past for the 8% of 16- and 17-year-olds who have left school without any qualifications (that is, those without even GCSEs) (Robinson, 1999). Indeed, unemployed young people, who disproportionately lack qualifications and confront a labour market that places a growing premium on accreditation, are spending increasing lengths of time on benefit and thereby becoming more susceptible to the negative consequences of unemployment feared by policy makers. This growing problem engendered political support for the New Deal for Young People, which was the first New Deal to be established nationwide (in April 1998). Nevertheless, its introduction still proved to be somewhat controversial because of its compulsory nature.

### Background to the New Deal for Disabled People

In the UK disability benefits are designed to meet a number of objectives, as reflected in the four main categories of benefit: (1) those replacing earnings for people judged incapable of work; (2) those compensating people for injury at work; (3) those designed to meet the extra costs of impairment; and (4) those supplementing income to a minimum level (Berthoud, 1998; Burchardt, 1999). (The latter are augmented by a tax credit paid to disabled people in work on low incomes.) The first category of benefits includes Incapacity Benefit, Severe Disablement Allowance, and the crediting of National Insurance (or social insurance) contribution records on grounds of incapacity. (Recipients of the latter do not receive a cash benefit, but their contributory records are credited to maintain their entitlement to other social insurance benefits, principally their state pension.) Recipients of these three benefit types together define the target group for the New Deal for Disabled People. Incapacity Benefit is the main contributory benefit paid to people assessed as incapable of work. These payments are not related to a worker's previous earning record and exceed what is paid under Jobseeker's Allowance. Severe Disablement Allowance, an equivalent benefit for people without an adequate contribution record, was subsequently abolished for new claimants in 2001, who now receive either Incapacity Benefit or social assistance depending on the age at which the impairment occurred.

The number of people claiming incapacity-related social security benefits increased from 1.1 million to 2.3 million between 1985 and 1999, and the mean period of benefit receipt rose from three years in 1985 to almost six years by the mid-1990s (DSS, 1997; DSS, 1998). As a result, spending on incapacity-related benefits increased dramatically, from £2.7 billion on Invalidity Benefit in 1978/99 to £7.2 billion in 1998/99 on its replacement, Incapacity Benefit (1998/99 prices; DSS, 2000). By 1998/99 expenditure on Incapacity Benefit was over twice that on Jobseeker's Allowance.

The political response to this expansion was generally one of alarm. Concern about these expenditure trends, allied to a belief that in reality growing take-up of incapacity-related benefits was a form of concealed unemployment, provided a significant part of the impetus to introducing the New Deal for Disabled People. It was argued that Incapacity Benefit provides an alternative support for the long-term unemployed, that too many of the long-term unemployed were moving from Jobseeker's Allowance onto Incapacity Benefit to take advantage of the higher benefit, and that, for some, Incapacity Benefit provides top-up income for early retirement (Cm4103, 1998a).

Some questioned whether alarm was justified. They argued that these trends reflected maturation of benefits that were only introduced in the 1970s. It was also argued that the trends could reflect changing attitudes towards, and increased awareness of, disability as well as to 'real' changes in the level of disability (Walker with Howard, 2000). Indeed, the proportion of the population recorded as having an impairment or illness does appear to have increased (from 3.3 million in 1984 to 5.8 million in 1996/97; Cousins et al, 1998). The proportion of disabled people in paid employment has increased rather than fallen (Walker with Howard, 2000). Moreover, since the change from Invalidity Benefit to Incapacity Benefit there has been a 6% fall in the number of recipients from 2.42 million in May 1995 to 2.28 million in May 1999.

Nevertheless, the contention underlying the New Deal for Disabled People was that a large number of people on incapacity benefits could, with appropriate help and support, obtain, and remain in, paid work (Pullinger, 2000). There was no public statement by the government that incapacity-related benefit recipients wanting to work were fraudulently claiming benefit. Rather it was argued that historically governments had failed to address the work aspirations of this group, and that the benefit system did not assist people with impairments or ill health tackle their barriers to entering the labour market (Cm3805, 1998c). Survey evidence, often quoted by ministers, was that over a million disabled people in receipt of benefit would like paid work now or in the future. Certainly, during winter 1999/00 people who reported disabilities were about seven times more likely to be out of work and claiming benefits than non-disabled people, and the ILO unemployment rate for long-term disabled people (10.7%) was double that of non-disabled people (5.2%) (DRC, 2000). The benefit system was seen as over-concentrating on what people could not do, their incapacity, as opposed to what work they could do, their potential. The challenge facing policy makers was that these people were not only not expected to work, but in the past jeopardised their benefit entitlement as soon as they sought to do so. In addition, ministers argued that, as with young people, paid work is the best route out of poverty for disabled people (Cm4103, 1998a).

## Looking closer

This section explores how a generic welfare-to-work model, as represented by the paradigm outlined above, has been translated into separate programmes for disabled and young people. The New Deal for Disabled People's pilot is compared with the New Deal for Young People to explore how the welfare-to-work model has been moulded to take account of both the characteristics of the target groups and political imperatives. The discussion focuses on: the target client groups, programme objectives; models of delivery; programme content; the degree of compulsion; and links with employers (see Table 6.1).

### Target client group

The most obvious difference between the two New Deals is, of course, the target group. Each creates its own political and policy imperatives, which help to explain differences in their rationales and structures. The New Deal for Young People targets a group traditionally required to seek employment: unemployed people aged 18 to 24 who are eligible to receive Jobseeker's Allowance. The New Deal for Disabled People, in contrast, is aimed at a group that has not traditionally been expected to work, people incapacitated for at least 28 weeks.

Both groups are disadvantaged in the labour market, but for different reasons. Young people necessarily lack work experience. Fifty five per cent have mainly been unemployed since leaving school and another 17% have mainly held casual or short-term jobs. While better educated than unemployed people generally, 21% have no qualifications and 12% admit to problems with literacy. Seventy per cent are male and 14% from ethnic minorities (Walker et al, 1999).

The target group for New Deal for Disabled People inevitably comprises individuals who are on average much older and who ostensibly had much more work experience. In the pilot, 78% were over 40, 53% over 50 (Loumidis et al, 2001b). Sixty one per cent had spent most of their lives in steady jobs, and 53% were in paid work immediately prior to claiming benefit. On the other hand, by definition, they all had some impairment or health condition making them officially incapable of work. Seventy four per cent had been affected by their illness or impairment for more than five years, and 65% had been limited in their ability to do paid work for a similar period. Fifty six per cent had claimed incapacity benefits for five years or more, and only 5% had claimed benefit for less than twelve months. Because of their age, the number with qualifications fell short of the national average: 57% had neither academic nor vocational accreditation. Men constituted 61% of the target group. Six per cent were from ethnic minorities. Some 27% of the target group believed that they could do some paid work – but of these, 56% would require work that was not too stressful, 52% work that was not too physical, and 23% required someone to help them at work. Given the range of impairments experienced by this group, it is probably safe to say that their employment needs and the

**Table 6.1: Features of the New Deal for Young People and New Deal for Disabled People**

| Characteristic | New Deal for Young People | New Deal for Disabled People – Personal Adviser Service Model |
|---|---|---|
| Introduction | January 1998 in 12 pathfinder areas; April 1998 nationwide | October 1998 in six areas April 1999 a further six areas |
| Coverage | Nationwide | Personal Adviser Service – 12 pilot areas |
| Entry requirements/target populations | 18 to 24-year-olds claiming Jobseeker's Allowance continuously for six months; earlier entry possible for disadvantaged groups | Incapacitated for work for 28 weeks or more and claiming Incapacity Benefit, Severe Disablement Allowance or National Insurance (social insurance) credits for incapacity. In addition, the service can be provided to people in employment and at risk of losing their jobs due to ill-health |
| Participation | The Gateway stage is voluntary, but clients may be sanctioned if they continually refuse opportunities and fail, when formally directed by an official, to attend interviews. The Option stage is compulsory and non-compliance can lead to sanctions. Sanctions involve loss of entitlement to benefit for two or four weeks | Voluntary, the Benefits Agency sent eligible claimants a letter of invitation. There are no sanctions for not participating or withdrawing from the programme |
| Number in target group | 0.4 million | 2.3 million people nationally, of whom 227,300 reside in the pilot areas |
| Budget 1997-2002 | £2,620m | £200m (for both PAS and Innovative Scheme pilots) |

**Table 6.1: contd.../**

| Characteristic | New Deal for Young People | New Deal for Disabled People – Personal Adviser Service Model |
|---|---|---|
| Delivery mechanisms | Personal Advisers. Three models of delivery: (a) Employment Service led – public sector agency that administers the Gateway and develops partnerships with external agencies to provide the Options; (b) private sector led – for profit companies administer most of the gateway and build partnerships with other agencies to provide the Options; and (c) consortia led – private, voluntary and public sector organisations (including the Employment Service) build partnerships with agencies to provide the Options. The Gateway is administered by the Employment Service | Personal Advisers. In six areas the pilots are delivered by the Employment Service, in the other areas by the private/voluntary sector |
| Programme characteristics | Three stages: Gateway (up to four months of advice and support); Options (subsidised employment, self-employment, work experience (voluntary work or Environmental Task Force), or full-time training or education; Follow Through. All Options include an element of training leading to an accredited qualification. The employment options lasts for up to six months, with the expectation that the position will become permanent. The work experience options last for up to six months. The full-time education/training option is expected to last nine months with a maximum of 12 months | Referral to specialist services. Innovation Fund can be used to meet the cost of services/goods not funded through more conventional schemes<br><br>No set menu of options<br><br>Education/training not provided as a matter of course, only when assessed to be necessary |

**Table 6.1: contd.../**

| Characteristic | New Deal for Young People | New Deal for Disabled People – Personal Adviser Service Model |
|---|---|---|
| Benefit/Wages paid to participants | Benefit paid during Gateway and Follow Through stages. Options: (a) participants in subsidised employment should receive terms and conditions similar to other employees. Their wage must at least equal the subsidy paid by the Employment Service. Participants are also entitled to in-work benefits. (b) Participants in the Voluntary Sector/Environment Task Force can receive a wage or a training allowance plus £15.38 per week. (c) full-time education/training – a training allowance equivalent to the amount of Jobseeker's Allowance paid before the course commenced. (d) Self-employment – an allowance plus a grant of up to £400 paid in instalments | Benefit |
| Subsidy | (a) Subsidised employment – public or private sector organisations receive a job subsidy and a contribution of £750 towards the cost of training for programme participants. The subsidy for full-time work is £60 per week and for part-time work £40 per week. (b) Voluntary Sector/Environment Task Force – providers receive a payment for delivering the option, and if a wage is offered a contribution equivalent to the average rate of Jobseeker's Allowance for 18 to 24-year-olds. (c) full-time education/training – a payment is made for each participant linked to attendance and achievement of qualifications | No subsidies available to employers under the programme. Service providers/training organisations will receive a payment for the services they provide |

barriers preventing employment were rather more heterogeneous than those of young unemployed people.

## Objectives

Formally, both New Deals seek to improve the employability of their clients and prioritise job placements. The New Deal for Young People aims both to remove barriers to immediate employment so participants move as quickly as possible into employment, and to enhance longer-term employability through provision of advice/support and training (Employment Service, 1997). Similarly, the aim of the New Deal for Disabled People is to reduce barriers to work, albeit of a group traditionally excluded from labour market participation. Specifically, it is intended not only to assist those disabled people that wish to work to do so but also, through local partnerships, to promote the abilities of people with long-term health problems and to extend the range of services available to them. An additional objective, to help those already in work to retain their employment, reflects a belief that it is easier to help a person remain with an employer who values their contribution than to support them in finding another job after a period of worklessness.

It is evident, therefore, that neither New Deal is a model 'work first' programme whereby clients are encouraged to take the first available job. Nor are they pure 'human development' initiatives, with the emphasis on improving the skills and knowledge of clients through training and education so as to increase employability and career prospects. Perhaps a little ironically, there was a sense in which the voluntary New Deal for Disabled People pilot was closer to a work first model than New Deal for Young People in that it did not prioritise accredited training (Millar, 2000). Indeed, some lobbyists – for example, the Royal National Institute for the Blind – even believed that the emphasis on job search and improving clients' employability in the New Deal for Disabled People was to the detriment of finding jobs (HC, 1999). They wanted welfare-to-work programmes to run alongside demand-side policies that created 'real' jobs for disabled people. The official evaluation also pointed to the need to target the employment practices of employers (Loumidis et al, 2001a).

There is no definitive evidence as to why the Labour government chose to give greater weight to human capital development in the New Deal for Young People than in the New Deal for Disabled People. However, the British government has traditionally seen it in their remit to offer remedial training to unemployed young people, and the new emphasis on quality and accreditation accords with Labour's goal of raising the skill base of the economy. Labour may also have considered that providing young people with basic work skills at the start of their careers, rather than offer disabled people retraining later in life, could be the more cost-effective option. It is also the case that the government was unclear precisely what policy package would best help disabled people secure work, and that the pilots were an attempt to find out.

In both programmes, the balance struck between work first and human capital development strategies appears to have changed over time, with the need for clients to obtain paid work increasingly being stressed. Because the early implementation of the New Deal for Young People was seen as too passive, an Intensive Gateway was piloted in 12 areas in August 1999 and rolled out nationally in June 2000 (HM Treasury, 2000a). This provides more help from personal advisers with job search and assistance in developing soft skills, including punctuality and team working. In addition, the last month of the four-month Gateway stage was made more intensive in July 1999. Participants are now told that remaining on benefit without activity is not an option and they are prepared for the next stage of the programme (Options). The New Deal for Disabled People pilot was initially very client-driven, providing a range of services in which the pace was largely dictated by the client. However this, too, has increasingly refocused on assisting clients to move more rapidly into paid work (Arthur et al, 1999; Loumidis et al, 2001a).

## Models of delivery

While the models of delivery used in the two New Deals (Table 6.1) have commonalities, differences are evident and perhaps have increased over time.

First, they share a caseworker approach in which a personal adviser takes responsibility for up to 100 clients. However, there are indications that while the New Deal for Young People personal adviser operated generically and sought to provide a comprehensive service (albeit some clients were referred to specialist services), the New Deal for Disabled People personal adviser had begun to specialise by function or, indeed, by nature of disability (Arthur et al, 1999; Loumidis et al, 2001a). This might reflect the substantially more heterogeneous needs of disabled people – resulting in a client group that was too diverse for a single caseworker to provide a comprehensive individualised service. Instead, referral to other personal advisers and agencies with specialist skills and knowledge was required (Loumidis et al, 2001a). Secondly, both programmes included a mix of delivery by public sector agencies (typically the Employment Service), by for-profit and not-for-profit sector organisations, or a mixture of both acting in consortia. And in both New Deals, partnership arrangements had evolved and were increasingly characterized by core or strategic partners together with a group of operational partners or service providers (Hasluck, 2000; Loumidis et al, 2001a).

For-profit and not-for-profit organisations were incorporated in the programmes with a view to introducing innovation in service delivery. Personal advisers were encouraged to exercise discretion in determining the help and assistance provided. On the one hand, clients can see this as positive when it addresses their expressed needs and improves their employability (Bryson et al, 2000). On the other hand, any discretionary system can lead to a spatial inequity in the delivery of services as clients with the same needs may be treated differently, with a risk that the quality of service provided becomes a lottery with prizes dependent upon where the client lives. The challenge, of course, is to provide a consistently high quality service while allowing staff the freedom to be innovative.

In practice, under the New Deal for Disabled People pilot the public, private, and voluntary sector agencies operated in very similar ways (Loumidis et al, 2001a). This was mainly because the client group, and the environment within which they performed, were essentially the same. Private and voluntary sector organisations always had to interface with public employment and benefit systems, and their bureaucracies constrained how and what could be achieved. Under the New Deal for Young People, however, a variety of local partnership arrangements have emerged in response to local labour market conditions, previous joint working relationships, and local networks (Hasluck, 2000). The performance of local offices – as measured by nine 'core performance measures' that include numbers moving into unsubsidised jobs, unit costs and satisfaction ratings – appears to reflect the type of delivery model adopted, the size of the caseload, and the nature of the local labour market. Early evidence suggested that: the performance of private sector-led schemes was relatively poor (Hasluck, 2000; HC, 2000); performance was generally higher in offices with small caseloads and those covering rural areas and small towns and lower in offices with a large number of clients or located in large urban areas (Hasluck, 2000) and caseload and type of labour market were likely to be associated with the composition of the client group and the resources available in each area. However, subsequent analysis of the performance of local units by the National Audit Office (NAO, 2002) found no significant relationships between a range of variables and unit performance – in particular no significant difference in the performance of private sector providers compared with the public sector.

Finally, both programmes rely on intermediaries or service providers to address specific barriers to work, such as drug or alcohol problems, poor literacy or numeracy skills or résumé preparation. And in both cases there has been criticism of the standard of service of some providers. In the case of New Deal for Young People the focus of concern has been on the type and quality of training. In the case of New Deal for Disabled People, the focus has been on the relative lack of suitable provision.

### Programme content

The programmes differ more in substantive content than in delivery model. The New Deal for Young People has a formal and linear structure. Clients who fail to find work progress through the three stages and, although some may re-enter the programme, the intention is that this should not need to happen. Following the initial Gateway stage, clients are presented with a menu of set Options, which are generally perceived by staff as a hierarchy, with jobs and training or education being preferable to placements in the voluntary sector or on the environment task force. The latter two in particular can be used as a 'threat' when confronted by 'uncooperative' clients (Stafford et al, 2000). Formally, clients leave Jobseeker's Allowance at the Options stage, and participants returning to unemployment within 13 weeks of the Options stage enter the Follow Through stage, which is similar to the Gateway.

The New Deal for Disabled People is potentially more tailored to the needs of individual clients. In the pilot, there were no set time limits after which clients had to progress from one activity to the next and, at least theoretically, no limit on the time clients could spend in the programme. These features of the pilot reflected policy makers' uncertainty about what works for disabled people, the heterogeneity of the client group's needs, and an unwillingness to be seen to require that a vulnerable group follow a set menu of Options. In practice, though, a growing emphasis on achieving employment outcomes caused personal advisers to be more selective in the cases admitted to the programme and more prepared to 'exit' clients who appeared unlikely to find work within the foreseeable future (Loumidis et al, 2001a).[5] This more flexible approach had a drawback, however, at least as operated in the pilot. It made some clients uncertain about the direction of their journey back to work and anxious about their progress (Arthur et al, 1999). An additional problem was failure to generate a significant increase in the type and volume of services available, which might have reflected a conflict between the short-term nature of the pilot and service providers' need for the security of long-term funding before investing in new services.

The voluntary nature of the New Deal for Disabled People also added recruitment of clients as a programme element. Whereas young unemployed people were in regular fortnightly contact with the Employment Service and moved automatically onto New Deal, recipients of incapacity-related benefits, which were (then) administered by a separate government agency (the Benefits Agency), had to be contacted and invited to join the programme.[6] The main approach adopted for this purpose was a single letter of invitation, with partnerships able to vary its content and presentation. Uptake was low, at 3%. A similar number of people with disabilities were either referred by other organisations or contacted the pilot service themselves. The challenge of reaching disabled people at risk of losing their employment was even greater, since potential clients are typically unknown to government agencies. For this reason, only limited priority was given to the goal of supporting job retention among persons with disabilities who were currently employed.

The low uptake appears to contradict survey (DRC, 2000) and other research evidence (Walker with Howard, 2000) that many people with impairments or illnesses at least claim to want paid work. And, indeed, the evaluation suggests that the marketing and targeting of the pilot could have been better. Qualitative evidence from staff and clients (Arthur et al, 1999; Loumidis et al, 2001a) attributes the low take-up to:

- lack of promotional material to follow up the letter of invitation;
- failure to promote the New Deal among relevant professionals;
- rejection by some potential clients of the 'disabled people' label associated with the programme and a consequent reluctance to take part;

- insufficient use of mass media to publicize the programme; and
- the belief held by many non-participants that they would never work again.

## Degree of compulsion

As already noted, the two New Deals differ significantly in their degree of compulsion. Participants in the New Deal for Young People must be available for work and demonstrate that they are actively seeking it. As recipients of Jobseeker's Allowance, they have to sign and follow an agreement that is repeatedly updated, specifying the activities they need to undertake in order to find work. Failure to follow the agreement provides prima facie evidence that the young person is not actively seeking work and grounds for the temporary removal of benefit. Likewise, if they reach the Options stage, participants must participate in an agreed Option or risk a benefit sanction of two or 26 weeks depending upon previous behaviour. Around one in eight young people at the Options stage are sanctioned (TEN, 2001), with the proportion sanctioned varying by type of Option. During the last quarter of 2000, for example, the proportion sanctioned ranged from 28% for those on the Environment Task Force to 6% for those in subsidised employment (TEN, 2001). (This further illustrates the hierarchy of Options.)

Case studies of unemployed young people (Saunders, 2001, quoted in Britton, 2002) shows that those sanctioned either did not wish to be on the New Deal, or were willing to participate provided the Option met their perceived needs, or were actively participating but were sanctioned through poor understanding or miscommunication. According to a survey of participants, those sanctioned were more likely to be male, have problems with basic skills, be younger entrants to the New Deal, have previous Jobseeker's Allowance claims, be in areas where operation of the Gateway was more intense (for instance, a larger number of interviews per client), have the service delivered by the private sector, live in northern England and attend the Environment Task Force Option (Bonjour et al, 2001).

The New Deal for Disabled People, in marked contrast, was entirely voluntary. Those meeting the entry conditions did not have to participate, and no penalties were imposed if they failed to undertake an agreed action or withdrew from the programme.

That compulsion was built into one but not the other reflects different political realities. Young people, especially single young people, are expected to work if they are not studying and, as already noted, politicians are fearful of the personal and social consequences of them not doing so. By giving young people 'no fifth option' – that is, of remaining on benefit and avoiding work experience and training – the government sought to ensure that those who would benefit from the scheme but who would not otherwise participate receive some help and assistance. Moreover, the judgement has been that public opinion will support the use of sanctions for young people, provided that the interests of any dependent children they may have are protected.

The government also recognised that past youth schemes had a poor reputation because the training and work experience provided could be of a very poor quality. It was, therefore, determined that young people on the programme would receive high quality service provision. The compulsory nature of the New Deal for Young People is, therefore, legitimised by the provision of 'decent' options (such as training, work experience, and subsidised employment) – thus ensuring that clients are not being required to participate in a process that might be ineffectual, stigmatising, or demeaning.[7]

More aggressive efforts to move disabled people into the labour market, in marked contrast, appear to have little public support. According to focus groups held with social insurance contributors there are two main reasons for this (see Stafford, 1998). First, the recipients have all been assessed as incapable of work on medical criteria. It would be quite a paradox if people entitled to benefit on the basis of their incapacity were required to participate in a workfare-like programme. Second, Incapacity Benefit is a social insurance benefit with entitlement based on National Insurance contributions. Thus, recipients, as contributors, are seen as having a 'right' to benefit. There is also widespread public sympathy for people with disabilities and a vocal lobby, which campaigned – though with limited success – to protect benefit levels when moves to tighten eligibility criteria were proposed by previous Conservative governments and also by Labour in 1997. Finally, people with disabilities believe that employers discriminate against them despite anti-discrimination legislation (Ritchie and Snape, 1993; Loumidis et al, 2001a). If discrimination is indeed substantial, such business attitudes and practices constitute yet another barrier to whatever good might come from the assertion of greater obligation for work effort among the disabled.

Even so, the Labour government introduced in 2002 a limited element of compulsion, by requiring all benefit recipients of working age, including Incapacity Benefit recipients, to attend a work-focused interview at the point of their initial claim and at other key events, such as when their incapacity is reassessed. These interviews address career ambitions and progression, the individual's barriers to returning to work, and the help and support that can be provided to ease a return to work. Only attendance at the interview is compulsory, however. There is no obligation on claimants of incapacity-related benefits to participate in any programme or even be available for, let alone actively seek, work.

## Links with employers

Employers are key customers for both the New Deal for Young People and the New Deal for Disabled People. Not only do they provide job vacancies and placements, but their continued involvement also helps to legitimate the programmes. When the New Deal for Young People was first implemented, government expended considerable effort in marketing and signing up employers to demonstrate that placements would be available during the Options stage.

Employers have generally supported the New Deal for Young People (Hasluck, 2000), although their initial awareness and enthusiasm for the programme has waned over time and some have even become critical of it. Large employers do not always want to replace their existing training programmes with those that meet the vocational qualification requirements of the New Deal for Young People, while small voluntary groups can find the programme difficult to administer. A common criticism of this New Deal is that young people referred to employers were not always 'job ready'. The government has responded by piloting in inner city areas the use of private and voluntary sector intermediaries to improve the match between employers' needs and participants' basic skill levels.

Financial support is available to employers and not-for-profit organisations that offer placements to young people under the terms of New Deal for Young People but not to disabled people (see Table 6.1). It is not clear how important these subsidies are to employers, but the fact that no equivalent subsidies were available for employers in the New Deal for Disabled People was cited by employers as an impediment to participation (Arthur et al, 1999).[8]

Another difference between the two programmes is the degree of outreach to employers. A major national advertising campaign aimed at employers accompanied the introduction of New Deal for Young People. Such promotion could not happen with the New Deal for Disabled People pilots because they were locally based, and associated publicity was often low key. An important objective of the local pilots was to educate employers about issues around the employment of disabled people. Some research (Ritchie and Snape, 1993; Arthur et al, 1999) has indicated that employers are often reluctant to employ disabled people for reasons that are empirically unjustified, and that this acts as a major barrier to employment. But other research (Meager et al, 1999) reveals that only 16% of disabled people of working age believe they experience discrimination in a work context because of their impairment or illness. Under the New Deal for Disabled People, personal advisers were assigned the multiple tasks of employer education, advice, job-placement, and in-work support; this combination sometimes proved difficult to accomplish effectively (Arthur et al, 1999). While some employers were actively involved in the pilot, some remained unaware of it, and some confused it with the other New Deals.

## Achievements

Both New Deals have been subject to extensive research and evaluation, mainly funded by government, the New Deal for Young People receiving particularly close attention. The size and uptake of the programmes is a key issue. For both New Deals, those that do not participate or drop out may suffer financially and be socially excluded – making broader governmental objectives, such as making the economy more competitive, more difficult to achieve. In addition, as welfare-to-work policies, estimates are required of their specific effects on movements into employment over and above those that would have occurred in their absence – that is, an estimate of their net impact (or additionality). Ideally, there would be evidence of the additionality of individual programme elements, notably of the Options in New Deal for Young People, whether some client sub-groups unduly benefit or are disadvantaged, and the overall cost-effectiveness of the two programmes. Of particular interest are movements into sustainable employment. The wider macro-economic impacts of the programmes, especially on wages and productivity, also merit attention. Moreover, since compulsion is used in the New Deal for Young People, the effectiveness of sanctioning in leading to behavioural changes and to sustained employment outcomes should also be assessed. Finally, the evaluations also need to consider implementation and delivery issues, in order to explore the mechanisms that lead to programme outcomes.

Evidence on some of these issues is not yet available. But there is some administrative data and non-experimental evaluation information on two issues: programme size (the volume of clients processed) for both programmes and the outcomes or effects for clients, at least for the New Deal for Young People. The flows of clients into the two programmes differ, reflecting differences in client group dynamics and programme structure. The principal outcome established for both programmes was a movement off benefit into paid work. However, this fails to recognise other socially valued contributions, such as voluntary work and caring for sick/disabled relatives. For the New Deal for Disabled People, in particular, non-paid work or intermediate outcomes should be accepted as valid outcomes for people who are distant from the labour market.

This section reviews the information that is available and outlines how, in light of the evidence available and other considerations, policy is being taken forward.

## Programme size

### The New Deal for Young People

This programme was much more generously resourced than the New Deal for Disabled People although the eligible population was smaller. It had a budget of £2,620m, compared with £200m for the New Deal for Disabled People pilot.

The New Deal for Young People caseload rose rapidly during the early months of the programme, as the large number of claimants who had already been unemployed for six months or more joined the programme. Numbers peaked at 149,500 in July 1999 and thereafter fell slowly to 98,400 in November 2000 (Figure 6.1) (DfEE, 2001). The caseload decline resulted from a significant fall in entrants (from a high of 83,000 in April-June 1998 to 11,100 in November

2000; DfEE, 2001 and ONS, 2000) as the number of clients available for recruitment from the stock of claimants declined, and an increasing number of young people left benefit altogether.

The numbers in the New Deal for Young People would have fallen even more, however, had some participants not remained in the Gateway for longer than the planned four months. The reasons for this, and why exit rates for each cohort of entrants have changed over time, are unclear (see Hasluck, 2000). It might be that an increasing emphasis on securing unsubsidised job placements causes clients to remain longer in the Gateway in order to increase their chances of employment. It is also possible that, as youth unemployment falls, the proportion of 'hard to place' participants who require longer on the Gateway increases. It might also be that resources available locally for the New Deal for Young People have been reduced as other initiatives and New Deals have come on stream.

What is unknown from the research and official data is the number of 18- to 24-year-olds who drop out of the system and live outside of the New Deal without jobs and in poverty. Attempts are made to encourage the homeless and others to engage. However, the scale of non-participation and how dropouts manage to survive financially is unknown.

### The New Deal for Disabled People

As noted, the level of take-up achieved by the New Deal for Disabled People pilot was low, even taking account of people who approached the programme without invitation. All told, the take-up for the twelve pilots up to 24 November 2000 was just 18,166 people – about 7% of the known population excluding people at risk of losing their jobs because of the onset of disability or ill health (Loumidis et al, 2001a).

**Figure 6.1: Numbers on New Deal for Young People, Great Britain**

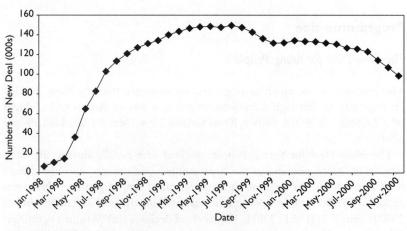

*Source:* DfEE (2001)

## Programme outcomes

### *The New Deal for Young People*

By November 2000 the Labour government felt able to declare that they had achieved their pre-election pledge of getting 250,000 young people back to work (Press release, 2000). While the research estimates reveal a more complicated story, they do point to quite considerable success.

The key outcome for government is a move into sustained unsubsidised employment. The government counts employment to be sustained if former participants do not return to Jobseeker's Allowance or another Option within 13 weeks. Sustained and non-sustained employment may be subsidized or unsubsidised. By the end of November 2000 the cumulative figure for the number of young people moving from the New Deal to employment was 269,210. Of these three quarters (206,530) had moved into sustained employment, most of them (87% or 180,230) holding unsubsidised jobs (DfEE, 2001). Of those entering employment of any kind, about a tenth (11% or 30,700) had subsidised jobs.

Figure 6.2 shows how the numbers moving into sustained and unsustained employment have fluctuated over the life of the New Deal for Young People. The proportion entering sustained employment has remained relatively high, ranging between 71 and 83%. The number of placements in subsidised and unsubsidised jobs has also remained relatively high. This implies that placement rates have increased, since the numbers on the programme have declined since July 1999 (see Figure 6.1). In fact, these figures probably under-estimate the numbers finding paid work, as 57% of those leaving the programme (before the Options stage) for unspecified destinations are known to have found paid unsubsidised jobs (Hales and Collins, 1999).

These official figures do not provide a measure of the net impact of the programme, however, because they do not take account of the number of young people that would have found employment had there been no New Deal for Young People. Evaluations that have attempted such estimates use one of two analytic approaches. The first consists of econometric techniques that compare actual numbers against those expected, by: (a) investigating the relationship between unemployment outflows (and inflows) and overall economic activity before New Deal for Young People was introduced; and (b) then forecasting the expected outflows (and inflows) to create 'counterfactual scenarios' for different age groups and/or geographical areas.[9] The second approach to get at the net impact of programmes is the difference-in-difference approach, which involves comparing differences in outflows between 18- to 24-year-olds and older age groups within the same areas and/or across different areas before and after the New Deal was introduced. The geographical comparisons are possible because the New Deal for Young People was trialed between January and March 1998 in Pathfinder areas, which had matched comparison areas. The difference-in-difference methodology has been used

**Figure 6.2: Numbers moving into employment from the New Deal for Young People**

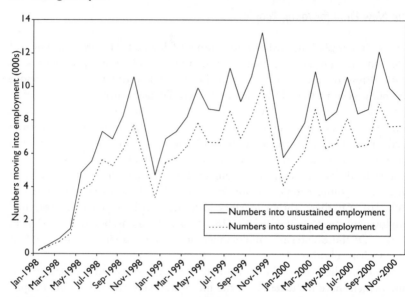

*Source:* DfEE (2000)

with actual data and simulated data for the 'after period'. Both approaches use administrative data and both run the risk that the estimates of additionality are biased because the comparison does not yield a 'perfect counterfactual'.[10]

There is a small number of econometric analyses that attempt to assess the impact of the New Deal by comparing various trends to a forecast of what would have occurred in the absence of the programme. Mainly undertaken by the National Institute of Economic and Social Research, this work suggests that:

- Long-term (that is, over six months) youth unemployment in Great Britain had been reduced by approximately 30,000 (or 40%) over the period April 1989 to April 1999 (including deadweight) (Anderton et al, 1999). Later estimates covering the first two years of the programme to March 2000 imply a reduction in long-term youth unemployment by 45,000 and an increase in short-term unemployment by 10,000 (Riley and Young, 2000, 2001a and 2001b). As the outflows are to all destinations – including the Options, inactivity, and moves back to short-term unemployment – it does not follow that youth employment increased by 35,000. Indeed, youth (subsidised and unsubsidised) employment is estimated to have increased by approximately 15,000. The National Audit Office (NAO, 2002) in its investigation of the programme highlighted the sensitivity of the latter estimates to the assumptions made. It proposed 'plausible ranges' for these estimates, and claimed the New Deal had reduced youth unemployment by between 25,000 and 45,000 and had increased youth employment by between 8,000 and 20,000.

- The deadweight – those who would have left unemployment in the absence of the New Deal – was 50% of the 500,000 expected to leave unemployment over the first four years. However, this may be an underestimate of deadweight as the calculation excluded those in unsustained jobs. Taking this into account gives a revised estimate of approximately 60% (Anderton et al, 1999).

A difference-in-difference analysis using longitudinal data reveals that the New Deal for Young People significantly increased outflows to employment by 17,250, mainly because of the subsidy paid to employers (van Reenen, 2001).

In addition, there is a consensus in the literature that employment placements resulting from the New Deal for Young People did not displace non-participants from jobs (that is, the substitution effects were zero) (Anderton et al, 1999; van Reenen, 2001; Riley and Young, 2001b).

A 1999 survey of young people six months after they had entered the programme suggests that non-white participants have been less successful than white clients in obtaining jobs (their employment rates were 34% and 39%, respectively) (Bryson et al, 2000). In particular, African Caribbeans were the least successful in securing paid work – the employment rate for those leaving the New Deal for Young People was only 18%. Racism, lack of skills and confidence, and low aspirations have been conjectured as possible causes of the lack of success among minority ethnic groups (HC, 2000). But there is relatively little published evidence on the effects of the New Deal for Young People on ethnic minorities.

More generally, concern has been expressed by commentators about the relatively high proportion of young people (23% up to November 2000; DfEE, 2001) who fail to find sustainable employment through the New Deal for Young People (HC, 2000). Policies may be needed to prevent clients alternating between New Deal programmes and brief periods of paid work.

Findings on the effects of sanctions are mixed. Research on the 26-week sanction indicates that clients increased their level of job search activity as a result (quoted in Britton, 2002). Indeed, some entered employment, but mainly casual and short-term jobs. Moreover, a national survey of participants showed that, controlling for other factors that can influence job entry, those sanctioned were as likely as other clients to enter work (Bonjour et al, 2001). However, sanctioned clients were more likely to still be on New Deal when re-interviewed for the survey; and the sanctioning had not encouraged them to leave for non-employment outcomes.

## The New Deal for Disabled People

The results of the New Deal for Disabled People pilot are much less clear-cut. There is some evidence about flows into and through the programme, but nothing that could be called impact evidence. The evaluation included a comparison between the outcomes for the clients in the 12 pilot areas and a nationally representative sample of disabled people living in 31 other areas who would have been eligible to participate had the Personal Adviser Service been available. However, the lower than expected take-up of the programme, together with small sample sizes, limit the use of the national survey as a counterfactual to assess the impact of the New Deal for Disabled People Personal Adviser Service.

Over the first 18 months or so of the pilot, the evaluation revealed little evidence that the programme had significantly increased the number of disabled people finding employment. Administrative data shows that 4,800 clients moved into work between September 1998 and November 2000 (Loumidis et al, 2001a). However, it may well take considerably longer than 18 months to equip a disabled person with sufficient work experience to secure employment.

During a two-year observation period, 24% of participants undertook some paid employment after meeting with a personal adviser and 22% of these claimed they would not have started work without the assistance they received. In addition, 60% of participants had started or increased their job search activity, 40% had started or applied for an education/training course and 16% had sought help from someone else after meeting with a personal adviser (Loumidis et al, 2001a).

Perhaps not surprisingly, participants were significantly more likely than non-participants to leave benefit and were disproportionately recent claimants and people with low impairment scores. The majority of clients reported satisfaction with the Personal Adviser Service. For example, 84% said their personal adviser had spent sufficient time with them, and listened to and understood their concerns and needs. However, a third (33%) also said they had not provided the advice and support desired. Of those who had left the programme, a quarter (25%) had done so because they were so dissatisfied with the service (Loumidis et al, 2001a).

### Policies update

So far, therefore, the application of the welfare-to-work model appears to have been more successful among young unemployed claimants than among disabled people. While the additionality is not great – although probably comparable to the generality of US welfare-to-work programmes for lone parents (Ashworth et al, 2001) – the New Deal for Young People is allegedly self-funding (Anderton et al, 1999) and benefits exceed costs (Reenen, 2001). Accordingly, the core of the programme, with its case working and the Options, remains in place. Only incremental changes are being made, to more effectively address the needs of those most difficult to place in employment. Indeed, since April 2001 the government has sought to bring the New Deal for people aged over 25 years more into line with the New Deal for Young People.

Recognising that any positive employment benefits might take longer to materialize for disabled people than for young people, the government extended the New Deal for Disabled People nationally, beginning in July 2001, in order to undertake further experimentation and innovation in service provision (HM Treasury, 2000b). The nationally extended New Deal for Disabled People, like its predecessor, is a voluntary programme. But unlike in the pilot programme, participants have a choice of provider. For-profit and not-for-profit organisations have bid to provide a job brokerage service for people with disabilities in local authority areas that they specify. Three-year contracts were awarded to 64 organisations, or Job Brokers. Bidders were asked to be innovative, and there is no requirement to follow the personal adviser model, or even case working. While individual Job Brokers may incorporate aspects of the Personal Adviser Service in their tenders, there is no close fit between the pilot and the new policy. This new service is complemented by the Employment Service, now merged with the Benefits Agency to form Jobcentre Plus, offering a single Gateway service to new incapacity-related benefit claimants that includes a mandatory work-focus interview that might lead to a referral to local Job Brokers or other services.[11]

## Conclusion

The UK, in contrast to the US, has gone beyond targeting welfare-to-work on lone parents and embraced other client groups. This chapter has explored how a generic, caseworker model of welfare-to-work has been applied in Britain to two of those other groups: young people and disabled people. While both programmes are members of the New Deal family they differ, as might be expected, in rationale, objectives, detail, size, and outcomes. These differences reflect the differences in the characteristics and needs of the client groups served and in their benefit status. The New Deal for Disabled People has to accommodate a more diverse client group, which it does by having a more flexible structure than the New Deal for Young People. Participants in the New Deal for Young People are mainly recipients of a means-tested cash benefit, while those of the New Deal for Disabled People are primarily recipients of a contributory cash benefit. This helps account for another important difference, the absence of mandatory options in the New Deal for Disabled People. Both New Deals are embedded in a welfare-to-work policy framework, but their degree of compatibility with it varies. In the case of New Deal for Disabled People, there is a tension between the formal, legal requirements of the benefit system – which demands that those entitled to benefit are medically assessed as incapable of work – and labour market policies that aim to move the same individuals into employment and by implication proclaim their capacity for work.

The irrationality of this is compounded by a system that classifies people rigidly into two mutually exclusive categories: either available for work or incapacitated. Neither the New Deal for Disabled People nor the benefit system for this group allows for a gradual return to work, whereby people can build up the hours worked to a level their impairments or health conditions enable them to sustain. The US uses a similar incapable/capable dichotomy. The fundamental problem is that allowing a gradual return to work would necessitate a relaxation of the distinction made between out-of-work benefits and in-work benefits and tax credits. The challenge for both systems is to find ways to reform the incapacity benefit regimes in ways that will address the needs of those with potential to move to greater capability and, with this change, to suitable employment.

In respect of compulsion, New Labour was able to overcome opposition to introducing it in the New Deal for Young People. The political, moral, and policy arguments for compulsion are less compelling for disabled people. Nevertheless, there is an element of creeping compulsion in the government's New Deal approach to disabled people, as there is to lone parents – and to other groups like carers. All are now required to attend a work-focused interview when making a benefit claim or at certain other key events (such as following receipt of medical test results for a claim for Incapacity Benefit). Whether giving information, training, and other support to disabled people (or to lone parents) is an alternative to workfare is unclear, but for now minimal compulsion will be a feature of the New Deals for those groups.

The government is also seeking to change people's attitudes towards benefit receipt. There is a new emphasis on clients' and the state's rights and responsibilities, with the New Deals playing a leading role in changing attitudes towards benefit receipt. The high profile given to the compulsory element of New Deal for Young People might mean that groups covered by voluntary programmes feel obliged to work. However, the evidence for this is not strong from the New Deal for Disabled People pilot, in which only 5% of participants thought the programme was compulsory and personal advisers actually explained to newly recruited participants that it was voluntary (Loumidis et al, 2001a). Nor is there any evaluation evidence that further compulsion is, in fact, required in the national New Deal for Disabled People.

The longer term effects of the New Deals are unknown. In the meantime, the government would seem to have learned much about the implementation and operation of welfare-to-work schemes, with the value of case and partnership working now firmly established. Even as, managerially, the programmes and test initiatives continue to be refined, both New Deals are now part of the landscape of welfare-to-work in the UK, and have already been influential in changing how benefit and employment services are delivered to workless people.

## Acknowledgements

The author was a member of the research team evaluating the New Deal for Disabled People Personal Adviser Service pilot. However, the views expressed in this chapter are those of the author and do not necessarily reflect those of other team members or the project's sponsors: the Department of Social Security and the Department for Education and Employment. An earlier version of this chapter was presented at the meeting of the Association of Public Policy Analysis and Management, 2-4 November 2000, Seattle, USA and the support of the Rockefeller Foundation is gratefully acknowledged. Thanks are also due to Maire Stafford and the editors for their helpful comments on the chapter. Angela Waite at CRSP helped to prepare the manuscript and Abigail Davis collected the data for Figure 6.1.

## Notes

[1] The rules on theraputic work have been ammended and the scheme is now known as permitted work.

[2] Further details about the Innovative Schemes pilots are given in Blackburn et al, 1999 and Hills et al, 2001.

[3] Although by the time it was released the New Deals for young people and lone parents had already been implemented and other New Deals had been announced, the consultation paper presents the policy framework that encompasses the portfolio of programmes.

[4] The International Labor Organisation definition of unemployment is a broader measure than a count of those registered as unemployed. It covers people who are: out of work, want a job, have actively sought work in the previous four weeks and are available to start work within the next fortnight; or out of work and have accepted a job they will start within the next fortnight (Office of National Statistics, 2000).

[5] Personal advisers in the New Deal for Disabled People pilot could also access an Intervention Fund to purchase other services or goods, such as travel costs to job interviews and expenses incurred in setting up a business (Arthur et al, 2000) – a degree of financial flexibility in meeting clients' needs that was not initially available in the New Deal for Young People.

[6] In April 2002 the Employment Service and those parts of the Benefits Agency dealing with people of working age merged to form a new government agency, Jobcentre Plus.

[7] Even so, politicians were initially wary of imposing sanctions and keen to avoid any suggestion that New Deal for Young People or Project Work, the very similar scheme piloted by the Conservative government, was 'workfare'. There is a strong attachment to the idea that benefits should be available as a social right, especially with regard to social insurance benefits, which may have been another reason why compulsion was initially restricted to young people. They are less likely than older people to receive Jobseeker's Allowance on the basis of their contribution record rather than because of demonstrable low income.

[8] Although personal advisers did have the option of using national funding schemes, such as Access to Work, to assist employers in employing people with disabilities.

[9] A counterfactual is an estimate of the situation that would have obtained had a new programme not been introduced.

[10] Differential time effects may also bias findings, and changes in outcome variables, which are caused by (unobserved) external factors, may be erroneously attributed to the intervention. The assessments also rely on data for the early years of the programme before programme delivery had had an opportunity to stabilize. There are no estimates of the long-term net impacts of the programme over the economic cycle, or of effects on job retention or job quality. Analyses of the wider impact of New Deal for Young People on the economy suggest that taking into account, for instance, wage effects is problematic, and that, in any event, the models produce similar results to those outlined in the text (Riley and Young, 2001b).

[11] The New Deal for Disabled People national extension also builds upon the Innovative Schemes pilot, where frontline staff worked directly with employers and sought to match clients to the requirements of employers. Underpinning their work was the notion of a 'pathway' along which clients progressed to employment. However, the extent to which Job Brokers will adopt the methods and techniques of the Innovative Schemes is, as yet, unknown. When going to press, the government was consulting on a further round of reform, considering, among other changes, increasing the number of mandatory interviews to five.

## References

Anderton, B., Riley, R. and Young, G. (1999) *The New Deal for Young People: First year analysis of the implications for the macroeconomy*, Research and Development Report ESR33, Sheffield: Employment Service.

Arthur, S., Corden, A., Green, A., Lewis, J., Loumidis, J., Sainsbury, R., Stafford, B., Thornton, P. and Walker, R. (1999) *New Deal for Disabled People: Early implementation*, DSS Research Report 106, Leeds: Corporate Document Services.

Ashworth, K., Cebulla, A., Davis, A., Greenberg, D. and Walker, R. (2001) 'Welfare-to-Work: establishing a basis in evidence', Paper submitted for presentation at the Annual Meeting of the Association of Public Policy Analysis and Management, Washington DC, November.

Berthoud, R. (1998) *Disability benefits: A review of the issues and options for reform*, York: York Publishing Services for the Joseph Rowntree Foundation.

Blackburn, V., Child, C. and Hills, D. (1999) *New Deal for Disabled People: Early findings from the innovation schemes*, DSS in-house Report no 61, London: DSS.

Blair, T. (1997) 'The will to win', Speech on the Aylesbury Estate, Southwark, 2 June.

Blunkett, D. (2000) 'On your side' the new welfare state as the engine of prosperity, London: DfEE.

Bonjour, D., Dorsett, R., Knight, G., Lissenburgh, S., Mukherjee, A., Payne, J., Range, M., Urwin, P. and White, M. (2001) *New Deal for Young People: National Survey of Participants: Stage 2*, Sheffield: Employment Service Research and Development Report ESR67.

Britton, L. (2002) 'Sanctions and the hard to help', *Working Brief*, no 130, London: Unemployment Unit and Youthaid.

Bryson, A., Knight, G. and White, M. (2000) *New Deal for Young People: National survey of participants: Stage 1*, Sheffield: Employment Service, Research and Development Report ESR44.

Burchardt, T. (1999) 'The evolution of disability benefits in the UK: re-weighting the basket', CASE paper 26, London: London School of Economics and Political Science.

Cm 4103 (1998a) *A new contract for welfare: Support for disabled people*, London: The Stationery Office.

Cm 4102 (1998b) *A new contract for welfare: The gateway to work*, London: The Stationery Office.

Cm 3805 (1998c) *New ambitions for our country: A new contract for welfare*, London: The Stationery Office.

Cm 5690 (2000) *Pathways to work: Helping people into employment*, London: The Stationery Office.

Cousins, C., Jenkins, J. and Laux, R. (1998 June) 'Disability data from the LFS: comparing 1997-8 with the past', *Labour Market Trends*, vol 106, no 6, pp 321-35.

Dearing, R. (1997) *Higher education in the learning society: Report of the National Committee*, National Committee of Enquiry into Higher Education, London: The Stationery Office.

DfEE (Department for Education and Employment) (1999) *Statistical first release: Participation in education and training by 16-17 year olds in England*: 1988 to 1998, London: DfEE.

DfEE (2001) *Statistical first release: New Deal for Young People and long-term unemployed people ages 25+*, Statistics to November 2000, London: DfEE.

DSS (Department of Social Security) (1997) *Welfare reform focus file 04: Benefits for sick and disabled people*, London: DSS.

DSS (1998) *Cross benefit analysis: Quarterly bulletin on the population of working age on key benefits*, London: Government Statistical Series.

DSS (2000) *The changing welfare state: Social security spending*, London: DSS.

Disability Rights Commission (2000) *DRC disability briefing*, May (www.drc-Great Britain.org), retrieved 20 August.

Employment Service (1997, November) *Operational vision*, Sheffield: Employment Service.

Gardiner, K. (1997) *Bridges from benefit to work*, York: York Publishing Services for the Joseph Rowntree Foundation.

Hales, J. and Collins, D. (1999) *New Deal for Young People: Leavers with unknown destinations*, Sheffield: Employment Service, Research and Development Report ESR21.

Hasluck, C. (1999) *Employers, young people and the unemployed: A review of the research*, Sheffield: Employment Service, Research and Development Report ESR12.

Hasluck, C. (2000) *The New Deal for Young People: Two years on*, Sheffield: Employment Service, Research and Development Report ESR41.

HC (House of Commons Social Security Select Committee) (1999) *Opportunities for disabled people, Volume 1: Report and proceedings, ninth report of the Select Committee on Education and Employment*, HC111-I, London: The Stationery Office.

HC (2000) *New Deal for Young People: Two years on, eighth report of the Select Committee on Education and Employment*, HC 510, London: The Stationery Office.

Hills, D., Child, C., Blackburn, V. and Youll, P. (2001) *Evaluation of the New Deal for Young People Innovative Schemes Pilot*, DSS Research Report No 143, Leeds: Corporate Document Services.

HM Treasury (1997) *Employment opportunity in a changing labour market: The modernization of Britain's tax and benefit system*, no 1, London: HM Treasury.

HM Treasury (2000a) *Budget 2000 prudent for a purpose: Working for a stronger and fairer Britain*, HC 346, London: The Stationery Office.

HM Treasury (2000b) *Spending review 2000 prudent for a purpose: Building opportunity and security for all*, London: The Stationery Office.

Loumidis, J., Stafford, B., Youngs, R., Green, A., Arthur, S., Legard, R., Lessof, C., Lewis, J., Walker, R., Corden, A., Sainsbury, R. and Thornton, P. (2001a) *New Deal for Disabled People: Evaluation of the Personal Adviser Service*, DWP Research Report, No 144, Leeds: Corporate Document Services.

Loumidis, J., Youngs, R. and Lessof, C. (2001b) *New Deal for Disabled People: National survey*, DWP Research Report No 160, Leeds: Corporate Document Services.

Maguire, S. (2000) 'Employers' diminishing demand for young people – myth or reality', Loughborough University: Centre for Research in Social Policy, Unpublished.

Meager, N., Bates, P., Dench, S., Honey, S. and Williams, M. (1999) *Employment of disabled people: Assessing the extent of participation* (revised edn), DfEE Research Report RR69, Nottingham: DfEE.

Millar, J. (2000) 'Keeping track of welfare reform: the New Deal programmes', Paper presented to JRF Seminar on Work, Security and the Single Gateway, 15 March, London.

NAO (National Audit Office) (2002) *The New Deal for Young People*, HC 639, London: The Stationery Office.

ONS (Office of National Statistics) (2000, July) *Labour market trends*, London: The Stationery Office.

Press Release (2000) 'New Deal hits target' (www.number-10.gov.uk), retrieved 8 December.

Pullinger, H. (2000) 'Background to the consultation', in Summary Report of the consultation on extension of New Deal for Disabled People, London: Employment Service, pp 22-3.

Riley, R. and Young, G. (2000) *The New Deal for Young People: Implications for employment and the public finance*, Sheffield: Employment Service Research and Development Report ESR62.

Riley, R. and Young, G. (2001a) *The macroeconomic impact of the New Deal for Young People*, London: National Institute for Economic and Social Research.

Riley, R. and Young, G. (2001b) *Does welfare-to-work policy increase employment? Evidence from the UK New Deal for Young People*, London: National Institute for Economic and Social Research.

Ritchie, J. and Snape, D. (1993) *Invalidity benefit: A preliminary qualitative study of the factors affecting its growth*, London: SCPR.

Robinson, P. (1999) 'Education, training and the youth labour market', in P. Gregg and J. Wadsworth (eds) *The state of working Britain*, Manchester: Manchester University Press, pp 147-67.

Sainsbury, R. (1999) 'The aims of social security', in J. Ditch (ed) *Introduction to social security*, London: Routledge, pp 34-47.

SEU (Social Exclusion Unit) (1999) *Bridging the gap: New opportunities for 16-18 year olds not in education, employment or training*, London: SEU.

Stafford, B. (1998) *National insurance and the contributory principle*, DSS in-house Report no 39, London: DSS.

Stafford, B., Cornwell, E., Smith, N. and Trickey, H. (2000) *Social integration through obligations to work? Current European 'workfare' initiatives and future direction: UK Report: New Deal for young people*, Working Paper 2328, Loughborough: Centre for Research in Social Policy, Loughborough University.

Stafford, B., Heaver, C., Ashworth, K., Bates, C., Walker, R., McKay, S. and Trickey, H. (1999) *Work and young men*, York: York Publishing Services for the Joseph Rowntree Foundation.

TEN (Training and Employment Network) (2001) *Welfare to work briefing*, Weekly Briefing No 145, London: Unemployment Unit and Youthaid.

van Reenen, J. (2001) *No more skivvy schemes? Active labour market policies and the British New Deal for the young unemployed in context*, IFS Working Paper WP01/09, London: Institute for Fiscal Studies.

Walker, R., Stafford, B., Youngs, R. and Ashworth, K. (1999) *Young unemployed people: (A) Characteristics of the New Deal target group (B) Labour market characteristics and outcomes*, Sheffield: Employment Service, Research and Development Report no 19.

Walker, R. with Howard, M. (2000) *The making of a welfare class? Benefit receipt in Britain*, Bristol: The Policy Press.

# SEVEN

# Shaping a vision of US welfare

*Robert Walker and Michael Wiseman*

This book is motivated by belief that the American debate can be both informed and challenged by greater understanding and appreciation of UK experience and accomplishments. Previous chapters document how Britain has addressed the common conundrums of social assistance policy and how it has taken, refined, and implemented lessons gleaned from US experience. In this chapter issues of outstanding concern that require the collective wisdom of policy makers and scholars on both sides of the Atlantic and elsewhere to resolve are identified. Even more importantly, this chapter illustrates how the book speaks directly to the failure of vision that characterised recent debates about the reauthorisation of the Temporary Assistance for Needy Families (TANF) and Food Stamp Program (FSP) that define US welfare and help to determine the current living standards and prospects of millions of American families.

While connecting with the 'How to?' questions of policy reform, British experience also directs attention to the 'Why?' and 'What for?' It encourages us not only to ask what is wrong with the present American system, a question that is both retrospective and narrow, but also to look ahead – to reflect on the kind of system that Americans might want and the opportunities that are available. A politically viable American vision of social assistance will surely differ markedly from the one guiding Britain's architects of reform. Nevertheless, the UK experience offers important policy lessons. Also it is the belief of the authors that the US response to this challenge could enhance the opportunities for future idea exchange between the two countries.

## Preparing the ground

As noted in Chapter One, Richard Rose (1993) has identified the importance of congruity in values, objectives, and structures when seeking to forge insights from policies in different jurisdictions. Alan Deacon convincingly argues in Chapter Three that sufficient congruity exists between Britain and the US to permit the exchange of policy ideas. Indeed, the evidence is the successful export of US policy models and rhetoric, such as those encapsulated in the mantras 'welfare-to-work' and 'making work pay', has in turn enhanced congruity and the relevance of British experience to the US. Institutions differ, and we are, as Mark Twain famously noted, separated by a common language – even 'welfare' means something different. Nevertheless, constructive policy dialogue is, with care, both possible and successfully practiced.

Perhaps the most important aid to dialogue is mutual recognition of the centrality of work and the place of obligations in welfare reform. Proactive, work-based policies were first pursued by Conservative governments under Margaret Thatcher and, after some soul-searching, developed as a unifying element within the current Labour government's reform strategy. Work-based obligations have always been a feature of Britain's welfare provision, although they were less evident in the 1970s when, partly under US influence, a social rights agenda was given greater prominence. The Conservative government led by John Major trialed a workfare scheme in the mid-1990s, but, as Deacon reports, it is the current Labour government, drawing on American communitarianism and the new paternalism, that has placed an emphasis on the duties and responsibilities of welfare recipients at the heart of reform.

Also providing a basis for dialogue is the longstanding goal of making work 'pay', that is assuring that persons moving from welfare-to-work secure higher incomes than are received when dependent on benefit. Concern about this problem reflects a reliance on means-tested assistance that is shared with the US, rather than with Britain's European partners. The antecedents of the current system of tax credits, introduced in 1999 and shaped by observation of the US Earned Income Tax Credit (EITC), were instigated by a Conservative government as long ago as 1972. Ironically, they were implemented as cash benefits after attempts to introduce a tax credit in Britain floundered. A national minimum wage was not introduced until 1998, when it was set at a level influenced by that in the US.

In acknowledging the need to reconcile what were once viewed as competing claims – rights versus responsibilities, promotion of enterprise versus eradication of poverty, and so on – the current Labour government, led by Tony Blair, has built upon, rather than reversed, changes introduced by successive Conservative governments. In so doing, it has distanced itself from earlier Labour governments and developed welfare institutions of considerable relevance to current US concerns. What is also apparent is strategic vision and a willingness to instigate incremental reform towards long-term goals, to specify policy targets and to learn from experience. But this is not to say that mistakes have always been avoided or that Labour has always retained the backing of its traditional supporters.

## Strategic vision

Mike Brewer and Paul Gregg spell out Labour's strategic vision in Chapter Four. The central ambition is to use the leverage of government to eradicate child poverty within a generation. Stated baldly, the goal smacks of naivety. More persuasive are the analysis of the problem and the comprehensiveness of the strategy. Both point to a need to break the confines of the US welfare reform debate and to ask not what can be done to get welfare mothers into work, or even how former welfare recipients can attain self-sufficiency, but what policies are there that foster self-sufficiency across the entire low-income population and how can they be made mutually supporting.

Child poverty in Britain, as in the US, was rising disproportionately quickly until the later 1990s and remains higher than in most comparable countries (see Vleminckx and Smeeding, 2001; Bradshaw, 2001). Analysis in Britain identifies the principal cause as the growth in adult worklessness and documents long-term and intergenerational social and economic consequences. Given this analysis, three strategic goals have been established: reduce the number of children in workless households; raise direct support for families with children; and limit the scarring effects by reducing the impact of deprivation.

The policies set in place to achieve these goals as described in the preceding chapters involve most central departments – Education and Skills; Work and Pensions; Transport; Environment; Food and Rural Affairs; and the Home Office with responsibility for law enforcement – and all levels of government. In recognition of the fact that social problems do not map well onto the structures of government in which departmental boundaries rapidly become barriers, new agencies have been created at the heart of the central government – located in the Treasury, the Cabinet Office and the Prime Minister's Office, with a remit to coordinate policy development across the traditional divisions of government.

The process is aided by a conceptualisation of poverty that is not limited to income deficiency and, with it, the danger of believing that cash transfers alone can address the problem. Rather, it embraces relative deprivation along a multiplicity of dimensions that reflect constraints on a person's full inclusion in society. While the difficulties of measuring poverty in this way are legion, even this brings some political and pragmatic advantages. The strategy towards eradicating poverty was announced without tying the government to a precise measure. What prevented this politically convenient exercise from being vacuous was the commitment to publish an annual poverty audit documenting the policies in place and recording progress made with respect to some 38 measures, typically expressed as movement towards specified targets (DSS, 1999).

Another aspect of Labour's strategic vision that speaks to US welfare reform is, as Deacon points out, recognition that much that is right on ethical grounds is also right for the economy. In seeking to eradicate childhood poverty and to promote equal opportunity, the British government has embarked on a long-term policy designed to raise the skill base of the labour force and to remove rigidities that have slowed economic change. The New Deal family of welfare-to-work programmes accords with this global vision, imparting work experience and – in the case of unemployed claimants – accredited training, so as to enhance the skills and advancement of the current generation of workers while providing, through their parenting, good role models and opportunities for the next.

In conceptualising and presenting welfare provisions as a positive agent of economic change rather than a constraint on economic performance, the Labour government is also aware that this can enhance public support and thereby free additional resources to invest in programmes. As in the US, the additional investment in tax credits to raise the incomes of the working poor has been considerable. In seeking to make welfare popular among the electorate, Labour learned from the US that welfare had to be seen to be working. In this regard, by embracing Conservative concerns about benefit fraud, Labour has sought not only to make welfare more effective but to convince public opinion that it is not money wasted.

In sum, Britain's strategy for what would be called welfare in the US is long-term and embracing. Social assistance and welfare-to-work measures are not viewed so much as independent programmes but as part of a panoply of policy instruments – the broader concept that 'welfare' encompasses in the UK – designed to eradicate child poverty and promote individual opportunity to the benefit of the economy and society as a whole.

## Working mothers

US welfare policies to edge single mothers from dependence on welfare into sustained economic independence have their structural counterparts in Britain: welfare-to-work schemes, tax credits, regulated child support, and a national childcare strategy. This is not solely the consequence of policy learning from the US and Australia, which is, as Jane Millar notes in Chapter Five, another model for British policy. It also reflects the circumstances in which lone parents find themselves in many societies. With limited skills and work experience, often burdened by guilt, self-doubt, and the scars of physical and emotional abuse, lone parents have to juggle the demands of parenthood with those of the breadwinner. Policy systems reflect a common response to this lack of security in employment, finance, and relationships confronted by lone parents, attempting to raise skills and income with varying success.

However, the apparent similarity in policies masks important differences that are instructive. While the TANF reforms in the US enforced work obligations on virtually all welfare mothers and provided a warrant for states to place time limits on financial support, neither condition applies in Britain. Indeed, Millar suggests that measures introduced in Britain during the last decade – including changes in child support policy and, since 1997, the Working Families' Tax Credit and New Deal for Lone Parents – have actually enhanced the ability of lone parents to choose whether or not to work. Certainly 20 years ago lone parents in Britain were expected to give priority to caring for their children rather than to paid employment, and until very recently they were denied access to job-search and training facilities available to other benefit recipients. Labour's welfare-to-work initiatives, building on a small pilot instigated by the last Conservative government, mean that lone parents are more able to draw on government resources to equip themselves for paid employment, should they wish to do so.

At present, public support in Britain would not condone policy that enforced lone parents with young children to take paid work. It seems that priority is given to the immediate care needs of children rather than to ensuring the role model of an employed parent or enforcing the conditionality of benefit receipt. Also, the public is sensitive to the high levels of poverty suffered by lone parents and, perhaps, is less condemnatory than in the US. Millar notes that lone parenthood is seen less as a threat to the traditional family than as an outcome of its demise. This may be because British society recognizes that most lone parenthood arises from the breakdown of marriage or previously stable cohabiting relationships. There has been a rise recently in the number of 'single' lone parents who have never enjoyed stable sexual relationships, but the level of teenage births, though high by international standards, is still much below the levels seen in the early 1970s when contraception was less widely practiced (Walker with Howard, 2000). Also, although lone parenthood is more common among certain ethnic minorities, notably those of West Indian descent, the linking of race, illegitimacy, and welfare receipt that so mars the US political debate is almost entirely absent in Britain.

Given that work obligations are not enforced in Britain, the country provides evidence of what can be achieved by a mixture of voluntary welfare-to-work programmes, childcare facilities, and financial incentives. Britain's national childcare strategy – the goal of which is to provide childcare places for all those wishing to use them – is by no means yet in place. The dramatic six-percentage-point increase in the employment rate of lone parents (to 50%) that was observed between 1997 and 2000 was therefore achieved without this basic support. Taking the results of the evaluations presented by Millar at face value suggests that financial incentives and voluntary employment and advice schemes are of equal importance in explaining employment growth set against a backdrop of buoyant labour demand. Two thirds of lone parents who returned to work through the New Deal felt themselves to be better off financially. Even though wages were generally low, relative poverty among lone parents fell from 38% in 1996/97 to 32% in 2000/01, and the poverty rate for all children dropped from 26% to 21% (CPAG, 2002; HBAI, 2002; these data use as the poverty standard 60% of median income before housing costs). Moreover, the proportion of lone parents rapidly returning to benefit – about 8% within eight months – has been low in comparison with American experience. This may be a selection effect: on average lone parents moving from welfare-to-work under Britain's voluntary system may be more motivated to continue. But it may also reflect the ready access such parents enjoy to in-work supports and the seamless healthcare coverage Britain provides.

These matters deserve more study. Our point is that like their counterparts in the US, lone mothers taking up paid work in the UK are typically entering the bottom of the labour market and assuming the economic risks such entry entails. In the context of America's post-reauthorisation debate, joint endeavour by the UK and US policy communities to devise effective measures to promote employment retention and career advancement does not seem a fanciful idea. Indeed it is happening already, with US consultants advising the UK Cabinet

Office on the design of a possible demonstration project to test ways of enhancing employment retention and human resource investment.

The British government has established the target of 70% of lone parents in work by the end of the current decade. While the way 'in work' is to be defined is unclear at this writing, the primary rationale is to contribute to the eradication of child poverty. The evidence is that lone parents in work in the UK are substantially better off financially than those on benefit. Policy makers are aware of the selectivity inherent in such comparisons – lone parents with the best prospects of enriching employment are likely already to be in work – and it will almost certainly prove more difficult to attain the new 70% target than the 50% one recently achieved. Indeed, Millar is not convinced that this will be attained without increasing compulsion. Ellwood (1988) has documented the trend to employment among married mothers that in the US legitimated and, indeed, helped to create the demand that lone mothers should also work. However, employment rates among married mothers in Britain already outstrip those attained in the US in the 1980s, so if compulsion is necessary, the British government will probably have to lead public opinion rather than to follow it as was possible in the US.

Perhaps aware of this conundrum, and yet intent on ending child poverty, the British government has embarked on a further strategy with purchase on the US goal of helping welfare families attain self-sufficiency. Plans discussed by Brewer and Gregg separate the support costs for adults from those for children in the payment of benefit. Britain – along with most other OECD countries, the US excluded – has long provided universal support to help offset the costs of children, as well as child dependency additions to means-tested benefits. In future, all benefits for children will be effectively amalgamated (even though for political reasons the universal support will retain a separate identity) and paid to the mother or nominated caregiver. Research evidence in Britain suggests that this is the best way to ensure that money allocated to children in two-parent households is in fact spent on them (Snape and Molloy, 1999). Accompanying this demogrant for children, which is withdrawn gradually as family income rises, means-tested benefits for adults will be more sensitively tuned to employment status and variations in income in a way that more clearly communicates the financial advantages of working.

It is somewhat ironic, therefore, that the British welfare-to-work scheme that the American reader might expect would bear most resemblance to the US – the New Deal for Lone Parents – is so very different. The similar goal of financial self-sufficiency for lone parents through work has to date been pursued by voluntary exhortation. More challenging to the US debate is the Labour government's decision to separate the earnings subsidy from basic financial support for children, and to deliver the earnings subsidy in the pay cheque. This allows a direct approach to contributing to the financial costs of children and makes the benefit of the earnings subsidy immediately apparent as it is earned.

## Extending the logic of welfare-to-work

The broader vision of UK-style welfare means that Britain has sought to employ US-style welfare-to-work models in a wider range of settings. The reasons for this lie both in distant history and the immediate past. Historically, British provisions are a legacy of mass unemployment rather than a response to the problem of fatherless families. In the contemporary context, child poverty and social inequality have been driven by the growth in workless families at a time when the social norm is for both parents to be in paid work. The latter is a phenomenon that Britain shares with the US, but in the US the reform issues are rarely cast with reference to worklessness. 'Dependency' is the more commonly cited primary concern.

### Youth unemployment

In Chapter Six, Bruce Stafford reports the considerable early success of a British welfare-to-work model with marked similarities to Wisconsin's W-2 but applied to young unemployed people. As in the US, unemployment among young people, especially young men, is associated in politicians' minds with crime, disorder, and thoughtless fatherhood. As Brewer and Gregg note, there is also statistical evidence in Britain that early experience of unemployment is causally related to poor employment records later in life. Add to these concerns the economic objective already mentioned of upgrading the skill base of the British economy and it is evident why New Deal for Young People was highlighted in Labour's 1997 election manifesto.

In Britain, as in the US, young unemployed people are typically very poorly educated and lack the soft skills work experience supplies. Turnover is also high as many young people inhabit the unstable fringe of the labour market. Unlike in the US, young people over the age of 18 in the UK who can demonstrate that they are both available for, and actively seeking, work have always been able to claim means-tested assistance even if their insurance record has been insufficient to allow them to receive unemployment benefit (contributory Jobseeker's Allowance, as this benefit is now called). Since 1998 benefit beyond six months has been conditional on enrolment in New Deal for Young People with its mix of job-search, work-experience and universal accredited training. Since 1999 the same obligations have applied to the partners of unemployed young people. Sanctions are mild compared to those that apply under TANF – up to four weeks loss of benefit for each instance of non-attendance in the participant's New Deal option but with a cumulative maximum of 26 weeks, compared to eventual total loss of benefit for non-compliance in most state TANF programmes (US General Accounting Office, 2000). However, these penalties are indeed applied: on average, 13% of young people assigned to options are sanctioned, either for refusing to attend or for non-completion; the rate ranges from 6% for subsidized employment to 27% for the Environmental Task Force (Bivand, 2002).

With this regime, the Labour government claims to have fulfilled its manifesto commitment to return 250,000 young people to work. The detail is inevitably more complex, not least because the political imperative to implement the scheme quickly on a national basis took priority over formal evaluation. The estimates available suggest 50% deadweight (measured in terms of youths in employment) but little substitution, net impacts after 18 months comparable with the median achieved in US demonstrations with lone parents, and zero net expenditure when viewed from the perspective of government (Ashworth et al, 2001). These results have encouraged the British government to extend the intensive welfare-to-work model represented by New Deal for Young People to other groups of unemployed people, replacing less intensive versions implemented earlier.

Clearly it is too soon to judge whether the New Deal succeeds in preventing long-term scarring or breaks cycles of criminality linked to worklessness. Moreover, the relevance of the UK experience to the US is likely to be limited while the focus of poverty policy remains on the fate of welfare mothers and their children rather than the employment prospects of fathers. But, if the policy focus were to shift from poverty relief to poverty prevention, then the case for experimenting with a benefit aimed at workless young men, conditioned on work activity, could be persuasive.

## Incapacity

Like Britain, the US has also witnessed a marked rise in the number of individuals claiming insurance benefits on the grounds of incapacity for work: the number of Disability Insurance beneficiaries increased by over 50% between 1990 and 1999 (Committee on Ways and Means, 2000, p 79; includes spouses and children). In the US this trend has gone largely unremarked in the political arena. In Britain it has been linked to concerns about the prevalence of worklessness and poverty and to worries about the prevalence of so-called hidden unemployment, both nationally and within specific localities that have been victims of structural economic change. Some commentators have also opined that the increased incidence of reported disability among working age people may be both a consequence of more stressful lifestyles and a by-product of demands for higher productivity within the workplace (Walker with Howard, 2000). Analysts have linked trends in the US, in contrast, to reduced stringency in eligibility screening and a rising earnings replacement rate at the bottom of the earnings distribution (Autor and Duggan, 2001).

Whatever the root cause, Britain is engaged in policy experimentation to find some model of work-oriented casework that might help disabled people back into employment. It has to be said that the experience to date is no more encouraging than the single comparable experiment run in the US that, in the American way, used random assignment (Kornfeld, 1999). The effort does, though, raise issues of more than parochial significance, as discussed in Stafford's chapter.

The first is the dichotomous nature of the distinction between whether a person is capable or incapable of working, which applies to insurance and assistance benefits in both Britain and the US. In fact, the role played by illness and disability in determining work opportunities is undoubtedly more complex, as is indicated by the prevalence of ill-health, disability and substance abuse among TANF recipients in the US and unemployment insurance beneficiaries in both countries (Dion et al, 1999; McKay et al, 1999; Moffitt and Roff, 2000; Zedlewski and Loprest, 2001). The medical assessment of incapacity in many cases imposes a finality that does not necessarily accord with the long-term capabilities or aspirations of recipients of incapacity benefits. In Britain, 30% of disabled people receiving benefits say they would like to work. But even under the current regime, taking steps to do so could debar them from receipt of incapacity benefits, which are more generous than work-related income support.

The second issue concerns the nature and flexibility of casework. Stafford explores how in Britain the application of the casework model was necessarily modified when extended to different groups. While a heavily structured model allowing on-going contact between caseworker and client was possible even with comparatively large caseloads of unemployed clients, the diversity and complexity of problems faced by disabled people triggered the growth of less structured specialization and referral. In the context of TANF, falling caseloads and their possibly changing composition raise issues concerning the meaning of casework; the most appropriate model to use; and mechanisms for optimising the fit between method, client, and circumstance (Hill, 2001). As in Britain there are also pertinent questions in the US about the lines of accountability and methods of redress, especially in circumstances where the quality and training of staff fit uneasily with their level of responsibility and the vulnerability of clients and their children.

The third issue is the tension inherent in supply-side strategies epitomized by welfare-to-work programmes, when limitations are posed by labour demand. This is perhaps most important when interpreting the apparent success of such initiatives in both the US and Britain during eras of unprecedented economic growth. If work focus and work requirements are to be sustained in periods of recession, governments will have to offer jobs of last resort, especially in the context of time limits that would unfairly penalise people whose welfare exits are delayed by macroeconomic conditions.

Finally, Stafford alerts readers to the importance of discrimination by employers against disabled people. This point is again generalisable to the US and to different groups. Great efforts have been made in both countries to sign up prestige employers to the mission of taking on ex-welfare recipients, with a large measure of success. Much less evident is the extent of engagement of small employers or even local managers of larger public companies. This becomes increasingly important (a) in times of recession, when employers have more choice in making appointments, and (b) when seeking jobs for the hard to place. Caseworkers engaged in job placement serve two clients, the welfare recipient and the employer. When confronted by employment discrimination, caseworkers can find themselves needing to influence attitudes and behaviours on both sides of the labour exchange.

## The next rounds of exchange

Before sketching out a vision of a next round of US welfare reform that is informed by the British experience documented in this volume, it is pertinent to consider what might be the next developments in the Anglo-American trade in social policy ideas. The congruity between British and American objectives in many areas of assistance policy and strategy should foster growing collaboration in development and evaluation of the building blocks of assistance strategy and the design of policies for addressing specific problems. References to such details – and the devils they shelter – abound in this volume. Here we highlight six of the most difficult ones.

### Incentives

Some problems never die. It is one thing to design a social assistance system that 'makes work pay', it is quite another to design a system that makes *more work pay more*. One of the purposes behind promotion of obligation to work is to compensate for the disincentives created by means-tested assistance systems. As is well known, multiplication of such systems multiplies the disincentives, and this interaction is particularly severe when benefits are large, as they are for benefit recipients in most subsidized housing. Not surprisingly, British authorities have shown particular interest in US programmes like JOBS-Plus (Riccio, 1999), which address the problem of raising employment rates among residents in the lowest-income public housing communities.

### Job retention and advancement

It is rapidly becoming apparent that while work-first policies succeed in reducing welfare rolls and increasing employment, they are much less effective in ensuring either substantial or sustained increases in income. Millar and Stafford both report worrying numbers of lone parents and formerly unemployed claimants in Britain returning rapidly to benefit. The story is repeated among former welfare recipients in the US, where research indicates that wage growth is typically very slow, with people's earnings not exceeding the poverty line even many years after leaving welfare (Primus et al, 1999; Pavetti and Arcs, 2001; Wavelet and Anderson, 2002). If policy is to achieve more than transforming the claimant poor into the working poor, let alone enabling working families to earn their way off in-work supplementation, strategies are needed to stimulate career advancement. Hotz and his colleagues (2002) have called this the next frontier in anti-poverty employment policy.

## The hard-to-serve

The precipitous decline of the welfare caseload in the US has generated great concern about the status of families who have either left welfare or, if poor, are not receiving assistance. So-called 'leavers' studies have been conducted in the US both by states and by independent researchers. Most report that a significant proportion – around 20% – of those exiting assistance do not sustain employment. Multiple problems ranging from lack of skills and credentials to drug addiction contribute to such experience. Families with barriers to self-support have always been part of the assistance caseload, but until recently they were generally passed over when targets for employment policy were selected. Struggling families are a problem on both sides of the Atlantic; there may be gains from partnership in evaluating strategies for helping this hard to serve population.

## Management

It is an article of faith in the US that the federal system allows better tailoring of policy to local situations than would a uniform nationwide policy. While the benefits actually realized from the American system may be questioned, it does seem to be true that activist social assistance policy requires local discretion and flexibility because both the character of labour markets and the needs and capacities of clients differ. The New Deals in Britain are now largely delivered through 'one-stop' centres based on American models and, as in the US, advisers/case workers working face-to-face with clients play central roles. Identifying the influence of programme organization and management on outcomes at the local level is essential for understanding sources of differences in performance across localities and for improving management incentives and performance capabilities. While details may differ from programme to programme, the core problems of governance are the same. Collaborative study of process could provide as much opportunity for mutual benefit as study of outcomes, in part because Britain's more centralized system may offer better opportunities and stronger motivation for systematic experimentation.

## Coping with scale

In passive benefit systems, neither geographic concentration nor the absolute scale of operations poses much of an administrative problem. If mail can reach families, so can checks, and administrative costs per capita may actually decline as the number of beneficiaries rises. Neither is true for more active interventions. It is generally easier to operate small programmes than large ones, and it is particularly difficult to involve dispersed rural recipients in employment-development efforts. Both countries need to find more effective ways to move from small-scale demonstrations to widespread implementation, and to extend access to employment assistance for rural or dispersed populations.

## Promoting evidence-based policy making

Despite strenuous efforts by the policy research community, the 2002 reform debate in the US was largely untouched by research evidence. Indeed, a prestigious panel established by the US National Research Council reviewed the research findings and concluded that the government had "largely failed" in its goal "to measure the effects of the policies it enacts so that policies can be improved in the future" (Moffitt and Ver Ploeg, 2001, p 3). Before PRWORA, the sweeping US federal welfare reform passed into law in 1996, states that wished to deviate from national requirements in their welfare programmes had to secure a federal waiver of regulations and to agree to evaluate the outcomes of the programmes. Waivers and evaluation are in most cases no longer required even for quite significant programme innovations. The ability of federal agencies to monitor state activities and promote evaluation has been curtailed; and state evaluations, if they are even undertaken, are often seriously flawed. The current Bush administration has taken steps to remedy this situation and to collect more systematic information on states' implementation of welfare, while the new cross-department waiver programme the administration has proposed should allow rigorous evaluation of strategies to coordinate provision. However, many of the interventions states are likely to propose will not be appropriate for evaluation by the random assignment methods that were the evaluation standard for earlier waiver programmes. This will strengthen interest from the US side in development of non-experimental evaluation techniques, an interest shared with British policy analysts.

## Towards the welfare we want

The intentions of PRWORA are to: (1) aid needy families so that children may be cared for in their homes or those of relatives; (2) end dependence of needy parents upon government benefits by promoting job preparation, work and marriage; (3) prevent and reduce out-of-wedlock pregnancies and establish goals for preventing and reducing their incidence; and (4) encourage the formation and maintenance of two-parent families. These are outcomes. If government can in fact do such things, they are accomplished through institutions. 'Ending welfare as we know it' is about changing an institution. But terminating one institution does not guarantee the birth of a more successful replacement. In the end, the real challenge posed to America by British reform is the 'vision thing': can American leadership come up with a vision for how the US system should evolve in order to promote such outcomes? The TANF and Food Stamp Program reauthorisation proposals made by the Bush administration talked about "pillars of reform": promoting work, strengthening families, the immense capacity of states, the importance of faith-based organisations. But pillars don't move, and reform is about change and the direction it should take.

Vision talk is cheap, and what is promoted as vision is often better termed a pipe dream. Nevertheless, it is vision that is missing from American policy. To return to a theme established in Chapter One, US politicians claim to have ended welfare as that country's citizens knew it. Now, the question is: what should new welfare be like? If America were to take its cue from Britain, it would be: (1) adequate, (2) coherent, (3) ambitious, and (4) dynamic.

## Adequate

What is adequate is socially determined. This is the foundation for defining poverty based on relative income, as Britain does. But regardless of the standard applied, the minimum provision made for those without other resources in most states was abominably low at the beginning of the 1990s, and it has since fallen. And for many Americans, especially those who are young and without children, there is virtually no safety net at all. British politicians have developed a political strategy for gaining public support for sustaining the safety net by recognizing need, linking benefit to work, and casting reform as one of multiple means toward attaining larger national goals of modernization and improved productivity. To be politically useful, visions for the welfare Americans might want must link change to what a better assistance system might do for the country as a whole. The first PRWORA goal – aiding needy families so that children may be cared for in their homes or those of relatives – is surely a worthy objective, but it fails to connect the objective of improving welfare to the aspirations of Americans in general.

## Coherent

Prime Minister Tony Blair's characterisation – work for those who can, security for those who cannot – usefully underscores the work orientation of social assistance while reaffirming the responsibility of government to preserve the social safety net given the central importance of employment. The four components of the US system – TANF, food stamps, the EITC and Medicaid – potentially provide everything to low-income American families that is available to poor families in Britain. What continues to be missing is a sense of how the four should combine to provide both security and incentive, either financial or through obligation, to work toward self-sufficiency. American politicians do not currently talk much about work and security as the *joint* foundation of reform, but a new vision might.

The proliferation in Britain of 'New Deals' for groups ranging from older workers to musicians has been for some an opportunity for ridicule. But the important message for the American vision is that promoting work, the first pillar of the Bush administration's reauthorisation plan, can become a theme that unifies a diverse set of social assistance and social insurance initiatives and, in the process, both reduces stigma associated with the receipt of assistance and links social assistance with national norms. 'Help to work' is an integrating concept that encourages reaching beyond the usual boundaries of US reform strategy.

Youth present an important opportunity for this type of reaching beyond. Many of the principal concerns of the 1996 reforms – notably promoting work and marriage, reducing non-marital births, encouraging the formation and maintenance of two-parent families – typically involve young people. Yet for the most part PRWORA-based programmes directly affect young adults only after events that substantially affect the life-course have transpired. Thus states worry about fatherhood after fathering has occurred, non-marital births among women who are already mothers, formation of two-parent families for people established as lone parents. Britain provides much more systematic support for people aged 18-25, support that promises opportunity and provides income to those who are willing to work, but is not linked to parenthood. Britain's experience with the New Deal for Young People is worthy of consideration as a model for experimentation in high-poverty areas in American cities or possibly rural areas. Milwaukee's New Hope programme, closely studied by British visitors, did offer earnings subsidy and job support for adults regardless of parental status, but no training or goal-oriented case management was included (Bos et al, 1999). New projects of this type offer an important opportunity for demonstrating how more integrated and comprehensive systems of social assistance would operate on the ground.

## Ambitious

British experience, as noted at the beginning of this chapter, directs attention to the welfare 'why?' and 'what for?' questions. In brief, Britain has welfare because there is need – the intention being to use welfare policy and related tools to promote national well-being through employment and, in a generation, to end child poverty.

The vision sought for the US focuses on institutions. Variation across states in both resources and administrative procedures means variation in security and opportunity. Americans might consider adopting, as an objective, assured access both to sufficient income if alternatives are not available and to the resources needed for job-finding and employment. No such assurance is now available; indeed basic income support for those without alternatives has declined. Lowering poverty rates is a long-term objective in the US. And assuring access to resources and opportunity is reasonably promoted by reformers as a means to attaining the poverty reduction goal. However, as emphasised in Chapter Two, progress in assuring such access awaits emergence of the political will necessary to address inequalities in intergovernmental transfers and in state fiscal commitment to securing social assistance.

## Dynamic

Perhaps the most astonishing feature of recent British welfare policy is its dynamism: things change. While 'continuation' seems to be the watchword for American policy, in Britain programme evolution continues apace. Indeed many of the programme and policy details outlined by the contributors to this volume no longer apply. The pace of policy change has been frenetic, arguably too frenetic, since 1997, but the change has rarely been for change's sake. Rather it has been a response to policy learning, to refined objectives and to evidence of policy failure indexed against publicly available performance standards. Moreover, cumulative change has been possible because of the existence of clearly stated, if not always precisely defined strategic goals. A genuine reform programme for the US would join up the federal government and the states to rethink the process whereby doing produces learning and learning changes policy. This does not mean that British change has always been, as claimed, 'evidence based'. What it does mean is that Labour has promoted its ongoing efforts at nationwide system improvement as a political asset. In America, the pretence of accomplishment too often serves as excuse for neglect.

The 1990s showed that running against welfare as America knew it could be politically useful. British experience may help American politicians in the new decade find a vision of welfare to run *for*, and not against. Such a transformation can only serve to enhance the international trade in policy ideas and practice.

## References

Ashworth, K., Cebulla, A., Davis, A., Greenberg, D. and Walker, R. (2001) 'Welfare-to-Work: establishing a basis in evidence', Paper submitted for presentation at the Annual Meeting of the Association of Public Policy Analysis and Management, Washington DC, November.

Autor, D.H. and Duggan, M.G. (2003) 'The rise in disability roles and the decline in unemployment', *Quarterly journal of economics*, vol 118, no 1, pp 157-205.

Bos, J.M., Huston, A.C., Granger, R.C., Duncan, G.J., Brock, T.W. and McLoyd, V.C. (1999) *New hope for people with low incomes: Two-year results of a program to reduce poverty and reform welfare*, New York, NY: Manpower Demonstration Research Corporation.

Bivand, P. (2002) *Rights and duties in the New Deal*, Working Brief, no 136, pp 15-17.

Bradshaw, J. (ed) (2002) *Children and social security*, York: Foundation for International Studies in Social Security.

Committee on Ways and Means (2000) *2000 Green book: Background material and data on programs within the jurisdiction of the Committee on Ways and Means*, Washington, DC: United States House of Representatives.

CPAG (Child Poverty Action Group) (2002) 'Poverty watch: Households below average income 1994/95-2000/1', *Poverty*, vol 112, p 20.

DSS (Department of Social Security) (1999) *Opportunity for all: Tackling poverty and social exclusion*, Cm 4445, London: The Stationery Office.

DWP (Department for Work and Pensions) (2002) *Households below average income 1994/5-2000/1*, London: DWP (available at www.dwp.gov.uk).

DWP (2002) *Measuring child poverty*, London: DWP (available on www.dwp.gov.uk).

Dion, R., Derr, M., Anderson, J. and Pavetti, L. (1999) *Reaching all job seekers: Employment programs for hard-to-employ populations*, Washington, DC: Mathematical Policy Research, Inc.

Ellwood, D. (1988) *Poor support: Poverty in the American family*, New York, NY: Basic Books.

Federal Interagency Forum on Child and Family Statistics (2002) *America's children: Key national indicators of well-being, 2002*, Washington, DC: US Government Printing Office.

Hill, C.J. (2001) *Casework job design and client outcomes in Welfare-to-Work programs*, Paper presented at the 59th Annual Meeting of the Midwest Political Science Association, Chicago, 19-22 April.

Hotz, V.J., Mullin, C.H. and Scholtz, J.K. (2002) 'Welfare reform, employment and advancement', *Focus*, vol 22, no 1, pp 51-5.

Loumidis, J., Stafford, B., Youngs, R., Green, A., Arthur, S., Legard, R., Lessof, C., Lewis, J., Walker, R., Corden, A., Thornton, P. and Sainsbury, R. (2001) *Evaluation of the New Deal for disabled people personal adviser pilot*, London: DSS, Research Report, no 144.

Kornfeld, R., Wood, M., Orr, L. and Long, D. (1999) *Impacts of the project NetWork demonstration, final report*, Cambridge, MA: Abt Associates Inc.

McKay, S., Smith, A., Youngs, R. and Walker, R. (1999) *Unemployment and jobseeking after the introduction of Jobseeker's Allowance*, Research Report no 111, London: DSS.

Moffitt, R. and Roff, J. (2000) *The diversity of welfare leavers*, Welfare, Children, and Families Study Policy Brief 00-2, Baltimore: Johns Hopkins University.

Moffitt, R.A. and Ver Ploeg, M., (eds) (2001) *Evaluating welfare reform in an era of transition*, Washington, DC: National Academy Press.

Pavetti, L. and Arcs, G. (2001) 'Moving up, moving out or going nowhere? A study of employment patterns of young women and the implications for welfare mothers', *Journal of policy analysis and management*, vol 20, no 4, pp 721-36.

Primus, W., Rawlings, L., Larin, K. and Porter, K. (1999) *The initial impacts of welfare reform on the incomes of single-mother families*, Washington, DC: Centre of Budget and Policy Priorities.

Riccio, J.A. (1999) *Mobilizing public housing communities for work: Origins and early accomplishments of the JOBS-Plus demonstration*, New York, NY: Manpower Demonstration Research Corporation.

Rose, R. (1993) *Lesson-drawing in public policy: A guide to learning across time and space*, Chatham, NJ: Chatham House Publishers, Inc.

Snape, D. and Molloy, D. (1999) *Financial arrangements of couples on benefit: A review of the literature*, in-house Report no 58, London: DSS.

US DHSS (Department of Health and Human Services) (2002) *Indicators of welfare dependence: Annual report to Congress 2002*, Washington, DC: DHHS.

US GAO (General Accounting Office) (2000) *Welfare reform: State sanction policies and number of families affected*, Report GAO/HEHS-00-44, Washington, DC: GAO.

Vleminckx, K. and Smeeding, T. (2001) *Child well-being, child poverty and child policy in modern nations: What do we know?*, Bristol: The Policy Press.

Walker, R. with Howard, M. (2000) *The making of a welfare class? Benefit receipt in Britain*, Bristol: The Policy Press.

Wavelet, M. and Anderson, J. (2002) 'Promoting self-sufficiency: what we know about sustaining employment and increasing income among welfare recipients and the working poor', *Focus*, vol 22, no 1, pp 56-62.

Zedlewski, S. and Loprest, P. (2001) *How well does TANF fit the needs of the most disadvantaged families?*, Washington, DC: New World of Welfare Conference, 2 February (www.fordschool.umich.edu).

# Index

Page references for figures and tables are in *italics*; those for notes are followed by n

## A

Abercedarian Project 84
Adam Smith Institute 14
Additional Person's Allowance (APA) 87-8
Adonis, Andrew 77n
Aid to Families with Dependent Children (AFDC) 2, 25, 31
  caseload decline 39-40, *39*, 46
  funding 43, *44*
  variation 45, 58
  waivers and reform 34, 35, 51
  welfare politics 33-4
Alaska 4
American Public Human Services Association (APHSA) 55
Anderson, J. 184
Anderton, B. 164, 165, 166
Arcs, G. 184
Arthur, S. 155, 157, 160, 169n
Arulampalam, W. 90
Ashworth, K. 92, 166, 182
Australia 14, 119, 178
Autor, D.H. 182

## B

Bane, Mary Jo 70
Barnes, H. 119
Battle, K. 109n
Baucus, Max 56
Benefits Agency (UK) 135n, 157, 167, 169n
benefits dependency 14, 33, 65, 67, 68, 76, 181
Berthoud, R. 148
Besharov, D. 76
Beveridge, W. 13
Bivand, P. 181
Blackburn, V. 169n
Blair, Tony 66, 71, 72, 176, 187
  Child Benefit 135n
  child poverty 20, 72-3, 74, 81, 84
  rights and responsibilities 69, 146
  third way 67
  young people 16, 147

Blank, R. 35, 66
block grants 35, 36, 43-4, *44*, 49-50, 57
Bloom, D. 43
Blundell, R. 101, 102, 109n
Blunkett, D. 146
Bonjour, D. 158
Borrie Commission 70
Bos, J.M. 188
Bradbury, B. 83, 106
Bradshaw, J. 131, 177
Brewer, M. 87, 93, *94*, 96, 100, 105, 109n, 132
British Cohort Study 84
Britton, L. 158, 165
Brown, Gordon 52, 66, 73-4, 96, 115-16
Bryner, G. 70
Bryson, A. 155, 165
Bryson, C. 119
Burchardt, T. 148
Bureau of Census (US) 85
Burke, V. 26, 61n
Bush, George W. 50

## C

California
combined benefit 29-30, *30*
  eligibility 45
  funding 44
Callan, T. 86
Canada 104
case management 89, 104, 122, 143, 155, 183
caseload decline 46, 61, 185
cause and effect 39-41, *39*, *40*
  and funding 44, 49-50
  and participation requirement 44
Census Bureau (US) 93
Chernick, H. 42
Child Benefit 4, *9*, 14, 86, 87, 104
  impact 94, *95*
  increases 20, 87
  withholding 135n
Child Care and Development Fund (CCDF) 43

child poverty 81, 176, 177, 179, 181
  future directions 103-5
  lone parents' employment change 101-3, *102*, *103*
  lone-parent families 116, 117, 125
  measuring and defining 84-6, 108n
  New Labour strategy 16, 20, 21, 66, 72-6, 86-92
  New Labour's motivation 81-4
  policy assessment 105-8
  reform package accomplishments 92-101, *93*, *94*, *95*, *97*, *98*, *99*, *100*
Child Poverty Action Group (CPAG) 179
child support
  UK 14-15, 119-20, 132, 133
  US 34, 53, 178
Child Support Act 1991 (UK) 119-20
Child Support Agency (CSA) (UK) 14-15
Child Tax Credit (UK) 87, 104-5, 106, 109n, 132, 133
childcare 89-90, 122, 124, 131, 133, 179
Childcare Tax Credit (UK) 86, 88-9, 90, 101, 124, 131-2
Children's Fund 20
Children's Tax Credit (UK) 86, 87-8, 94, 97, 100, 109n
Clark, 109n
Clark, T. 82
Clinton, Bill 16, 20, 33, 35, 67
Collins, D. 163
Colorado 44
Committee on Ways and Means (US) 36, 61n, 97, 182
communitarianism 69, 176
compulsion 169n
  New Deal for Disabled People 158-9
  New Deal for Lone Parents 132-3, 134
  New Deal for Young People 145, 158-9, 161
Congress 55-6, 57-8
Congressional Budget Office 61n
Congressional Research Service (CRS) 61n
Connecticut 44, 45
Conservative Party
  benefit fraud 178
  disabled people 159
  lone parents 115, 119-21, *120*, 134
  welfare policies 13-15, 71, 176
  young people 169n
Council of Economic Advisors 41, 42, 61n
Council Tax Benefit (CTB) 5, 7, *10*, *11*, *12*, 95, 96

Cousins, C. 149
Currie, J. 84, 91

**D**

Dalaker, J. 83
Davies, H.T.O. 124
Davies, J. 121
Dawson, T. 124, 130
Deacon, A. 65
Dearing, R. 148
Democratic Party 54-5, 56, 66-8
Department of Agriculture (US) *27*
Department for Education and Employment (DfEE) 122, 124, 126, 147, *162*, 163, *164*
Department for Education and Skills (UK) 177
Department of Employment (UK) 14
Department of the Environment, Transport and the Regions (UK) 177
Department of Health, Education, and Welfare (US) 34
Department of Health and Human Services (DHHS) (US) *27*, *28*, 32, 33, 45, 46
  appointments 50, 52
  job reductions 38
  resignations 36
  waivers 56-7
Department of Housing and Urban Development (US) *28*
Department of Labor (US) 32
Department of Social Security (DSS) (UK) 20, 71, 74-5, 117, 148
  National Childcare Strategy 131
  *A new contract for welfare* 69-70, 146, 149
  WFTC 132
Department of Trade and Industry (DTI) (UK) 124
Department of the Treasury (US) *27*
Department for Work and Pensions (UK) 85, *102*, 109n, 130, 177
  New Deal for Lone Parents 122, 124, 125, 129
  poverty audit 136n
dependency 14, 33, 65, 67, 68, 76, 181
deregulation 13, 15
Desai, T. 102
Dickens, R. 82, 83
Dion, R. 183
Disability Insurance 14, 182
Disability Rights Commission (DRC) 149, 157

disabled people 22
  benefits 4, 31
  welfare-to-work 16, 182-3
  *see also* New Deal for Disabled People
District of Columbia 31
Dolowitz, D.P. 119
domestic violence 42
Driver, S. 67-8
Duggan, M.G. 182
Duncan, S. 117, 121
Dwyer, P. 69
dynamism 189

**E**

Early Excellence Centres 90
Earned Income Tax Credit (EITC) (US)
    17, 21, 25, *27*, 29, 30, *30*, 58-9, 176, 187
  adults without child dependents *12*
  Clinton 35
  eligibility 31
  focal unit 26
  impact on child poverty 96-7, 98
  importance 47, 49
  increase 39
  lone parents *10*
  phase-out 88, 95
  two-parent families *11*
  uniformity 32
earnings inequality 82
economy, UK 81, 82
education 20, 90-2, 147-8
  and child poverty 74-5
  lone parents 117, 132, 133
Education Zones 17
Educational Maintenance Allowances
  (EMAs) 20, 90, 91-2
Edwards, R. 117, 121
Ellwood, David 68, 70, 71, 83, 98, 109n,
    133, 136n, 180
employment 176
  job retention and advancement 184
  lone parents 47, *48*, 101-3, *102*, *103*, 115-
    16, 117, 118-19, 130, 131, 134, 135,
    178-80
  New Labour emphasis 69-71
  young people 90
  *see also* making work pay
Employment Service (UK) 124, 135n, 154,
    155, 157, 167, 169n
Employment Zones 17
ethnic minorities 5
  lone parents 117, 121, 127, 179
  New Deal for Young People 165

Evans, M. 124, 126, 127, 134
evidence-based policy making 186

**F**

Falk, G. 36, 44, *44*
*Families and children survey* 132
family caps 43
Family Credit 13, 87, 96
  childcare costs 89
  eligibility 15, 120
  replacement 17, 122
  take-up 109n, 131, 132
  threshold 89
Family Income Supplement 15
Family Support Act (FSA) 1988 (US) 34,
    35, 60
Farm Bill 2002 (US) 21, 54
Field, Frank 135n
Finch, H. 124
Finer Report 115, 119, 121, 133-4
Finlayson, L. 90
Food Resource Action Center (FRAC)
    61n
Food Stamp Program (FSP) 4, 25, *27*, 29,
    30, *30*, 41, 187
  adults without child dependents *12*
  caseload decline 46
  eligibility 31-2, 37
  focal unit 26
  importance 49
  lone parents *10*
  reauthorisation 1, 21, 54, 58-9, 175, 186
  two-parent families *11*
  uniformity 32
fraud 72, 77n, 178
Free School Meals *8*
Freedman, S. 134
Freeman, R. 16

**G**

Gabe, T. 46, 47
Gale, W. 87
Gardiner, K. 146
Gateway 16
GCSEs 91, 147
General Accounting Office (GAO) (US)
    44, 61n, 181
General Assistance *12*, 21, 25, *28*, 31, 32
Germanis, P. 76
Giannarelli, L. 45, 46
Giddens, Anthony 68, 74
Giuliani, Rudolph 52

Glennerster, H. 133, 136n
Gordon, D. 86
Gosling, A. 82
Gregg, P. 82, 83, 84, 90, 101, 132
Griswold, Heckel & Kelly Associates, Inc
    (GHK) 124, 130
gross domestic product 3

**H**

Hales, J. 124, 125, 127, 128, 129, 163
Hamblin, M. 124, 130
Hamilton, G. 60
Handler, J.F. 13
Hasenfeld, Y. 13
Haskey, J. 116, *117*
Haskins, R. 66
Hasluck, C. 124, 127, 132, 147, 155, 156,
    160, 162
Hawaii 4
Head Start 17, 84, 91
Health Action Zones 17
health care 4, 35
    *see also* Medicaid; Medicare; National
        Health Service; State Children's
        Health Insurance Program
Heron, E. 69
Hill, C.J. 183
Hillman, N. 134
Hills, D. 169n
Hills, J. 70, 119, 121
Holtermann, S. 117
Home Office 177
home/school agreements 69
homelessness 90
Horn, Wade 66
Hotz, V.J. 184
House of Commons Social Security Select
    Committee 120, 145, 147, 154, 156, 165
Households Below Average Income
    (HBAI) 135n, 179
housing assistance 25, 26
Housing Benefit (HB) 4, 5, 7, *10, 11, 12*
    and WFTC 95, 96, 101
    withholding 135n
Howard, M. 5, 14, 149, 157, 179, 182
Hoynes, H. 102
human capital development 154-5

**I**

Illegitimacy Reduction Bonus 56
incapacity *see* disabled people
Incapacity Benefit *8*, 14, 148, 149, 159, 168

incentives 184
income distribution
    UK 77n, 82, 93-4, *93, 94*
    US 47
Income-Related Jobseeker's Allowance 4
Income Support (IS) 4, *6, 11, 12*, 86, 87,
    104-5
    eligibility 15
    impact 94, *95*
    lone parents *10*, 14, 117, 122, 125, 126,
        127, 128, 130, 132, 133, 136n
income tax 86, 87
Inland Revenue 87, 96, 105, 132
Innovation Fund 132
Innovative Schemes 170n
Institute of Economic Affairs 14, 121
International Labor Organisation (ILO)
    147, 169n
Invalidity Benefit 14, 75, 149
Ireland 85, 86, 106

**J**

Jantti, M. 83, 106
Jarvis, L. 121
Jenkins, S. 70, 117
Jenny, N.W. 57
Job Brokers 167, 170n
job retention 184
Jobcentre Plus 104, 126, 132, 134, 135n,
    167, 169n
JOBS (Job Opportunities and Basic Skills)
    34, 43
JOBS-Plus 184
*Jobs study* (OECD) 14
Jobseeker's Allowance (JSA) 4, 7, *11, 12*,
    14, 87
    disabled people 145
    young people 144, 158, 169n, 181
Johnson, P. 82

**K**

Kiernan, K. 117
King, D. 65, 68-9
Klein, R. 67
Knox, V. 55
Kornfeld, R. 182

**L**

labour exchanges 13
labour market 13, 14, 15, 17, 20, 21
Labour Party 76, 143, 176

child poverty 72-6, 81, 86-101, *93, 94, 95, 97, 98, 99, 100*
  and Democratic Party 66
  disabled people 159
  fraud 77n
  lone parents 115, 122, *123*, 133
  obligations 68-9
  paid work 69-71
  third way 66-8
  unemployment 118
  US influence 65
  welfare policy 15-17, *18-19*, 20, 22, 71-2, 176 8
  young people 154, 163
  *see also* New Deals
Land, H. 14, 120, 131
Layard, R. 90
learning 60
Leicester, A. 82
Leisering, L. 70
Lelkes, O. 119, 121
Lessof, C. 124, 128, 130
lesson-sharing 2, 21
Lewis, J. 14, 116, 124, 130
Liebman, J. 98, 109n
Lister, R. 117, 119, 120, 121
lone parents *10*, 22, 178-80
  UK 4, 5, 14-15, *19*, 115-21, *118, 120*
    employment change 101-3, *102, 103*
    Labour Party policy 122, *123*, 124
    New Deal for Lone Parents 16, 124-30, *127*, 130-2
    policy moving on 132-5
    unemployment 83
  US
    combined benefit 26, 29-31, *30*
    employment 47
    income distribution 47
    poverty 47-8, *48*
long-term unemployment 16, *18*, 32
Loprest, P. 183
*Losing ground* (Murray) 33
Louisiana 44
Loumidis, J. 150, 154, 155, 156, 157, 159, 162, 166, 168
Low Pay Commission 131

**M**

Machin, S. 82, 84
Maguire, S. 148
maintenance of effort (MOE) requirements 36, 37
Major, John 121, 176

making work pay 16, 17, 20, 65, 70, 175, 176
  lone parents 122, 131-2, 133
  tax and benefits structure 89, 184
Mandelson, Peter 73
marginal deduction rates 99-101, *99, 100*, 109n
Marquand, David 66
marriage 53, 56, 121
Married Couple's Allowance (MCA) 87, 88
Marsh, A. 90, 109n, 117, 131, 134
Marsh, D. 119
Martell, L. 67-8
Maryland 44
matching grants 36
material deprivation 86
McClements scale 108n
McGuire, T.J. 42
McKay, S. 109n, 131, 132, 183
McLaughlin, E. 118
Mead, Lawrence 14, 34, 68, 75-6
Meager, N. 160
means-tested benefits 184
  UK 4-5, *6-9*, 13, 15, 176
  US 25-6, *27-8*
Medicaid *10, 11*, 25, 26, *28*, 31, 41, 187
Medicare 25
Mendelson, M. 109n
Michigan 40, 44
Millar, J. 119, 120, 125, 131, 135, 135n, 146, 154
Milwaukee 188
minimum wage 17, 20, 86, 131, 176
Minnesota Family Investment Plan (MFIP) 55
Moffitt, R. 183, 186
Molloy, D. 180
Morgan, P. 121
Moynihan Report 68
multiplication 41
Murray, Charles 14, 33, 68

**N**

National Assistance 13, 14
National Audit Office (NAO) (UK) 156, 164-5
National Child Development Survey (UK) 84
National Childcare Strategy 89-90, 122, 124, 131, 179

National Evaluation of Welfare-to-Work
   Strategies (NEWWS) 60
National Governors' Association (NGA)
   50, 51, 55, 61n
National Health Service 4
National Institute of Economic and Social
   Research 164
National Insurance 86, 148
National Minimum Wage (NMW) 17, 20,
   86, 131, 176
Naughtie, J. 66
Neighbourhood Childcare Centres 90
Nelson A. Rockefeller Institute of
   Government 57
*New ambitions for our country* 146, 149
*new contract for welfare, A* (DSS) 69-70, 146,
   149
New Deal for Communities 17
New Deal for Disabled People *19*, 22, 143,
   144, 145, 160-1, 167-8
   background 148-9
   changes 167, 170n
   compulsion 158-9
   delivery models 155-6
   features *151-3*
   links with employers 159-60, 170n
   objectives 154-5
   outcomes 165-6
   programme content 156-8, 169n
   programme size 162
   target client group 150, 154
New Deal Evaluation Database 124, 126,
   *127*
New Deal for Lone Parents *19*, 22, 89, 122,
   124-5, 143, 178, 180
   outcomes 126-8, *127*
   participation and take-up 125-6
   Personal Advisers 135n
   process 129-30
   success 130-2
New Deal for the Long-Term
   Unemployed *18*
New Deal for Partners *19*, 89
New Deal for Young People 16, *18*, 22, 90,
   143, 144-5, 160-1, 167-8, 181-2, 188
   background 147-8
   budget 130-1
   changes 166
   compulsion 69, 158-9, 169n
   delivery models 155-6
   features *151-3*
   links with employers 159-60, 170n
   objectives 154-5
   outcomes 163-5, *164*, 170n

   programme content 156-8
   programme size 161-2, *162*
   target client group 150, 154
New Deals 71, 76, 143, 177, 187
   case management 89, 104
   obligations 68-9
New Democrats 66-8
New Labour *see* Labour Party
new paternalism 33-4, 69, 176
New York 29, *30*, 44, 52
Nickell, S. 82
Nightingale, D.S. 52
Nolan, B. 86

**O**

obligations 15, 65, 68-9, 72, 146, 176
Office of National Statistics (ONS) (UK)
   82, 117, 169n
open-ended grants 36
Oregon 44
Organisation for Economic Co-operation
   and Development (OECD) 3, 14, 82,
   83
Orloff, A.S. 119, 135

**P**

Page, Robert 77n
paid work *see* employment
part-time work 132, 133
paternalism 33-4, 58, 69, 176
Pavetti, L. 184
Peck, J. 3, 65
pensions 25
personal advisers 155
   New Deal for Disabled People 145, 160,
      166
   New Deal for Lone Parents 122, 129, 130,
      135n
   New Deal for Young People 144, 145
Personal Responsibility and Work
   Opportunity Reconciliation Act
   (PRWORA) 1996 (US) 1, 25, 35-6, 76
   block grants 36
   end of entitlement 37
   Federal role 38
   goals 186, 187
   outcomes 39-50, *39*, *40*, *44*, *48*
   state latitude 36-7
   time limits 37
   work requirements 38, 52
Personal Responsibility, Work, and Family
   Promotion Act 2002 (US) 53-4, 56

Pettigrew, N. 126
Piachaud, D. 93
policy transfer 2, 65-6, 76, 175
poverty
  UK 82, 146, 177, 179
  US 31, 47-8, *48*
  *see also* child poverty
Poverty and Social Exclusion Survey 86
Price, David 13, 71
Primus, W. 184
Project Work 14
Pullinger, H. 149

**R**

Rafferty, A.M. 67
Rainwater, L. 68
Ramey, C. 84
Ramey, S. 84
Randall, V. 124
reauthorisation 22, 25, 29, 50, 61, 175, 186
  learning 60
  opposition 54-6
  outcome 57-8
  Senate proposal 56-7
  White House proposal 50-4, 66
Reed, H. 101
rent assistance 4
Republican Party 57, 66
responsibility 15, 65, 68-9, 72, 146, 176
Restart 13-14
Riccio, J.A. 184
Ridge, T. 131
Riley, R. 164, 165, 170n
Ritchie, J. 159, 160
Robinson, P. 148
Roff, J. 183
Rose, Richard 2, 21, 175
Rosso, R. 46

**S**

Sainsbury, R. 146
Sawhill, I. 66
Senate 54-7
Senate Finance Committee (SFC) 56
Severe Disablement Allowance 148
Shaw, A. 90
single parents *see* lone parents
Single Regeneration Budget 17
Smeeding, T. 177
Smith, John 70
Smithers, R. 135n
Snape, D. 159, 160, 180

social exclusion 16, 17, 20, 73, 76, 146
Social Exclusion Unit (SEU) 90, 148
Social Fund 7
social insurance 13, 159
Social Security (US) 25
Social Security Administration (US) *28*
Social Services Block Grant (SSBG) 43
South Carolina 29, *30*, 31, 40, 58
spin 41
Stafford, B. 147, 156, 159
State Children's Health Insurance Program
  (S-CHIP) *28*
super waiver 51, 55, 57
Supplemental Security Income (SSI) 21,
  25, *28*, 31, 32
Sure Start 17, 90, 91
Sutherland, H. 93

**T**

tax credits 86-7, 104-5, 148, 176, 178
  *see also* Childcare Tax Credit; Children's
    Tax Credit; Earned Income Tax
    Credit; Working Families' Tax Credit
Taylor-Gooby, P. 121
teenage pregnancy 53, 90
Teles, Stephen 67, 68
Temporary Assistance for Needy Families
  (TANF) 2, 4, 20-1, 25, *27*, 29, 35, 49,
  58-61, 143, 187
  access 37, 42-3
  block grants 36
  caseload decline 39, *39*, 40, *40*, 46, 183
  Clinton's strategy 41
  compulsion 181
  focal unit 26
  funding 43
  and health care 4
  lone parents 5, *10*
  reauthorisation 1, 50-8, 66, 175, 186
  two-parent families *11*
  variation 29-32, *30*, 45-6
  work requirements 38, 178
Texas 29-30, *30*, 31, 44
Thatcher, Margaret 14, 176
Theodore, N. 3, 65
third way 66-8
Thomas, D. 84, 91
Thomas, A. 55
Thompson, Tommy 35, 50, 52
time limits
  TANF 36, 37, 43
  UK 105

Training and Employment Network (TEN) (UK) 158
Transfer Income Model (TRIM) 46
HM Treasury 16, 74, 75, 77n, 81, 85, 87, 93, 101, 105, 130, 132, 146, 147, 155, 167
Twain, Mark 175-6

**U**

underclass 14, 16
unemployment 13, 14, 82, 117-18, 169n
  and child poverty 83
  young people 147, 150, 181
unemployment benefit (UK) 4, 13
unemployment insurance (UK) 13, 14
Unemployment Insurance (UI) (US) 4, 31-2
UNICEF 20
United Kingdom
  child poverty 72-6
    assessment 105-8
    future directions 103-5
    measuring and defining 84-6
    New Labour strategy 86-92
    New Labour's motivation 81-4
    reform package accomplishments 92-101, *93*, *94*, *95*, *97*, *98*, *99*, *100*
  dynamism 189
  future policy sharing 184-6
  lone parents 115-21, *118*, *120*, 178-80
    Labour Party policy 122, *123*, 124
    New Deal for Lone Parents 124-30, *127*, 130-2
    policy moving on 132-5
  making work pay 176
  New Deals 143-4, 146
  obligations 68-9
  paid work 69-71
  policy transfer 2-3, 65-6, 76, 175
  third way 66-8
  welfare 3-5, *6-9*, *10-12*, 21-2, 71-2
    history 5, 13-17, 20
  welfare-to-work 175-6, 181-3
  young people 188
  *see also* New Deal for Disabled People; New Deal for Young People
United States
  child poverty 73, 83, 84
    measuring 85
    strategies 91, 96-8, *97*, *98*, 119
  disabled people 182-4
  future policy sharing 184-6
  lone parents 116, 121, 133, 134, 178-80

marginal deduction rates 99
  obligations 68-9
  policy transfer 2-3, 16-17, 65-6, 76
  PRWORA 35-8, 39-50, *39*, *40*, *44*, *48*
  reauthorisation 1, 50-8
  social assistance system 3-5, *10-12*, 13, 14, 20-1, 22, 25-6, *27-8*
  tax system 87
  third way 66-8
  vision 186-9
  welfare politics 33-5
  women's employment 119
  young people 181, 182
Urban Institute 46, 61n

**V**

van Reenen, J. 165, 166
Ver Ploeg, M. 186
Vincent, J. 120
vision 61, 186-9
Vleminckx, K. 177

**W**

Wadsworth, J. 82
wage loss 82
waivers 2, 34-5, 39-40, 51, 55, 56-7, 60, 186
Walker, A. 117
Walker, R. 2, 3, 5, 14, 17, 34, 65, 70, 97, 149, 150, 157, 179, 182
Wallace, G. 35
Wavelet, M. 184
Weaver, K. 33, 66, 68, 70
Webb, S. 82
Webster, D. 131
welfare dependency 14, 33, 65, 67, 68, 76, 181
Welfare Employment Program (WEP) 52
Welfare Rules Database (WRD) 61n
welfare-to-work 16, 167, 175-6
  UK 16-17, 20, 71, 106, 143, 178, 181-4
  US 32
  *see also* New Deals; Temporary Assistance for Needy Families
Welfare to Work Partnership 41
Whelan, C.T. 86
White, M. 65
Whiteford, P. 119, 131
Wickham-Jones, M. 65, 68-9
Wilde, P. 46
Wilkens, A. 43

Willetts, David 77n, 134
Wilson, William Julius 68, 75
Wintour, P. 135n
Wisconsin 16, 35, 44, 52
Wisconsin Works (W-2) 16
Wiseman, M. 2, 17, 35, 43, 45, 46, 52, 97
women 131, 135
  *see also* lone parents
Work and Responsibility Act 1994 (US)
  35
Work, Opportunity, and Responsibility for
  Kids (WORK) Act 2002 (US) 56
workfare 14, 34, 169n, 176
Working Families' Tax Credit (WFTC) *6*,
  17, 86, 88, 104-5, 122, 178
  and EITC 96-7
  impact 94, 95-6, *95*
  lone parents *10*, 101-2
  marginal deduction rates 99-101, *99*,
    *100*, 109n
  take-up 109n, 131, 132
  two-parent families *11*
Working Tax Credit 105, 133
*Working toward independence* (White House)
  50-4


**Y**
Yancey, W. 68
Young, G. 164, 165, 170n
young people 188
  UK
    Educational Maintenance Allowances
      20, 90, 91-2
    employment 90
    New Deal for Disabled People 145
    unemployment 118
    welfare-to-work 16, *18*, 181-2
  US 31
  *see also* New Deal for Young People


**Z**
Zedlewski, S. 183